JUST ENOUGH UNIX

JUST ENOUGH UNIX

THIRD EDITION

Paul K. Andersen

New Mexico State University
Las Cruces, NM

Boston   Burr Ridge, IL   Dubuque, IA   Madison, WI   New York   San Francisco
St. Louis   Bangkok   Bogotá   Caracas   Lisbon   London   Madrid   Mexico City
Milan   New Delhi   Seoul   Singapore   Sydney   Taipei   Toronto

McGraw-Hill Higher Education

*A Division of **The McGraw-Hill** Companies*

This book is printed on acid-free paper.

domestic   1 2 3 4 5 6 7 8 9 0 DOC/DOC 9 0 9 8 7 6 5 4 3 2 1 0 9
international 1 2 3 4 5 6 7 8 9 0 DOC/DOC 9 0 9 8 7 6 5 4 3 2 1 0 9

ISBN 0-07-230297-6

Publisher: *Tom Casson*
Executive editor: *Elizabeth A. Jones*
Developmental editor: *Michelle Flomenhoft*
Senior marketing manager: *John T. Wannemacher*
Senior project manager: *Beth Cigler*
Senior production supervisor: *Heather D. Burbridge*
Freelance design coordinator: *Pam Verros*
Printer: *R.R. Donnelley & Sons Company*

http://www.mhhe.com

TABLE OF CONTENTS

PREFACE

What is UNIX?

Mention computers, and most people tend to think of computer hardware—the physical device, consisting of circuit boards, a central processing unit (CPU), memory chips, and so on. Equally important, however, is the software—the programs that tell the hardware what to do. Without software, a computer is just a box with wires attached to it.

An operating system is an important kind of software that manages the resources of the computer. You might think of the operating system as the master control program for the entire computer system, hardware and software.

In this book you will learn about the UNIX operating system. UNIX is fast becoming the standard computer operating system in industry, government, and education. It is especially popular in academia: according to AT&T, where UNIX was developed, every major university in the United States now has at least one computer system running under UNIX.

Which Version of UNIX?

Although UNIX originated at the AT&T Bell Laboratories, much of its subsequent development has occurred at the University of California, Berkeley. Computer manufacturers, too, have gotten into the act, producing their own variations on the UNIX theme. Examples include AIX, from IBM; A/UX, from Apple Computer; HP-UX, from Hewlett-Packard; Solaris, from Sun Microsystems; ULTRIX, from Digital Equipment Corporation; and XENIX, from Microsoft.

These versions of UNIX are quite similar. Most can trace their ancestry to either AT&T UNIX or Berkeley UNIX; some are amalgams of both. This book presents features that are found on almost all UNIX systems, with special emphasis on those that are common to AT&T System V and Berkeley System Distribution (BSD) 4.3 UNIX.

Who Should Read This Book?

This book is intended for anyone who wants to acquire a working knowledge of UNIX without having to become a UNIX expert. It is especially appropriate for students of science, engineering, or business who are taking their first computer programming course.

What Does This Book Cover?

This book covers the basics of the UNIX operating system. It has eight main parts:

I   INTRODUCTION TO UNIX

II   UNIX FILE SYSTEM

III   UNIX SHELL

IV   TEXT EDITORS

V   UNIX NETWORKING

VI   STARTUP FILES

VII   SHELL SCRIPTS

VIII PROGRAMMING UNDER UNIX

INTRODUCTION. In Part I, you will find an overview of the UNIX operating system, and you will learn what you will need to start using it. Three different approaches are presented: traditional (command-line) UNIX; the X Window System with Motif; and the Common Desktop Environment (CDE).

UNIX FILE SYSTEM. UNIX organizes information in collections called files. You will learn how to create, name, rename, copy, and delete files in Part II. You will also learn how UNIX keeps track of your files.

UNIX SHELL. The part of UNIX that interprets user commands and passes them on to the computer is called a shell. Many different shells have been written for UNIX; the three most prevalent are the Bourne Shell (standard on AT&T System V UNIX), the C Shell (standard on Berkeley UNIX), and the Korn Shell. These shells are considered in Part III.

TEXT EDITORS. You can create or modify UNIX files using a utility program called an editor. The most popular UNIX editors are vi ("vee-eye"), emacs, pico, and CDE Text Editor, which are discussed in Part IV.

UNIX NETWORKING. The recent growth of the Internet and World Wide Web around the world has been phenomenal. UNIX systems are a considerable part of this development. Internet and Web tools are presented in Part V.

STARTUP FILES. One of the great advantages of the UNIX operating system is its flexibility. A startup file contains commands for the shell to execute when it begins running. Startup files are examined in Part VI.

SHELL SCRIPTS. The UNIX shell is also a sophisticated programming language. A file containing a program for the UNIX shell is called a shell script. Shell scripts are described in Part VII.

PROGRAMMING UNDER UNIX. Most UNIX systems include the programming languages C and Fortran. Many also include Pascal and other languages such as C++, BASIC, Lisp, and COBOL. UNIX also offers a selection of software tools that are used in programming. UNIX programming is discussed in Part VIII, with emphasis on C, Fortran, and Pascal.

What's New in the Third Edition

Seven new chapters have been added; several chapters have been revised extensively. Most of the new material has to do with the Common Desktop Environment (CDE). The new chapters are

* Getting Started with CDE (Chapter 5)

* Using File Manager (Chapter 9)

* Editing with emacs (Chapter 14)

* Editing with pico (Chapter 15)

* Editing with Text Editor (Chapter 16)

* Processing Mail with pine (Chapter 19)

* Processing Mail with Mailer (Chapter 20)

A chapter on gopher has been deleted. It appears that gopher, if not yet extinct, is seriously endangered by Web browsers such as Netscape Navigator.

How to Use This Book

Anyone who is just starting with UNIX should read straight through Parts I, II, III, and IV. The remaining parts may be read in any order. If your interest is in the Internet and the World Wide Web, read Part V. If you would like to learn about shell scripts and startup files, read Parts VI and VII. If you are interested primarily in using UNIX to program in C, FORTRAN, or Pascal, read Part VIII.

Each part of this book begins with a chapter that explains the material without requiring the use of the computer. Other chapters are called "tutorials." These are intended to be read at the computer terminal. You should plan to spend about an hour at the terminal to cover each tutorial.

At the end of each section, you will find some short exercises. To derive the maximum benefit from this text, be sure to work through all of the exercises.

Acknowledgments

Many persons helped in the preparation of this and previous editions. The following reviewers read the manuscript at various stages in its development and provided helpful comments and suggestions:

John Thomas Berry
Foothill College

Eric P. Bloom
Boston University

Goranka Bjedov
AT&T

John Carroll
San Diego State University

Tat W. Chan
Fayetteville State University

Richard J. Easton
Indiana State University

John K. Estell
University of Toledo

Charles Frank
Northern Kentucky University

Donald L. Greenwell
Eastern Kentucky University

Scott Gever
Foothill College

Joe Hagarty
Raritan Valley Community College

Vasant G. Honavar
Iowa State University

Jack S. Kaye
University of Wisconsin—Milwaukee

Bill Manaris
University of Southwest Lousiana

J. Fernando Naveda
Rochester Institute of Technology

Evelyn Obaid
San José State University

Harapan Sinaga
Oklahoma State University

John Slimick
University of Pittsburgh—Bradford

Alexander Stoffel
Mayville State University

J. William A. Ward
University of South Alabama

This book could not have been produced without the invaluable assistance of Dr. M. G. Scarbrough, colleague and friend.

PART I:
INTRODUCTION TO UNIX

1 INTRODUCTION TO UNIX

Read a computer magazine, and you are sure to find an advertisement like this:

Blow the doors off the competition with the latest MegaMicro Daytona 500 workstations! Our 64-bit, 333-MHz AlphaBeta CPU delivers astounding 500-MIPS power that leaves the others in the dust. With 128 MB of RAM and an enormous 20-GB disk, the MegaMicro Daytona 500 is easy on your budget too ....

And so on. Or perhaps something like this:

MICROFRIENDLY takes you to the next level of user-friendly computing with the latest release of the HARMONIX® operating system. Featuring the X Window System with Motif and the Common Desktop Environment, MICROFRIENDLY HARMONIX® is a fully POSIX-compliant version of System V UNIX® with Berkeley utilities. MICROFRIENDLY HARMONIX® makes client-server computing easy, harmonious, and FRIENDLY.

In this chapter, you will learn what these ads mean. You will also get an overview of UNIX—what it is, how it works, and what it can do for you.

1.1 Computer Hardware

Computers come in a bewildering range of shapes, sizes, and types. Despite their differences, almost all have the following four essential components (see Figure 1–1):

- *Central processing unit (CPU).* The CPU performs calculations and manipulates data.

- *Main memory (primary memory, internal memory, RAM).* This is the place where the CPU looks for instructions and data to process. Main memory—also

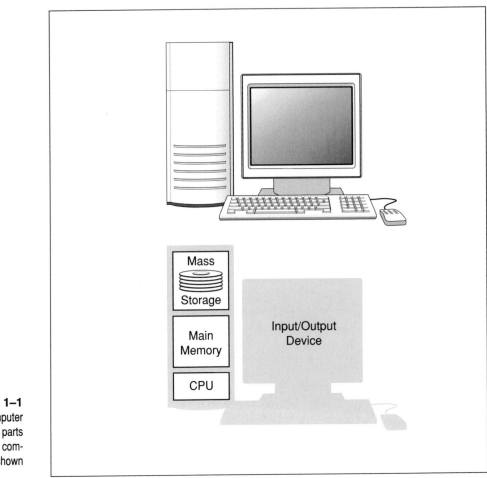

Figure 1–1

A typical computer system. The four parts of a single-user computer are shown

called *random-access memory* or *RAM*—is fast but limited in how much it can hold.

- **Mass storage (external memory, secondary memory).** Information that is not immediately needed by the computer is placed in mass storage or secondary memory, which is usually slower than main memory but can hold much more. The most common mass storage devices are magnetic disks.

- **Input/output (I/O) device.** I/O devices are used to move information to and from the computer. The most common I/O devices include the keyboard, mouse, video display, and printer.

Other devices—such as terminals, printers, scanners, and so on—are sometimes attached to the computer. These are generally called *peripherals*.

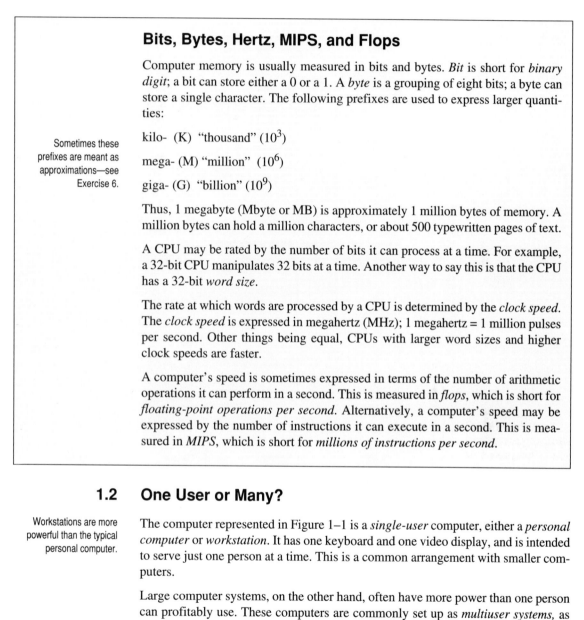

Bits, Bytes, Hertz, MIPS, and Flops

Computer memory is usually measured in bits and bytes. *Bit* is short for *binary digit*; a bit can store either a 0 or a 1. A *byte* is a grouping of eight bits; a byte can store a single character. The following prefixes are used to express larger quantities:

Sometimes these prefixes are meant as approximations—see Exercise 6.

kilo- (K) "thousand" (10^3)

mega- (M) "million" (10^6)

giga- (G) "billion" (10^9)

Thus, 1 megabyte (Mbyte or MB) is approximately 1 million bytes of memory. A million bytes can hold a million characters, or about 500 typewritten pages of text.

A CPU may be rated by the number of bits it can process at a time. For example, a 32-bit CPU manipulates 32 bits at a time. Another way to say this is that the CPU has a 32-bit *word size*.

The rate at which words are processed by a CPU is determined by the *clock speed*. The *clock speed* is expressed in megahertz (MHz); 1 megahertz = 1 million pulses per second. Other things being equal, CPUs with larger word sizes and higher clock speeds are faster.

A computer's speed is sometimes expressed in terms of the number of arithmetic operations it can perform in a second. This is measured in *flops*, which is short for *floating-point operations per second*. Alternatively, a computer's speed may be expressed by the number of instructions it can execute in a second. This is measured in *MIPS*, which is short for *millions of instructions per second*.

1.2   One User or Many?

Workstations are more powerful than the typical personal computer.

The computer represented in Figure 1–1 is a *single-user* computer, either a *personal computer* or *workstation*. It has one keyboard and one video display, and is intended to serve just one person at a time. This is a common arrangement with smaller computers.

Large computer systems, on the other hand, often have more power than one person can profitably use. These computers are commonly set up as *multiuser systems,* as depicted in Figure 1–2. Note that the multiuser computer has the same four basic parts as the single-user computer: CPU, main memory, mass storage, and input/output devices. (The I/O devices shown in Figure 1–2 are terminals, which consist of a keyboard and a video monitor.)

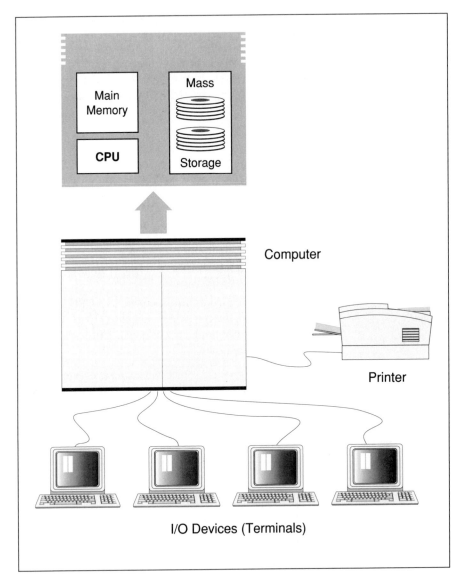

Figure 1–2
Multiuser computer system. This system is set up to handle as many as four users at a time. Some systems can serve hundreds of users simultaneously.

1.3 Computer Networks

A server is computer hardware (or software) that provides a service to other hardware (or software).

Another way to accommodate multiple users is to link two or more computers together to form a *network*. Figure 1–3 shows a network consisting of three workstations (called *hosts*), a printer, and another computer called a *file server* that has no video display device but does have magnetic disks. In this case, each of the three hosts has only limited secondary memory, relying instead on the magnetic disks attached to the server. (The server serves the workstations by providing mass storage for them.)

Computer networking has become very popular in recent years. One reason for this—as for many other things—is simple economics. By allowing users to share expensive resources such as printers, a network can be relatively economic to set up and operate.

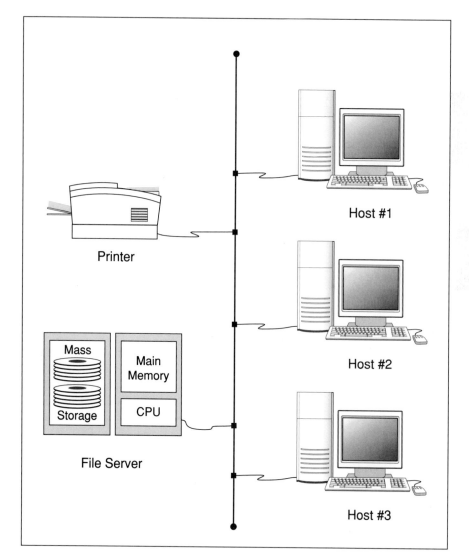

Printer

Mass Storage

Main Memory

CPU

File Server

Host #1

Host #2

Host #3

Figure 1–3
Computer network. This network includes four computers, one of which is a server providing disk storage for the other three.

1.4   The Operating System

As important as the computer hardware is, it can do nothing without *software*, the coded instructions that tell the CPU what to do. An especially important type of software is the *operating system* (OS), which performs three vital functions:

- The OS controls all of the various peripheral devices (printers, disk drives, terminals, and so on) that are attached to the computer.

- The OS handles communications between the user and the computer, passing commands from the user to the computer and returning messages from the computer to the user.

- The OS manages the way other programs are stored and run.

Some operating systems are *proprietary*, meaning that they are designed to work only on certain types of computers. For example, MS-DOS—the most popular operating system of the 1980s—was designed for machines having an Intel CPU. Likewise, the original Apple Macintosh System ran only on machines using a Motorola CPU.

Software is said to be portable if it can be moved from one type of computer to another with minimal changes.

In contrast, the UNIX operating system is nonproprietary—it will run on a wide variety of computer systems. One way to express this is to say that UNIX is a *portable* operating system. You will also hear people say that UNIX is an *open* system. However you choose to put it, UNIX is the leading portable (or open) operating system in the world today.

1.5   Multitasking and Time-Sharing

UNIX is a *multitasking* operating system, meaning it enables the computer to work on more than one task at a time. With UNIX, you can run several programs "in the background" while you work on another task "in the foreground."

How does multitasking work? Although some computers actually can perform more than one task at a time, others cannot. However, by switching rapidly back and forth between tasks, performing a little here and a little there, a computer can create the illusion of doing many things simultaneously. This technique is called *time-sharing*, and it is feasible only because (a) the computer is very fast and (b) UNIX takes care of scheduling what is to be done and when.

UNIX is also capable of interacting with more than one user at a time—in other words, it is a *multiuser* operating system. This capability is especially important on large mainframe computers that must serve a large number of users; without it, everyone would have to wait his or her turn to use the computer.

The Origins of UNIX

The UNIX story begins with a failed operating system, some fun-loving computer scientists with time on their hands, and a computer game named *Space Travel*. The failed operating system was Multics, a joint venture involving General Electric, MIT, and the AT&T Bell Laboratories. Multics was envisioned as a great technological leap forward: an interactive, multiuser operating system that would be years ahead of anything then available. But the project was too ambitious, and by 1969 it was clear that Multics was in big trouble. Reluctantly, Bell Labs withdrew from the project, leaving the Bell researchers with nothing to do.

One of those researchers, Ken Thompson, had written *Space Travel*, a computer game that allowed a Multics user to pilot an imaginary spacecraft to the major bodies of the solar system. While awaiting approval from Bell management for several new research projects, Thompson decided to keep busy by rewriting *Space Travel* to run on a little-used PDP-7 minicomputer in the lab. He enlisted the aid of Dennis Ritchie, another Bell computer scientist who had worked on the Multics project.

It was no easy task. All programming had to be done on another machine, then transferred to the PDP-7 using punched paper tape. It did not take long for Thompson to wish that the PDP-7 had its own operating system, similar in some respects to Multics, but much simpler. So he wrote one. This was the first UNIX operating system, although it did not acquire that name until the following year. (The name was originally "Unics," a pun on the name Multics. Later this was changed to UNIX.)

The PDP-7 had only about 9 Kbytes of main memory, less than some of today's handheld calculators. Thompson and Ritchie requested a larger computer. In exchange, they offered to produce a UNIX-based word-processing system for the Bell Labs patent department. They got their new computer—a PDP-11 having 24 K of main memory—and delivered the word-processing system in 1971. It was an immediate success, and UNIX was launched.

UNIX was originally written in assembly language, a kind of primitive programming language. Since each type of computer has its own assembly language, early versions of UNIX could run only on PDP-7 and closely related machines. But in 1973, UNIX was rewritten in C, a high-level programming language invented by Dennis Ritchie. It was much easier to write programs in C; just as important, C was designed to be a portable language, not tied to any particular type of computer hardware. As a result, UNIX itself became a portable operating system.

1.6 Major Components of UNIX

The UNIX operating system consists of four main parts:

- **Kernel.** The *kernel* is the master control program of the computer. It resides in the computer's main memory, and it manages the computer's resources. It is the kernel that handles the switching necessary to provide multitasking.

- **Shell.** The part of UNIX that interprets user commands and passes them on to the kernel is called the *shell.* Three different shells are commonly used today: the Bourne Shell, the Korn Shell, and the C Shell, all of which are discussed in this book.

- **File System.** UNIX organizes information into collections called *files.* You can put just about any kind of information into a file—a program you have written, a memo, data waiting to be analyzed, the manuscript for your next novel, even a letter to your mother. Files may be grouped together into collections called *directory files*, usually called *directories.*

- **Utilities.** A *utility* is a useful software tool that is included as a standard part of the UNIX operating system. Utilities are often called *commands.* UNIX provides utilities for text editing and formatting, programming, database management, communications, and so on.

1.7 Windows and Graphical User Interfaces

It is difficult to take full advantage of a multitasking operating system like UNIX if you can only see output from one process at a time on your monitor. Fortunately, most recent UNIX systems have the ability to divide the monitor screen into multiple areas called *windows* (Figure 1–4), each of which acts as if it were a separate monitor. Using a windowing system, you could read your electronic mail in one window, compose a reply in another window, and run a spreadsheet program from a third window, all at the same time.

The typical windowing system also offers what is called a *graphical user interface* (GUI or "gooey"), which allows you to work with pictures as well as character data. To run a particular program under a GUI, you might use a pointing device such as a mouse to select an *icon* (a symbol) that represents that program, rather than having to remember and type a command. Because most people find it easier to work with pictures and pointing devices, GUIs have become very popular.

If you have used an Apple Macintosh or a PC running either Microsoft Windows or OS/2, you are already familiar with windows and GUIs. On UNIX systems, the GUI is usually based on the X Window System ("X" for short), which was originally developed at the Massachusetts Institute of Technology.

Windows

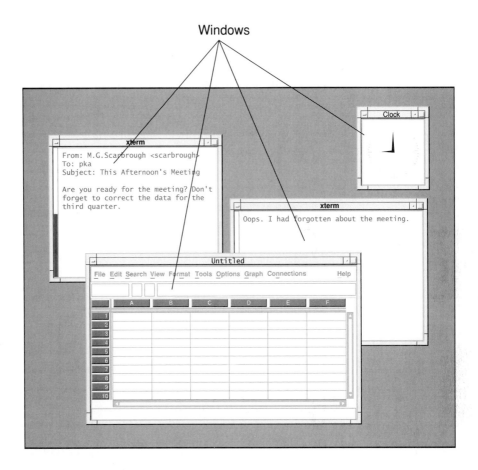

Figure 1–4
A windowing display.
Four windows are
shown; each window
acts as an independent output device.

A server is software (or
hardware) that provides a
service to other software (or
hardware).

The X Window System works according to what is called a *client-server model.* In other words, X acts as a server for other programs (the clients) by providing a graphical user interface for them. This makes X especially well suited to networked computing because the clients and server can run on separate computers.

1.8 The Window Manager

Although the X Window System makes it possible to create a graphical user interface, X does not specify what the windows must look like or how they are manipulated by the user. That is the job of a program called the *window manager.* The window manager determines the "look and feel" of the GUI, controlling the appearance of the windows and determining how those windows are opened, closed, sized, resized, and moved.

Four window managers are in common use:

- *Tab Window Manager* (`twm`). Originally developed at MIT and supplied as part of the X Window System, `twm` is a "plain vanilla" window manager that offers few frills. Even so, experienced UNIX programmers like `twm` because it can be configured to suit their personal tastes.

- *Open Look Window Manager* (`olwm`). Sun Microsystems has been the strongest promoter of Open Look, which has generally not been adopted by other manufacturers.

- *Motif Window Manager* (`mwm`). Motif was developed by the Open Software Foundation (OSF), a consortium of several leading UNIX vendors. Motif was designed to have a "look and feel" similar to that of the IBM Presentation Manager and Microsoft Windows, two widely used GUIs for personal computers.

- *Desktop Window Manager* (`dtwm`). Based on Motif, the Desktop Window Manager was developed for the Common Desktop Environment (discussed below).

This book features the Motif Window Manager (`mwm`) and the Desktop Window Manager (`dtwm`) because these are standards in the UNIX world.

1.9   Common Desktop Environment

The plethora of UNIX windowing systems has been a cause of confusion for system administrators and users. In 1993, six of the largest UNIX vendors started the Common Open Software Environment (COSE) initiative to address this problem. The result of this initiative was the Common Desktop Environment (CDE).

CDE is designed to provide a consistent look and feel, regardless of the variety of UNIX being used. The CDE user interface is organized around the idea of a "desktop," using icons to represent items—such as documents, files, and file folders—that might be found on a real desk. This approach is familiar to users of the Apple Macintosh and the Microsoft Windows operating systems. CDE also provides a new set of standard software tools, including a text editor, a calendar/datebook, and an electronic mail tool, in addition to the traditional UNIX utilities.

1.10 X Terminals

The X Window System was designed to be portable. As a result, X runs on virtually every kind of computer, from Macintoshes and PCs to supercomputers. This has contributed greatly to its success.

Character-based terminals are often called dumb terminals.

However, X will not run on a conventional character-based terminal, because considerable computing power is required to support a graphical user interface. This has led to the development of a hybrid input/output device called an *X terminal*, which has a CPU and enough internal memory to run X, but is not a complete computer in itself. An X terminal is more expensive than a character-based terminal, but less expensive than a complete UNIX workstation.

1.11 Exercises

1. Be sure you can define the following terms:

hardware	mega-	multitasking
software	giga-	time-sharing
CPU	word size	kernel
main memory	clock speed	shell
secondary memory	flops	file
mass storage	MIPS	file system
external memory	server	directory
I/O device	client	utility
peripheral	host	command
network	operating system	window
bit	proprietary	GUI
byte	portable	icon
kilo-	open system	window manager

2. What are the four main hardware components of most computer systems?

3. What are the main components of the UNIX operating system?

4. Name the most commonly used X window managers.

5. Name the most common UNIX shells.

6. When referring to the capacity of a computer's memory, computer scientists often use prefixes like kilo-, mega-, and giga- only approximately. For example, a kilobyte of memory is not exactly 1,000 bytes, but rather 2^{10} bytes. Likewise,

a megabyte is really 2^{20} bytes, and a gigabyte is really 2^{30} bytes. What is the difference between a thousand and 2^{10}? A million (10^6) and 2^{20}? A billion (10^9) and 2^{30}?

2 YOUR UNIX ACCOUNT

In one respect, UNIX is like your local bank. Just as you need a bank account to withdraw money (legally) from a bank, you also need an account to use a UNIX computer. In this chapter, you will learn what you need to know to obtain and begin using a UNIX account.

2.1   Your System Administrator

Every bank has a manager who sets bank policy, opens and closes customer accounts, balances the books, and generally sees that the bank operates smoothly. Of course, the manager does not necessarily do all of these things personally, but the manager is responsible to see that someone does.

Similarly, most UNIX installations have a *system administrator*, who sees that the system runs smoothly (most of the time, anyway). The system administrator's duties include

* Setting up the hardware.

* Installing software, including the UNIX operating system.

* Starting up the system (and shutting it down when necessary).

* Monitoring system usage.

* Backing up users' files.

* Creating new user accounts.

* Troubleshooting.

The system administrator does not necessarily do all of these things personally—large computer installations typically divide these duties among several persons. Thus, when you read "system administrator," think "the system administrator or one of his or her assistants."

2.2   Your Account Name

A large UNIX installation may serve hundreds or thousands of users, each having his or her own account. To identify these accounts, each is given a unique name, which is typically based in some way on the user's real name or nickname. For example, the following would all be likely account names for a user named John P. Jones:

```
jpjones
```

```
jonesjp
```

```
jones
```

```
johnp
```

```
jpj
```

```
sparky
```

The policies for assigning account names vary. In some organizations, the system administrator chooses the name for you; in others, you may choose your own, subject to certain rules. The following rules are fairly typical:

- Select a name that is at least three characters long, but no more than eight characters long.

- Be sure that no other account has the same name.

- Choose an account name that is related in some way to your real name or a nickname.

- Use only numbers and lowercase letters; do not include uppercase letters or punctuation.

When you start a work session on the computer, you will be asked to *log in* by giving your account name:

```
login:
```

Because you use your account name when logging in, your account name is often referred to as your *login name* or *login.*

2.3   Your Password

Your login name is public knowledge. To prevent unauthorized use of your account, the computer also asks you for a secret *password*:

```
password:
```

By entering your password, you verify to the computer that you really are the person to whom the account belongs.

The system administrator will probably choose your first password for you. After that, you can (and should) choose your own passwords. A good password is one that is easy for you to remember, but difficult for someone else to guess. Here are some good general guidelines for selecting a password:

Your particular computer installation may have other rules as well—consult your system administrator.

- Choose a password that is at least six characters long. (Passwords can be as long as you like, but some systems only examine the first eight characters.)

- Combine numbers, upper- and lowercase letters, and punctuation.

- Make the password memorable, but avoid common names and words.

- Do not use your social security number, your telephone number, your login, or any variation (forward or backward) of your login.

- Make sure a new password differs significantly from the old one.

A number of strategies exist for choosing a password. One is to misspell an easily remembered word or name. For example, neither `Chicago` nor `chicago` would be acceptable as passwords. But the following deliberate misspellings would be:

Do not use these examples—think up your own password.

`chiKagoh`

`Chi.CAGO`

`Sheekago`

`She?kago`

Another strategy is to form a password from the first letter of each word in an easily remembered phrase. Including punctuation is a good idea. For example:

`NiMyyd!`   (*Not in My yard you don't!*)

`Ihnybtf`   (*I have not yet begun to fight*)

`H,hotr`   (*Home, home on the range*)

`wtdatap`   (*where the deer and the antelope play*)

Your password is the main line of protection for your account. Anyone who discovers your password can do nearly anything to your account—including deleting all of your files. Therefore, it is extremely important that you keep your password secure.

WARNING	MEMORIZE YOUR PASSWORD—DO NOT WRITE IT DOWN. AND NEVER DIVULGE YOUR PASSWORD TO ANYONE.

You will see how to change your password in the next chapter.

If you suspect that someone else has learned your password, you should change it immediately. In fact, it may be a good idea to change your password occasionally in any case, just to be safe.

2.4   Other Account Information

When your account is created, the system administrator sets up the following information in addition to the login name and password:

*   ***Home Directory.*** Your home directory is the place where all of your other files and directories reside. The home directory has a name, which is the same as your login name.

*   ***Group ID.*** You may be assigned to a group of users. In some organizations, groups are set up so that users in the same department or working on the same projects can easily share files.

*   ***Login Shell.*** Three UNIX shells are commonly used: the Bourne Shell, the C Shell, and the Korn Shell. The system administrator will select one of these to start up automatically whenever you log in.

When you receive your UNIX account, be sure to ask what groups (if any) you have been assigned to and what your login shell is.

2.5   More Questions to Ask

There are a number of additional questions you should ask your system administrator:

*   Which version of UNIX will I be using?

*   What kind of terminal will I be using? What is its `terminfo` code?

*   What are the erase, interrupt, stop, and continue keys?

*   Which printer(s) may I use?

*   How can I gain access to the system?

The rest of this chapter will explain what each of these questions means.

2.6 Versions of UNIX

When we say UNIX, we are really talking about a family of operating systems. Most can trace their ancestry to AT&T System V or Berkeley Software Distribution (BSD) UNIX:

Name	Supplier	Based on
AIX	International Business Machines	AT&T System V
A/UX	Apple Computer	AT&T System V
Dynix	Sequent	BSD
HP-UX	Hewlett-Packard	BSD
Irix	Silicon Graphics	AT&T System V
Linux	Free Software Foundation	
NextStep	Next	BSD
OSF/1	Digital Equipment Corporation	BSD
SCO UNIX	Santa Cruz Operation	AT&T System V
Solaris	Sun Microsystems	AT&T System V
SunOS	Sun Microsystems	BSD UNIX
Ultrix	Digital Equipment Corporation	BSD UNIX
Unicos	Cray	AT&T System V
UnixWare	Novell	AT&T System V
XENIX	Microsoft	AT&T System III

Ask your system administrator whether your system is based on AT&T or BSD UNIX.

Keep in mind that these UNIX versions are very similar; if you learn to use one, you should have little trouble with any of the others.

Why So Many Versions of UNIX?

When UNIX was under development at AT&T's Bell Laboratories in the 1970s, AT&T was still prevented by federal law from competing in the computer industry. Since the company could not make a profit on UNIX, they gave it away, essentially free of charge.

UNIX became very popular at colleges and universities, where it was used for both teaching and research. (The low price tag undoubtedly had something to do with this popularity.) The early versions of UNIX were still quite crude, so academic computer scientists introduced their own improvements. Especially prominent in this effort was the Computer Systems Research Group at the University of California at Berkeley, which began producing its own versions of UNIX. By 1982, Berkeley Software Distribution (BSD) UNIX rivaled the AT&T versions in popularity.

Meanwhile, many computer companies produced their own versions of UNIX, often borrowing features from both AT&T and Berkeley UNIX. Of course, each version had its own name, usually ending in *x* (AIX, A/UX, HP-UX, Irix, Ultrix, and XENIX, to mention a few.) At one time there were as many as 200 variants of UNIX on the market.

Although similar in most respects, the many versions of UNIX had enough differences to cause headaches for programmers, vendors, and users. To make life easier for everyone, an industry group was formed to define a UNIX standard. The first Portable Operating System Interface (POSIX) standard was formally adopted in 1988. Since then, most of the major vendors of UNIX operating systems have modified their systems in accordance with the POSIX standards.

AT&T was also conscious of the need for standardization. In 1989, AT&T System V ("System 5") Release 4 appeared. System V Release 4 (abbreviated "SVR4") combined the best features of the four most popular UNIX derivatives, which were SVR3, 4.3BSD, SunOS, and Microsoft XENIX.

In 1991, a 21-year Finnish graduate student named Linus Torvalds created Linux, a UNIX clone for personal computers. Linux is available at no charge from the Free Software Foundation. Hundreds of volunteer programmers worldwide work to maintain and extend Linux.

In 1993, the Computer Systems Research Group at Berkeley announced it would cease operations with the release of 4.4BSD. However, the Open Software Foundation (OSF)—a consortium of major computer manufacturers that includes IBM, Digital Equipment Corporation, and Hewlett-Packard—continues work on operating systems based on BSD UNIX.

2.7 Terminal Type and Terminfo Code

As an open system, UNIX must be able to work with a wide variety of I/O devices. The UNIX system includes a database describing the operating characteristics of the many different terminals it can use. This is called either the `terminfo` ("terminal information") or `termcap` ("terminal capabilities") database. When you log in, your system may request that you indicate the type of terminal device you are using by specifying its `terminfo` (or `termcap`) code. Here are the codes for some common terminals:

Manufacturer	Model	Code
Digital Equipment Corporation	VT100	vt100
Hewlett-Packard	2621	hp2621
International Business Machines	3164	ibm3164
Lear-Siegler	ADM 3	adm3
Sanyo	55	sanyo55
Televideo	925	tvi925
Tektronix	4015	tek4015
Wyse Technology	50	wyse50

Ask your system administrator which `terminfo` code(s) you should use.

2.8 Special Keys

Figure 2–1 shows a typical computer keyboard. It has the same letter, number, and punctuation keys as a typewriter. It also has a number of special keys not found on the traditional typewriter. The following five keys are of particular interest:

*   (RETURN) Also called the (ENTER) or (NEWLINE) key, this is used to send commands to the shell.

*   (ESCAPE) This key, which may be labeled (ESC), is usually found near the upper left corner of the keyboard.

*   (ERASE) Various keys are used to erase characters. On many systems, this function is performed by a (BACKSPACE) or (DELETE) key, or by a combination of keys.

*   (BREAK) This key is sometimes used during the login procedure.

*   (CONTROL) This may be labeled (CTRL) on some terminals. It is used in combination with other keys to perform special functions.

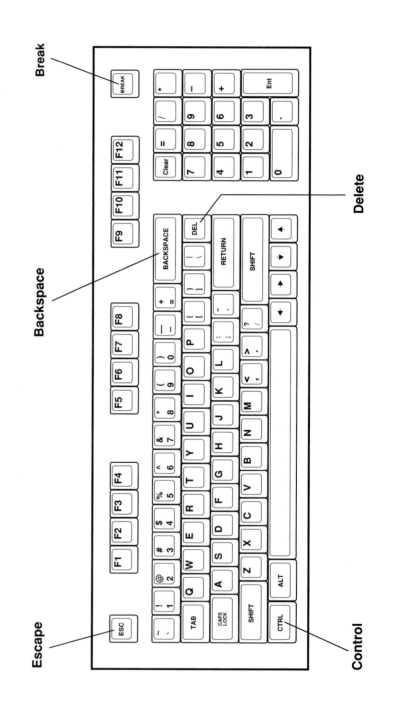

Figure 2–1
A computer keyboard,
showing some of the
special keys

Of these, the (CONTROL) key deserves special mention. A large number of UNIX commands are executed by holding down the (CONTROL) key while simultaneously pressing another key. For example, on many terminals the erase function can be invoked by the key combination

(CONTROL)-(H)

When referring to this combination of keys in print, you will often see the notation ^H, where the caret (^) stands for the (CONTROL) key.

Later in the book, you will learn about many of the functions that involve the (CONTROL) key. For now, there are four special functions that you should ask about:

Function	Purpose	Key Combination	Alternative
erase	deletes a character	(CONTROL)-(H) (^H)	(BACKSPACE)
interrupt	stops a program	(CONTROL)-(C) (^C)	(DELETE)
stop	freezes the terminal	(CONTROL)-(S) (^S)	?
continue	unfreezes the terminal	(CONTROL)-(Q) (^Q)	?

Your system administrator can tell you which keys perform these functions.

Note that there may be more than one way to delete a character or interrupt a program. As shown in Appendix A, UNIX provides a way for you to change the keys that invoke these functions.

2.9   Printer Codes

Almost every UNIX system has a printer for producing paper output. (Paper output is called *hardcopy*.) A large computer installation may have many printers. Individual printers are identified by a code name, which typically reflects the type and location of the device. For example, suppose that one of the printers connected to your UNIX system were an Apple LaserWriter 360, located in Room 12. The system administrator might give this printer one of the following code names:

```
alw360-12
```

```
lw360r12
```

```
room12lw
```

You get the idea. There are no standard rules on naming printers, so it is a good idea to ask your system administrator for the names of the printers that are part of your system.

Teletypes and Terminals

When Thompson and Ritchie rewrote UNIX to run on the PDP-11 for the Bell Patent Department, the primary input/output devices were Teletype terminals. These were slow, noisy electromechanical devices that produced their output on rolls of paper.

The Teletype keyboard had the usual typewriter keys for upper- and lowercase letters, numbers, and punctuation. It also had a special "Control" key that was used in combination with other keys to perform special functions. (For example, holding down the Control key and typing the letter *B* caused a bell to ring.)

Although Teletypes are now obsolete, they are not entirely forgotten. The keyboards of newer I/O devices still have a Control key that is used in combination with other keys to perform special functions. In the vocabulary of UNIX, the abbreviation `tty` (short for Teletype) is still used to mean "terminal." And "print" is still used to mean "display output on a terminal," even though most terminals today print to a video screen rather than paper.

2.10   Exercises

1. Be sure you can define the following terms:

system administrator	home directory	`termcap` code
account name	group	control key
login name	login shell	interrupt
login	BSD	`tty`
logging in	System V	print
password	`terminfo` code	hardcopy

2. What version of UNIX will you be using? Is it based on AT&T or on BSD UNIX?

3. How are login names assigned for users on your system? Are you allowed to choose your own login, or is one chosen for you?

4. What are the rules for choosing a password on your system? Keeping those rules in mind, choose two or three passwords to use later. (Do not write down your passwords or divulge them to anyone.)

5. Which of the following would be good passwords for someone named Glynda Jones Davis, whose login name, phone number, and social security number are gjdavis, 555-2525, and 632-10-6854, respectively? Explain your reasoning.

cat	Glynda7	tylerTwo
Smith	sivagjg	t555s632
5552525	Jones	532106854
KRoo2	jones	kangaroo
7cattz	NotSmith	trouble
Glynda	tiPPecanoe	trubble

6. What kind of terminal will you be using? What is its terminfo (or termcap) code?

7. Which keys are used to erase input, interrupt a program, freeze the terminal, and unfreeze the terminal?

8. Which printer may you use? What is its code name?

3 TUTORIAL: GETTING STARTED

In this chapter, you will learn how to log into your UNIX account, change your password, and try out some UNIX commands using a character-based terminal. If you are working with an X terminal or workstation, you may wish to skip this chapter.

If you haven't done so already, ask your instructor, system administrator, or consultant about setting up an account. You will need the following information:

- Your login name
- Your password
- The name of the computer you will be using

3.1 Switching on the Power

Skip to Section 3.2 if your terminal is already on.

Some terminals are meant to be left on at all times, and should not be turned off. You cannot always tell by looking at the screen—your system may have a screen-saver program that blanks the display when it has been idle for a time. Therefore, the first step is to try to "wake up" the screen:

1   **Press the spacebar or** (RETURN) **key.** This is usually enough to cancel the screen-saver. If it does, go on to Section 3.2, "Obtaining a Login Prompt."

2   **Find the power switch and turn it on.** The switch may be hidden under the front edge of the keyboard or on the back panel of the terminal. (See if you can find the power cord—the switch may be close to the point where the cord enters the terminal.) Turn on the terminal.

3   **Allow the terminal to warm up.** After a while, you should see a small, blinking line or rectangle on the terminal screen. This is the *cursor*. It shows where the next typed character will appear.

3.2　Obtaining a Login Prompt

Now you must get the computer's attention. What you want is for the computer to show you a *login prompt*, indicating that it is ready for you to log in:

```
login:
```

If you already see this on the terminal screen, skip to Section 3.3.

How you get a login prompt depends on whether your terminal is connected to one or many computer hosts. *If your terminal is connected to one host*, try the following procedure for obtaining a login prompt:

1　**Press** (RETURN) **several times.** This may be enough to cause the computer to display a login prompt:

```
login:
```

2　**If the login prompt does not appear, try pressing** (BREAK) or (RESET). Some systems may require that you press (BREAK) then (RETURN).

3　**If Steps 1 and 2 do not work, see your system administrator.**

If your terminal is connected to a terminal server, it will be necessary for you to select a host computer. How this is done depends on your system. The following procedure is fairly typical:

1　**Press** (RETURN) **several times.** Often this will suffice to get the terminal server to display its prompt. Terminal-server prompts vary from system to system; here are some examples:

```
Which computer?
```

```
Dial:
```

```
UNIVERSITY-NET>
```

2　**Enter the name of the host computer at the prompt.** If you wanted to work with a machine named `merlin`, you would enter this name at the prompt:

```
Which computer?merlin (RETURN)
```

The chosen host computer should respond with a login prompt:

```
login:
```

3　**If Steps 1 and 2 do not work, consult your system administrator.**

3.3　Logging In

If you have reached this point, you should see a login prompt on the screen:

```
login:
```

1   **Enter your login name and press** (RETURN). If your login name were jsmith, you would enter this after the prompt:

Do not enter jsmith
(unless that is your login).
Enter *your* login here. ────────────

```
login:jsmith (RETURN)
```

The computer will respond by prompting you for your password:

```
password:
```

2   **Enter your password and press** (RETURN).

Enter your password here;
it will not appear on the
screen. ────────────

```
password: ▨▨▨▨▨▨▨
```

Note that YOUR PASSWORD DOES NOT APPEAR ON THE SCREEN. The idea is to prevent others from looking over your shoulder and learning your password. (You will see how to change the password later.)

3   **If you made an error typing either your login name or password, repeat Steps 1 and 2.** The computer will tell you that your login is incorrect, and it will give you the chance to log in again:

```
Login incorrect
login:
```

3.4   Messages

Once you gain access to the computer, it may print a variety of messages, including

- Type of UNIX.

- Message of the day from the system administrator.

- Mail alert, telling you there is electronic mail waiting for you.

If you have mail, you will see how to read it later.

3.5   Setting the Terminal Type

Some UNIX systems are set up to ask you to specify your terminal type when you log in. If yours is such a system, it will show you a prompt like

```
Set terminal type (vt100):
```

Or perhaps

```
TERM (vt100):
```

The `terminfo` code in the parentheses represents the *default terminal type*; the computer assumes that this is the terminal you are using.

1 **If your terminal matches the default type, simply press** (RETURN). Then skip to the next section, "UNIX Shell Prompt."

2 **Otherwise, enter the** `terminfo` **code for the type of terminal you are using.** (This is something you should have obtained from your system administrator.) Be sure to press (RETURN) after the code.

3.6 UNIX Shell Prompt

At this point, you should see a *shell prompt*, which is simply the shell's way of telling you that it is ready to receive your instructions. If your login shell is the C Shell, the prompt is probably a percent sign:

%

If you are using the Bourne Shell or the Korn Shell as a login shell, the usual prompt is a dollar sign:

$

Other symbols are occasionally used for shell prompts, including the pound sign (#), the "greater than" sign (>), the asterisk (*), the "at" symbol (@), and the colon (:). Some systems are set up to include the host name as part of the prompt, like this:

`merlin %`

In this book, we will use the following as our "generic" prompt, to take the place of either the percent sign or the dollar sign:

In the examples that follow, do not enter the prompt symbol.

§

3.7 Terminal Troubles

Sometimes your terminal will not behave as you expect it to. Two problems are especially common:

- *Everything you type appears in uppercase letters.* The UNIX system acts as if your terminal cannot handle lowercase letters.

- *The usual erase key does not work.* For example, you may wish to use the (BACKSPACE) key to erase characters.

If either of these problems occurs, you should refer to Appendix A, "Taming Your Terminal."

3.8   Changing Your Password

Review Section 2.3 on selecting a password.

A good password is one that is easy for you to remember but difficult for someone else to figure out. Often the initial passwords assigned by system administrators fail these criteria. It is a good idea to change your password frequently to prevent unauthorized use of your account. If you have not already done so, you should take a minute to think about a password.

1   Enter the `passwd` command at the shell prompt. Note that this is `passwd`, not `password`:

§ passwd ⟨RETURN⟩

The system will prompt for your old password:

Old password:

2   Enter your old password, then press ⟨RETURN⟩. As usual, your password will not appear on the screen:

Old password:▒▒▒▒▒▒▒

The computer will then ask you to enter your new password:

New password:

3   Enter your new password, then press ⟨RETURN⟩. As usual, your password will not appear on the screen:

New password:▒▒▒▒▒▒▒

To ensure that you have made no mistakes, the computer will ask you to repeat your new password:

Retype new password:

4   Repeat your new password. If this is not done exactly as before, the system will not accept the new password, and you will have to start over:

Retype new password:▒▒▒▒▒▒▒

You will know that the new password has been accepted when the shell prompt appears:

§

3.9 Trying Out Some UNIX Commands

Next, try a few UNIX commands to see how they work.

1 Start with the date command. Type date after the prompt, and press (RETURN) :

§ date (RETURN)

The computer will respond with the date and time. For example, if you were to give this command on Monday, August 13, 2001, at 8:35 pm (Eastern Standard Time), the output would be something like

Mon Aug 13 20:35:41 EST 2001

Note that this is the time for the host computer's locale, and that time is given on the 24-hour clock.

2 Next, try the who command. Type who, followed by (RETURN) :

§ who (RETURN)

The computer will respond with a list of the users who are currently logged into the system. For example,

root	console	Aug 13	08:11
aadams	tty16	Aug 13	07:01
pgw	tty03	Aug 13	18:15
ben	tty18	Aug 13	11:32
jeff	tty12	Aug 13	09:45

The user's login name is listed first, followed by a code that identifies the line or *port* to which the user is connected. The date and time that the user logged in are also shown.

3 Try the who am i command. This command prints your login name on the screen:

§ who am i (RETURN)

3.10 Reading Your Mail

Skip this section if you have not received e-mail.

If you received a message telling you that you had received electronic mail, now is the time to read your mail.

1 Enter the command to start the mail program. The command depends on whether you are using a UNIX system based on AT&T System V or Berkeley (BSD) UNIX:

AT&T System V:

§ mailx (RETURN)

BSD:

§ Mail (RETURN)

The system will respond with a list of the messages. For example,

```
U  1 wards  Fri Aug 10 15:27  554/26358  "Class Roster"
N  2 aadams Mon Aug 13 8:59  40/1527  "Lunch"
N  3 gwc  Mon Aug 13  9:47  15/440  "Research Notes"
&
```

A *U* in the first column indicates an unread message left over from the last time you logged in; an *N* indicates a new message. The messages are numbered (from 1 to 3 in this case). The login name of the sender is shown, along with the date and time the message was received and the number of lines and characters the message contains (lines/characters). Finally, the subject of the message is given in quotes. The ampersand (**&**) on the last line is the *mail prompt*.

2　**Read your message(s).** Simply enter the message number after the mail prompt and press (RETURN) :

&2 (RETURN)

This will cause the second message to appear:

```
Message 2:
From aadams Mon Aug 13 8:59:01 2001
Date: Mon Aug 13 8:59:01
From: aadams (Abigail Adams)
To: (Your login name)
Subject: Lunch

Let's get together for lunch at 12:45 today. Okay?
&
```

3　**Leave the mail utility.** Typing *x* (for "exit") at the mail prompt will take you out of the mail utility, leaving the message(s) in the mailbox:

&x (RETURN)

Electronic mail—including the ways to send, save, and delete mail—is discussed in more detail in Part V.

3.11 Reading the UNIX Manual

Many UNIX systems come equipped with a detailed on-line manual that you can read using the man command. The manual describes the commands that are available on the system. To see how this is done, try the following command:

§ man cal (RETURN)

The cal command is one that we will use in later chapters; it displays a calendar on the screen. If your system has the on-line manual, you should see a description of cal. (For more information on how to make sense of the manual, see Appendix B.) Otherwise, you will see the message

man: Command not found.

3.12 Logging Out

When you are finished working on the computer, you must "log out." This tells the system that you are finished using it.

WARNING	NEVER LEAVE THE TERMINAL WITHOUT LOGGING OUT FIRST. On some UNIX systems, your account will remain open even if your terminal is turned off. This invites the unscrupulous to get into the system and cause trouble.

1 If you are using the C Shell, try the logout **command:**

% logout (RETURN)

2 If you are using the Bourne or Korn Shell, try the exit **command:**

$ exit (RETURN)

3 If neither logout **nor** exit **works, try** ^D. Remember, the notation ^D means you should hold down the (CONTROL) key and type the letter *D*:

§ (CONTROL)―(D)

4 If necessary, log out from the terminal server. If you had to log onto a terminal server before selecting a computer host, you may also have to log out from the terminal server.

5 If nothing seems to work, ask for help. Do not leave without logging out first.

3.13 Command Summary

Each of the commands listed here is entered at the shell prompt.

Changing Your Password

passwd (RETURN)   change password

Miscellaneous UNIX Commands

date (RETURN)   print current date and time

who (RETURN)   print a list of users currently logged in

who am i (RETURN)   print your login

man cal (RETURN)   show the manual page describing the cal command

Logging Out

logout (RETURN)   logout for C Shell

exit (RETURN)   logout for Bourne or Korn Shell

^D   optional logout command

3.14 Exercises

1. Be sure you can define the following terms:

cursor	login shell	shell
default	mail prompt	shell prompt

2. What kinds of terminals are connected to your UNIX system? Examine several different terminals and locate the (RETURN), (CONTROL), (BACKSPACE), (ESCAPE), and (BREAK) keys, and the ON/OFF switch.

3. See if your terminal has a key labeled "NO SCROLL." This key is supposed to "freeze" the terminal display. Press it and type your name. What happens on the screen? Now press the key again. What do you see?

4. On many terminals, the ^S key combination "freezes" the terminal. Try this key combination and type something on the keyboard. What happens? The key combination ^Q "unfreezes" the terminal, reversing the effects of ^S. Try this.

5. Does your keyboard have a key labeled "CAPS LOCK" or "CASE"? If so, press it and type something on the keyboard. What does this key do?

6. UNIX is *case-sensitive:* it distinguishes between upper- and lowercase letters. Try the commands listed below and note what each one does (if anything):

WHO (RETURN)

CAL 2001 (RETURN)

DATE (RETURN)

WHO AM I (RETURN)

4 Tutorial:
Getting Started with Motif

Skip this chapter if your terminal does not run X, or if your system runs the Common Desktop Environment (CDE).

In this chapter, you will learn how to use an X terminal or workstation to log into your UNIX account, change your password, and try out some UNIX commands. If you haven't done so already, ask your instructor, system administrator, or consultant about setting up an account. You will need the following information:

- Your login name

- Your password

- The name of the computer you will be using

If necessary, you can start X yourself—see Appendix C.

This chapter assumes that your system is set up to start the X server and window manager automatically. If this is not true for your system, you will have to start them yourself. In that case, you should log in according to the procedure presented in Sections 3.1 through 3.7; then refer to Appendix C, "Starting X and Motif."

4.1 Logging into the Display Manager

The X program that controls your login procedure is called the *display manager.*

1   **Wake up the display.** Most X terminals are equipped with a *screen saver*, a program that blanks out the screen when it has been idle for a time. Pressing a key or moving the mouse is usually enough to cancel the screen saver.

The display manager will produce a login screen that may look something like Figure 4–1.

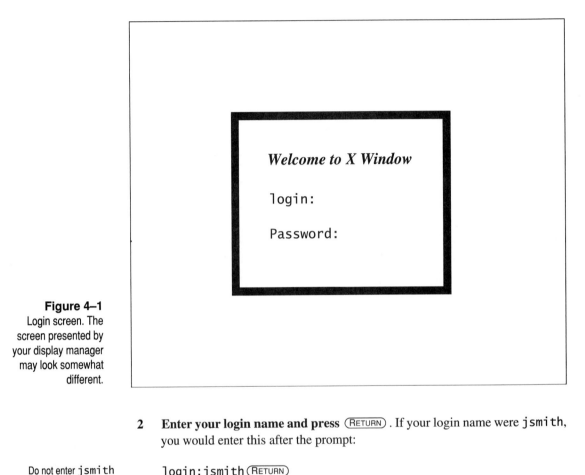

Welcome to X Window

```
login:

Password:
```

Figure 4–1
Login screen. The
screen presented by
your display manager
may look somewhat
different.

2 **Enter your login name and press** (RETURN) . If your login name were jsmith,
you would enter this after the prompt:

Do not enter jsmith
(unless that is your login).
Enter *your* login here.

```
login:jsmith (RETURN)
```

3 **Enter your password and press** (RETURN) .

Enter your password here;
it will not appear on the
screen.

```
password:
```

Note that YOUR PASSWORD DOES NOT APPEAR ON THE SCREEN. The
idea is to prevent others from looking over your shoulder and learning your
password. (You will see how to change the password later.)

4 **If you made an error typing either your login name or password, repeat Steps 2 and 3.** The computer will inform you that your login is incorrect, and it will give you the chance to log in again:

```
Login incorrect
login:
```

Although this says "login incorrect," the same message is given if your password is incorrect.

4.2   Root Window

The root window is also called the *desktop*.

Once you have successfully logged in, it may take the computer a minute or so to start up the Motif window manager (mwm). Eventually, a window should appear, as shown in Figure 4–2. The background is called the *root window*. The smaller window is an xterm window. (You may also see a number of other windows, depending on how your system administrator has configured the window manager.)

Figure 4–2
Root and xterm windows.

4.3 The xterm Window

You will do most of your work in the xterm window. The name xterm is short for "X Terminal," and as the name suggests, the xterm window acts like a conventional terminal screen. Some of the parts of the xterm window are shown in Figure 4–3. (Later in this chapter, you will learn what these do.)

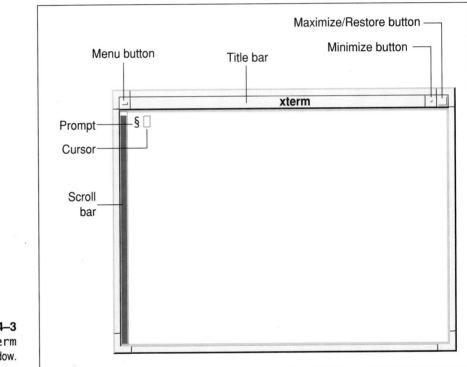

Figure 4–3
Parts of the xterm window.

4.4 Getting Acquainted with the Mouse

If you have previously worked with a personal computer, you are undoubtedly familiar with the use of a mouse with a GUI. As you move the mouse on its pad or the table top, an arrow-shaped pointer also moves on the screen.

Unlike many personal computers—which typically work with a mouse having just one or two buttons—the Motif Window Manager is designed to operate with a three-button mouse (Figure 4–4).

Unfortunately, there is no universally accepted standard that sets the functions of the mouse buttons—each system can be configured according to the administrator's (or user's) personal preferences. The following arrangement is fairly typical:

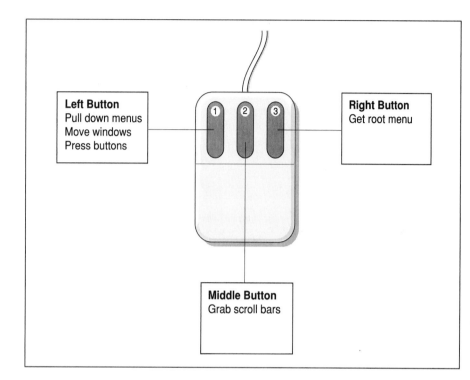

Left Button
Pull down menus
Move windows
Press buttons

Right Button
Get root menu

Middle Button
Grab scroll bars

Figure 4–4
Three-button mouse.
The functions of the
buttons may be differ-
ent on your system.

You may have to
experiment to discover how
the buttons work on your
mouse.

- **Left Button (#1).** The left button is generally used for command selection and activation. This includes pulling down menus, selecting menu items, moving windows, and pressing on-screen buttons.

- **Middle Button (#2).** On some systems, this button is used to grab and manipulate window scroll bars.

- **Right Button (#3).** This button has traditionally been used to obtain pop-up menus.

There are three ways to activate a mouse button:

- *Click.* Press and quickly release the button.

- *Double-click.* Press and release the button twice in rapid succession.

- *Drag.* Press and hold the button while moving the mouse.

4.5 Pulling Down the Window Menu

The window menu provides a number of useful commands for changing the size and position of the window. To see how this menu works—and to practice using the mouse—try resizing the xterm window:

1 **Move the pointer to the window menu button.** This button is found at the upper left corner of the xterm window:

Click here

2 **Click once with the left mouse button.** A menu will appear:

This is called a *pull-down menu* because you pull it down from the window frame.

Menu items in gray cannot be selected

Underlined letter is a shortcut for this command

Restore	Alt+F5
Move	Alt+F7
Size	Alt+F8
Minimize	Alt+F9
Maximize	Alt+F10
Lower	Alt+F3
Close	Alt+F4

Shows an alternate key combination for this choice

3 **Click once on Maximize with the left mouse button.**

Minimize	Alt+F9
Maximize	Alt+F10
Lower	Alt+F3
Close	Alt+F4

The Maximize command makes the xterm window grow to its full size. Note that you could have performed the same action by using either the one-letter command shortcut or the alternate key combination.

4   Click once on Restore with the left mouse button.

The xterm window will return to its previous size. Note once again that you could have performed the same action by using either the one-letter command shortcut or the alternate key combination.

You will learn more about the other window menu options in the next section. For now, you should just close the menu.

4.6   Window Menu Options

Before going on, let's review the meaning of the various options offered on the window menu:

- **Restore.** Returns a window to its original size once it has been maximized.

- **Move.** Allows you to move the window to a different position in the root window. (This option is not often used.)

- **Size.** Allows you to change the size of the window. (This option is not often used.)

Remember, an icon is a small picture or symbol.

- **Minimize.** Converts the window into an icon. (This is sometimes called the "iconify" command.) You can restore the window by double-clicking on the icon.

- **Lower.** Moves current window behind other windows.

- **Close.** This command closes and eliminates the window, usually stopping any program that was running in it. Be careful not to confuse this with the Minimize command, which shrinks the window into an icon. (To confuse matters, on some windowing systems, "Close" does work just like "Minimize.")

4.7   Getting the Pop-Up Menus

Another kind of menu—a "pop-up" menu—appears when you click on the root window. The choices presented by such a menu depend on how the system administrator has configured your system. Take a minute to examine these menus:

1   **Move the pointer to the root window.**

2   **Open a menu using the right button (#3).** Depending on how your system is set up, you may have to hold down the mouse button. (If no menu appears, try another button.) Note what you see on the menu. It might look something like this:

The root menu on your system might look very different from this.

Before going on, be sure that you understand the various options offered on the window menu:

- **New Window.** This option starts another window, usually an `xterm` window.

- **Shuffle up.** Just as you would shuffle a deck of cards, shuffling the windows puts some windows behind others. The shuffle up command takes the top window and places it behind the others in the root window. The second window then becomes the active one.

- **Shuffle down.** This brings the rearmost window forward and places it in front of the others in the root window. This window then becomes the active window.

- **Refresh.** Sometimes the images on the screen get jumbled. Refresh causes the computer to redraw the windows.

- **Restart.** This stops the current `mwm` session and starts another one in its place.

- **Logout.** You would use this command when you want to quit working on the machine. This closes all windows and stops any programs you have running.

3   **Close the menu.** On some systems, you do this by simply releasing the button. Other systems require that you click on the menu's title bar.

4   **Open a menu using the left button.** With the pointer on the root window, press (and if necessary, hold) the left button. Note what you see on the pop-up menu.

5   **Close the menu and open another using the center button.** Note again what you see. On many systems, this menu gives you options for logging into other machines on the network.

4.8   X Utilities

An application is a program that performs some useful function.

In your survey of the various pop-up menus, you may have discovered a menu that allows you to select various X utilities (also called X tools or clients). Some of the more common X utilities are listed below:

xbiff   Informs you when e-mail has arrived

xcalc   Brings up an on-screen calculator

xclock   Starts a clock in its own window

xedit   Starts a simple text editor

xterm   Starts another xterm window

4.9   Starting xterm from the Root Menu

Skip this section if there is no xterm or New Window menu option.

Now that you have seen how to get the root pop-up menus, you are ready to start another xterm window:

1   **Move the pointer to the root window.**

2   **Press and hold the button that brings up the proper menu.** This would be the menu showing an xterm or New Window option.

3   **Without releasing the button, slide the pointer down to the New Window or xterm command.** The command will be highlighted.

4   **Release the button.** Be patient—it may require a few seconds for the window to start up.

Starting one of the other X utilities listed on the menu—such as xcalc, xclock, and so on—is done similarly. (We leave it as an exercise for you to try these.)

4.10 Keyboard Focus

Although you may have multiple `xterm` windows open simultaneously, only one of these windows can receive input from the keyboard at a time. The window that gets the input is said to have the *keyboard focus*; this is sometimes called the *active window*. Most window managers change the color or shading of the frame and/or title bar of the active window to distinguish it from other windows.

There are two ways to select the window that will get the keyboard focus:

- **Point-to-focus method.** On some systems, merely moving the pointer to an `xterm` window changes the focus to that window. (This is also referred to as the *point-to-type method.*)

- **Click-to-focus method.** Some systems require that you point to a window and click the left mouse button. (This is also called the *click-to-type method.*)

Take a moment now to determine which method your system employs.

4.11 UNIX Shell Prompt

If you examine the contents of the `xterm` window, you will see a *shell prompt*, which is simply the shell's way of telling you that it is ready to receive your instructions. If your login shell is the C Shell, the prompt is probably a percent sign:

```
%
```

If you are using the Bourne Shell or the Korn Shell as a login shell, the usual prompt is a dollar sign:

```
$
```

Other symbols are occasionally used for shell prompts, including the pound sign (#), the "greater than" sign (>), the asterisk (*), the "at" symbol (@), and the colon (:). Some systems are set up to include the host name as part of the prompt, like this:

```
merlin %
```

In this book, we will use the following as our "generic" prompt, to take the place of either the percent sign or the dollar sign:

In the examples that follow, do not enter the prompt symbol.

```
§
```

4.12 Starting xterm Using a Command Line

You have already seen how to start a new `xterm` window using a pop-up menu. There is another way to open a new window:

1   **Select one of the** xterm **windows to be the active window.**

2   **Enter the** xterm **command at the shell prompt.** Note the ampersand (&) at the end of the command. This tells the shell to run the command "in the background":

Be sure to include the
ampersand. —————————

§ xterm &(RETURN)

3   **Wait for the new window to start up.**

4.13   Resizing a Window

You can easily change the size or shape of a window by dragging its corner:

1   **Move the pointer to the bottom right corner of the window frame.** The shape of the pointer will change.

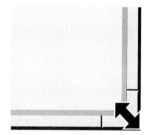

2   **Drag the corner of the window.** You should see an outline of the new window position.

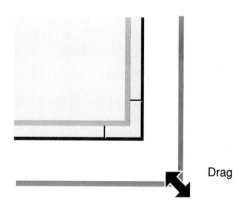

Drag

3 Release the mouse button.

4.14 Moving a Window

Moving an `xterm` window is also very easy:

1 Move the pointer to the window's title bar.

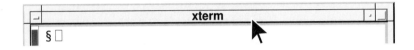

2 Drag the window to the new position. You should see an outline of the new window position.

3 Release the mouse button.

4.15 Minimizing and Restoring a Window

In Motif, Minimize means iconify a window; Close means eliminate the window.

Under the Motif Window Manager, the Minimize command on the Window menu converts the window into an icon. This is sometimes called "iconifying" the window. This operation is not to be confused with the Close command, which eliminates the window entirely. (Not all window managers conform to this usage. If you use a different window manager, you may find that the Close command iconifies the window.)

1 Select one of the `xterm` windows to be the active window.

2 Open the window menu. Remember, this is done by clicking on the window menu button in the upper left-hand corner of the window frame.

3 Select the Minimize option. The window will shrink to an icon.

4 Double-click on the icon. This will restore the window to its previous size.

4.16 Changing Your Password

Review Section 2.3 on selecting a password.

A good password is one that is easy for you to remember but difficult for someone else to figure out. Often the initial passwords assigned by system administrators fail these criteria. It is a good idea to change your password frequently to prevent unauthorized use of your account. If you have not already done so, you should take a minute to think about a password.

1 Select an `xterm` window to be the active window.

2 Enter the `passwd` command at the shell prompt. Note that this is `passwd`, not password:

§ passwd (RETURN)

The system will prompt for your old password:

Old password:

3 **Enter your old password, then press** (RETURN). As usual, your password will not appear on the screen:

Old password:▩▩▩▩▩

The computer will then ask you to enter your new password:

New password:

4 **Enter your new password, then press** (RETURN). As usual, your password will not appear on the screen:

New password:▩▩▩▩▩

To ensure that you have made no mistakes, the computer will ask you to repeat your new password:

Retype new password:

5 **Repeat your new password.** If this is not done exactly as before, the system will not accept the new password, and you will have to start over:

Retype new password:▩▩▩▩▩

You will know that the new password has been accepted when the shell prompt appears:

§

4.17   Trying Out Some UNIX Commands

Next, try a few UNIX commands to see how they work.

1 **Select one of the xterm windows to be the active window.**

2 **Enter the date command.** Type date after the prompt, and press (RETURN):

§ date (RETURN)

The computer will respond with the date and time. For example, if you were to give this command on Monday, August 13, 2001, at 8:35 pm (Mountain Daylight Time), the output would be something like

Mon Aug 13 20:35:41 MDT 2001

Note that this is the time for the host computer's locale, and that time is given on the 24-hour clock.

3   Next, try the who **command.** Type who, followed by (RETURN):

§ who (RETURN)

The computer will respond with a list of the users who are currently logged into the system. For example,

root	console	Aug 13	08:11
aadams	tty16	Aug 13	07:01
pgw	tty03	Aug 13	18:15
ben	tty18	Aug 13	11:32
jeff	tty12	Aug 13	09:45

The user's login name is listed first, followed by a code that identifies the line or *port* to which the user is connected. The date and time that the user logged in are also shown.

4   Try the who am i **command.** This command prints your login name on the screen:

§ who am i (RETURN)

4.18   Reading Your Mail

Skip this section if you have not received e-mail.

If you have received electronic mail, now is the time to read it.

1   Select an xterm **window.**

2   Enter the command to start the mail program. The command depends on whether you are using a UNIX system based on AT&T System V or Berkeley (BSD) UNIX:

AT&T System V:

§ mailx (RETURN)

BSD:

§ Mail (RETURN)

The system will respond with a list of the messages. For example,

```
U  1 wards  Fri Aug 10 15:27  554/26358  "Class Roster"
N  2 aadams Mon Aug 13 8:59   40/1527    "Lunch"
N  3 gwc  Mon Aug 13  9:47   15/440    "Research Notes"
&
```

A *U* in the first column indicates an unread message left over from the last time you logged in; an *N* indicates a new message. The messages are numbered (from 1 to 3 in this case). The login name of the sender is shown, along with the date and time the message was received and the number of lines and characters the message contains (lines/characters). Finally, the subject of the message is given in quotes. The ampersand (&) on the last line is the *mail prompt*.

3   Read your message(s). Simply enter the message number after the mail prompt and press (RETURN) :

&2 (RETURN)

This will cause the second message to appear:

```
Message 2:
From aadams Mon Aug 13 8:59:01 2001
Date: Mon Aug 13 8:59:01
From: aadams (Abigail Adams)
To: (Your login name)
Subject: Lunch

Let's get together for lunch at 12:45 today. Okay?
&
```

4   Leave the mail utility. Typing x (for "exit") at the mail prompt will take you out of the mail utility, leaving the message(s) in the mailbox:

&x (RETURN)

Electronic mail—including the ways to send, save, and delete mail—is discussed in more detail in Part V.

4.19   Reading the UNIX Manual

Many UNIX systems come equipped with a detailed on-line manual that you can read using the man command. The manual describes the commands that are available on the system. To see how this is done, try the following command:

§ man cal (RETURN)

The cal command is one that we will use in later chapters; it displays a calendar on the screen. If your system has the on-line manual, you should see a description of cal. (For more information on how to make sense of the manual, see Appendix B.) Otherwise, you will see the message

man: Command not found.

4.20   Logging Out

When you are finished working on the computer, you must "log out." This tells the system that you are finished using it.

WARNING	NEVER LEAVE THE TERMINAL WITHOUT LOGGING OUT FIRST. On some UNIX systems, your account will remain open even if your terminal is turned off. This invites the unscrupulous to get into the system and cause trouble.

Unfortunately, the process for logging out varies from system to system. (When in doubt, check with your system administrator.)

- **If Logout or Exit appears on the root menu, select this option.** You may have to wait a minute, but eventually the login screen should appear.

- **If you see an icon labeled Logout, double-click on this icon.** This will either log you out or open up another window in which you can log out.

- **If you see a window labeled Logout, double-click on this window.** Wait to see if the login screen appears.

When the login screen appears, the system is ready for the next user.

4.21   Command Summary

Each of the commands listed here is entered in an xterm window at the shell prompt symbol.

Changing Your Password

passwd (RETURN)   change password

Opening an xterm Window

xterm & (RETURN)   start another xterm window

Miscellaneous UNIX Commands

date (RETURN)   print current date and time

who (RETURN)   print a list of users currently logged in

who am i (RETURN)   print your login

man cal (RETURN)   show the manual page describing cal command

4.22   Exercises

1. Be sure you can define the following terms:

display manager	screen saver	desktop
root window	mouse	click
double-click	drag	menu
pull-down menu	maximize	minimize
pop-up menu	root menu	icon
keyboard focus	active window	

2. See if your terminal has a key labeled "NO SCROLL." This key is supposed to "freeze" the terminal display. Press it and type your name. What happens on the screen? Now press the key again. What do you see?

3. On many terminals, the ^S key combination "freezes" the terminal. Try this key combination and type something on the keyboard. What happens? The key combination ^Q "unfreezes" the terminal, reversing the effects of ^S. Try this.

4. Does your keyboard have a key labeled "CAPS LOCK" or "CASE"? If so, press it and type something on the keyboard. What does this key do?

5. UNIX is *case-sensitive:* it distinguishes between upper- and lowercase letters. Try the commands listed below and note what each one does (if anything):

   WHO (RETURN)

   CAL 1999 (RETURN)

   DATE (RETURN)

   WHO AM I (RETURN)

6. The xbiff utility notifies you of the arrival of electronic mail by beeping and raising the flag on a mailbox icon. Try it. If xbiff is not available as a menu option, you can start it by entering the command

   ```
   xbiff &
   ```

7. Experiment with the xcalc client program. If it is not available as a menu option, you can start xcalc with the command

   ```
   xcalc &
   ```

8. Try the xclock client program. If it is not available as a menu option, you can start xclock with the command

   ```
   xclock &
   ```

5 TUTORIAL: GETTING STARTED WITH CDE

Skip this chapter if your system does not run CDE.

In this chapter, you will learn how to begin working with the Common Desktop Environment (CDE). If you haven't done so already, ask your instructor, system administrator, or consultant about setting up an account. You will need the following information:

- Your login name

- Your password

- The name of the computer you will be using

5.1 Logging In

The CDE program that controls your login procedure is `dtlogin`. You do not have to start this program; it should already be running, waiting for you to log in.

1 **Wake up the display.** Most workstations are equipped with a *screen saver*, a program that blanks out the screen when it has been idle for a time. Pressing a key or moving the mouse is usually enough to cancel the screen saver. You should then see a login screen that may look something like Figure 5–1.

Figure 5–1
Login screen. The screen presented by your display manager may look somewhat different.

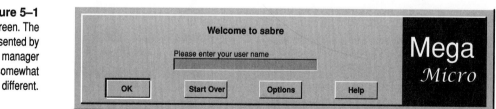

2 **Enter your login name and press** (RETURN). If your login name were `jsmith`, you would enter this in the box. A password screen then appears.

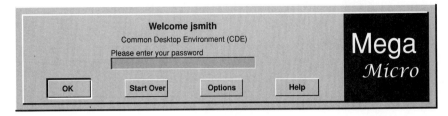

Figure 5–2
Password screen.

3 **Enter your password and press** (RETURN). Note that YOUR PASSWORD DOES NOT APPEAR ON THE SCREEN. The idea is to prevent others from looking over your shoulder and learning your password. (You will see how to change the password later.)

4 **If you made an error typing either your login name or password, repeat Steps 2 and 3.** The computer will inform you that your login is incorrect, and it will give you the chance to log in again:

```
Login incorrect; please try again.
```

Although this says "login incorrect," the same message is given if your password is incorrect.

After you log in, your screen should look something like Figure 5–3. The background is called the *workspace*. Against this background is a `dtterm` or Terminal window and the CDE *Front Panel*. (You may see other windows or objects as well, depending on how your system administrator has set up your system.)

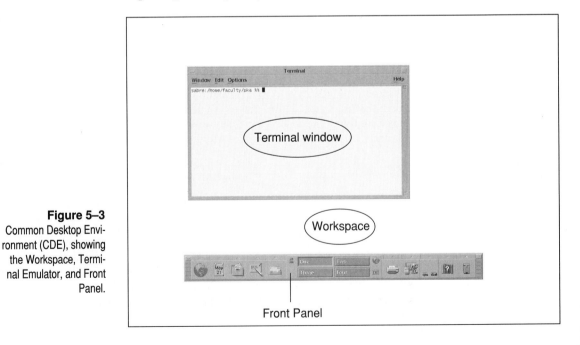

Figure 5–3
Common Desktop Environment (CDE), showing the Workspace, Terminal Emulator, and Front Panel.

See Exercise 2 for information on changing and naming workspaces.

The Common Desktop Environment allows you to switch between four (or more) workspaces. This can be useful if you are working on multiple projects. By reserving a different workspace for each project, you can readily organize the tools and applications you need.

5.2   Getting Acquainted with the Mouse

If you have previously worked with a personal computer having a graphical user interface (GUI), you are undoubtedly familiar with the use of a mouse. As you move the mouse on its pad or the table top, an arrow-shaped pointer also moves on the screen.

Unlike many personal computers—which typically work with a mouse having just one or two buttons—the Desktop Window Manager is designed to operate with a three-button mouse (Figure 5–4).

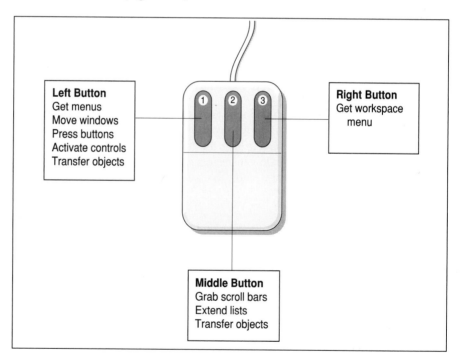

Left Button
Get menus
Move windows
Press buttons
Activate controls
Transfer objects

Right Button
Get workspace
menu

Middle Button
Grab scroll bars
Extend lists
Transfer objects

Figure 5–4
Three-button mouse. The functions of the buttons may be different on your system.

See Exercise 6 for information on changing your mouse's behavior.

There is no universally accepted standard that sets the functions of the mouse buttons—each system can be configured according to the administrator's (or user's) personal preferences. The following arrangement is fairly typical:

You may have to experiment to discover how the buttons work on your mouse.

- **Left Button (#1).** The left button is generally used for command selection and activation. This includes pulling down menus, selecting menu items, moving windows, and pressing on-screen buttons.

- **Middle Button (#2).** This button is typically used to grab and move windows and scroll bars, to extend lists, and to transfer objects.

- **Right Button (#3).** This button is often used to obtain pop-up menus.

There are several ways to activate a mouse button:

- *Click.* Press and quickly release the button. This is done to select a window, icon, or menu option.

- *Double-click.* Press and release the button twice in rapid succession. Double-clicking is done to start certain programs, to restore windows to their original size, and to close windows.

- *Drag.* Press and hold the button while moving the mouse. This action is used to move objects—such as windows and icons—around the desktop.

- *Drop.* Release the button after dragging an object to a new position.

5.3 Keyboard Focus

Although you may have multiple windows open simultaneously, only one of these windows can receive input from the keyboard at a time. The window that gets the input is said to have the *keyboard focus*; this is sometimes called the *active window*. Most window managers change the color or shading of the frame and/or title bar of the active window to distinguish it from other windows.

There are two ways to select the window that will get the keyboard focus:

The CDE Style Manager allows you to change the focussing method—see Exercise 5.

- *Point-to-focus method.* On some systems, merely moving the pointer to a window changes the focus to that window. (This is also referred to as the *point-to-type method*.)

- *Click-to-focus method.* Some systems require that you point to a window and click the left mouse button. (This is also called the *click-to-type method*.)

Take a moment now to determine which method your system employs.

5.4 The Terminal Emulator

You can open additional Terminal windows—see Exercises 7 and 8.

You will do much of your work in this book using the Terminal Emulator, also called `dtterm`. As its name suggests, the Terminal Emulator acts like a conventional terminal screen—in particular, a DEC VT220 terminal. Some of the parts of the Terminal window are shown in Figure 5–5.

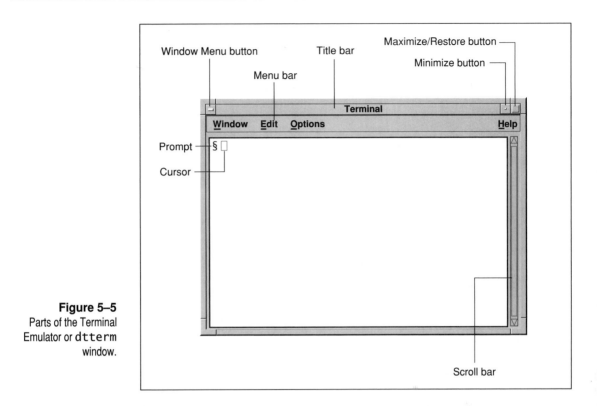

Figure 5–5
Parts of the Terminal
Emulator or `dtterm`
window.

5.5   Pulling Down the Window Menu

The Window Menu provides a number of useful commands for changing the size
and position of the window. To see how this menu works—and to practice using the
mouse—try resizing the Terminal window:

1 **Move the pointer to the Window Menu button.** This button is found at the
upper left corner of the Terminal window:

Click here

2   **Click once with the left mouse button.** A menu will appear:

This is called a *pull-down menu* because you pull it down from the window frame.

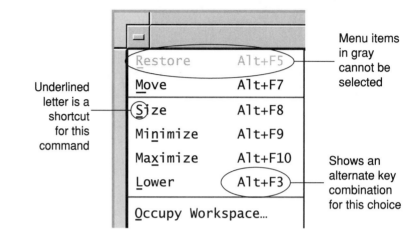

Menu items in gray cannot be selected

Underlined letter is a shortcut for this command

Shows an alternate key combination for this choice

3   **Click once on Maximize with the left mouse button.**

The Maximize command makes the Terminal window grow to its full size. Note that you could have performed the same action by using either the one-letter command shortcut or the alternate key combination.

4   **Click once on Restore with the left mouse button.**

The Terminal window will return to its previous size. Note once again that you could have performed the same action by using either the one-letter command shortcut or the alternate key combination.

You will learn more about the other Window Menu options in the next section. For now, you should just close the menu.

5.6   Window Menu Options

Before going on, let's review the meaning of the various options offered on the Window Menu:

- **Restore.** Returns a window to its original size once it has been minimized or maximized.

- **Move.** Allows you to move the window to a different position in the workspace.

- **Size.** Allows you to change the size of the window.

Remember, an icon is a small picture or symbol.

- **Minimize.** Converts the window into an icon. (This is sometimes called the "iconify" command.) You can restore the window by double-clicking on the icon.

- **Maximize.** Enlarges the window to fill the entire screen.

- **Lower.** Moves current window behind other windows.

- **Occupy workspace.** Puts the window into another workspace.

- **Occupy all workspaces.** Puts the window into all workspaces.

You can also close a window by double-clicking on the Window Menu button.

- **Close.** This command closes and eliminates the window, usually stopping any program that was running in it. Be careful not to confuse this with the Minimize command, which shrinks the window into an icon.

5.7   Resizing a Window

You can easily change the size or shape of a window by dragging its corner:

1   Move the pointer to the bottom right corner of the window frame. The shape of the pointer will change.

2   Drag the corner of the window. You should see an outline of the new window position.

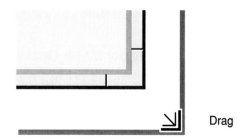

Drag

3   **Release the mouse button.**

5.8   Moving a Window

Moving a Terminal window is also very easy:

1   **Move the pointer to the window's title bar.**

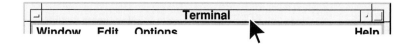

2   **Drag the window to the new position.** You should see an outline of the new window position.

3   **Release the mouse button.**

5.9   Minimizing and Restoring a Window

Minimize means iconify a window; Close means eliminate the window.

The Minimize command on the Window menu converts the window into an icon. This is sometimes called "iconifying" the window. This operation is not to be confused with the Close command, which eliminates the window entirely.

1   **Make the Terminal window active.**

2   **Open the Window menu.** Remember, this is done by clicking on the Window Menu button in the upper left-hand corner of the window frame.

3   **Select the Minimize option.** The window will shrink to an icon. The icon will be placed off to the left edge of the workspace.

4   **Double-click on the icon.** This will restore the window to its previous size.

5.10 UNIX Shell Prompt

If you examine the contents of the `dtterm` window, you will see a *shell prompt*, which is simply the shell's way of telling you that it is ready to receive your instructions. If your login shell is the C Shell, the prompt is probably a percent sign:

%

If you are using the Bourne Shell or the Korn Shell as a login shell, the usual prompt is a dollar sign:

$

Other symbols are occasionally used for shell prompts, including the pound sign (#), the "greater than" sign (>), the asterisk (*), the "at" symbol (@), and the colon (:). Some systems are set up to include the host name as part of the prompt, like this:

`merlin %`

In this book, we will use the following as our "generic" prompt, to take the place of either the percent sign or the dollar sign:

In the examples that follow, do not enter the prompt symbol.

§

5.11 Trying Out Some UNIX Commands

In this section, we will try some traditional UNIX commands to see how they work.

1 **Make the Terminal window active.**

2 **Enter the `date` command.** Type `date` after the prompt, and press (RETURN):

§ `date` (RETURN)

The computer will respond with the date and time. For example, if you were to give this command on Monday, August 13, 2001, at 8:35 pm (Eastern Standard Time), the output would be something like

`Mon  Aug 13  20:35:41  EST  2001`

Note that this is the time for the host computer's locale, and that time is given on the 24-hour clock.

3 **Next, try the `who` command.** Type `who`, followed by (RETURN):

§ `who` (RETURN)

The computer will respond with a list of the users who are currently logged into the system. For example,

root	console	Aug 13	08:11
aadams	tty16	Aug 13	07:01
pgw	tty03	Aug 13	18:15
ben	tty18	Aug 13	11:32
jeff	tty12	Aug 13	09:45

The user's login name is listed first, followed by a code that identifies the line or *port* to which the user is connected. The date and time that the user logged in are also shown.

4   **Try the** who am i **command.** This command prints your login name on the screen:

§ who am i ⬭RETURN⬭

5.12   Changing Your Password

Review Section 2.3 on
selecting a password.

A good password is one that is easy for you to remember but difficult for someone else to figure out. Often the initial passwords assigned by system administrators fail these criteria. It is a good idea to change your password frequently to prevent unauthorized use of your account. If you have not already done so, you should take a minute to think about a password.

1   **Make the Terminal window active.**

2   **Enter the** passwd **command at the shell prompt.** Note that this is passwd, not password:

§ passwd ⬭RETURN⬭

The system will prompt for your old password:

Old password:

3   **Enter your old password, then press** ⬭RETURN⬭. As usual, your password will not appear on the screen:

Old password:▓▓▓▓▓▓▓

The computer will then ask you to enter your new password:

New password:

4   **Enter your new password, then press** ⬭RETURN⬭. As usual, your password will not appear on the screen:

New password:▓▓▓▓▓▓▓

To ensure that you have made no mistakes, the computer will ask you to repeat your new password:

```
Retype new password:
```

5 **Repeat your new password.** If this is not done exactly as before, the system will not accept the new password, and you will have to start over:

```
Retype new password:
```

You will know that the new password has been accepted when the shell prompt appears:

§

5.13 Reading the UNIX Manual

Many UNIX systems come equipped with a detailed on-line manual that you can read using the man command. The manual describes the traditional UNIX commands that are available on the system. To see how this is done, try the following command:

```
§ man cal (RETURN)
```

The cal command is one that we will use in later chapters; it displays a calendar on the screen. If your system has the on-line manual, you should see a description of cal. (For more information on how to make sense of the manual, see Appendix B.) Otherwise, you will see the message

```
man: Command not found.
```

5.14 The Front Panel

The Front Panel provides ready access to the powerful tools offered by the CDE. Figure 5–6 shows the parts of a typical Front Panel. (Because the Front Panel is readily customized, yours may appear somewhat different.)

5.15 Using a Control

The icons on the Front Panel are called *controls*. The behavior of a control depends on how it is used:

- *Click behavior.* Clicking on the icon may launch a software application or open a window. For example, clicking on the Calendar control starts the Calendar application; clicking on the Trash control opens a window showing the contents of the Trash Can.

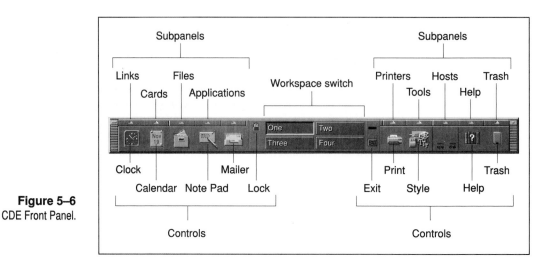

Figure 5–6
CDE Front Panel.

- *Drag-and-drop behavior.* In some cases, an object—such as a file—can be processed in some way by dropping it onto the icon. For example, an appointment file dropped on the Calendar icon will be entered into the appointment calendar; a file dropped on the Trash control will be placed in the Trash Can.

- *Indicator behavior.* Some controls provide information. Thus, the Calendar control displays the current date; the Trash control changes its appearance to show whether the Trash Can is empty or not.

Not all controls exhibit all three kinds of behavior. For instance, you can click on the Exit control to end your current computing session; but there is no drop or indicator behavior associated with the Exit control.

Let's see what happens when you click on the Calendar control:

1   Click on the Calendar icon.

A calendar window will appear.

2   Explore the Calendar. Take some time to figure out how the calendar works. (See if you can change calendar views—daily, weekly, monthly, and yearly.)

3   Close the Calendar window. Double-click on the Window Menu button. (Or pull down the Window menu and select Close.)

5.16   Opening and Closing a Subpanel

A *subpanel* is a menu accessible from the Front Panel that lists additional controls. The following subpanels are typically available:

- **Links.** This subpanel generally provides access to frequently used web applications, such as a browser. The clock application is often put here as well.

- **Cards.** The controls for the Calendar, Address Manager, and other personal productivity applications may be listed here.

- **Files.** Controls for various file- and disk-management tools are listed here.

- **Applications.** Frequently used applications—including the Text Editor and Applications Manager—can be started from this subpanel.

- **Mail.** The Mailer and other electronic mail tools are controlled from this subpanel.

- **Printers.** Controls related to printing are grouped together on this subpanel.

- **Tools.** Controls for frequently used software tools may be placed on this subpanel.

- **Hosts.** The Terminal and Console controls are available on this subpanel.

- **Help.** Various on-line Help viewers are listed here.

- **Trash.** The Trash Can and Empty Trash controls are found on this subpanel.

It is easy to open and close a subpanel:

- **Click the up-button to open.**

The subpanel opens and the up-button becomes a down-button.

- **Click the down-button to close.**

The subpanel closes and the down-button becomes an up-button again.

There are two other ways to close a subpanel. You can double-click on the Window menu button. Or you can click on one of the controls listed on the subpanel, which will activate the control and, at the same time, close the subpanel.

5.17 Tearing Off a Subpanel

You can "tear off" a subpanel and drag it to another location. One advantage of this is that the subpanel will remain open even after you click on one of its controls.

1 Open the subpanel.

2 Grab the top of the subpanel.

3 Drag the subpanel away from the Front Panel.

5.18 Promoting a Control to the Front Panel

You have probably noticed that every control shown on the Front Panel also appears on the underlying subpanel. You can "promote" a frequently used control from the subpanel to the Front Panel:

1 Open the subpanel. Try the Applications subpanel.

2 Move the pointer to the control you want to promote. You will use the Text Editor frequently in later chapters; let's promote it to the Front Panel.

3 Press and hold the #3 mouse button.

Another menu will appear.

4 Select Promote to Front Panel.

5 Release the mouse button.

The subpanel will close and the promoted icon will appear on the Front Panel.

5.19 Adding a Control to a Subpanel

It is easy to add a control to a subpanel:

1 Open and tear-off the Applications subpanel. Remember, tearing-off a subpanel keeps it open.

2 Click on the Applications control.

The Applications Manager window will appear.

3 Double-click on Desktop_Apps. You may have to scroll up or down (or resize the window) to find the Desktop_Apps icon in the Applications Manager window. Double-clicking on this icon opens the Desktop Applications window.

4 Find the Calculator icon.

5 Drag and drop the Calculator on Install Icon in the Applications subpanel.

Install Icon

The calculator control will appear on the subpanel.

5.20 Getting Help

The Common Desktop Environment provides an extensive on-line Help System. Help information is organized in *volumes*, like books in a library. Each of the standard CDE applications has its own Help volumes; other applications may also have volumes in the system. There are several ways to obtain help:

- *Help key.* On most systems, this is the *F1* key. Pressing it provides help that is appropriate for the particular application or window you are using. (This is called *context-sensitive* help.)

- *Help menu.* Most application windows include a pull-down Help menu on the Menu bar. This is usually linked to the help volumes for that application.

- *Help Manager.* Help Manager allows you to examine any volume in the Help System.

Let's use Help Manager to search for a particular topic:

1 Double-click on the Help Manager control. If you do not see the control on the Front Panel, look for it on the Help subpanel.

We leave it as an exercise for you to explore the Top Level Help volume.

The Help Viewer will appear. The viewer is open to the *Top Level Volume*, which provides an overview and introduction to the Common Desktop Environment.

2 Click on the Index... button.

The Index Search dialog box will appear.

3 Select the All Volumes button. Note that you can search the current volume, selected volumes, or the entire Help library.

4 Select the Entries With: button.

5 Enter a topic or keyword in the box. To find information on the Calendar Manager, for example, enter *calendar* in the box.

6   Press Start Search.

Help Manager will list index entries that contain the word *calendar*. A typical item in the list will look like this:

+87   Calendar Help

This means that the requested topic appears 87 times under the index entry for the Calendar. The plus sign (+) indicates that the topics themselves are not shown.

7   Click on the index entry to expand the list.

The plus sign changes to a minus sign (–), and the topics appear under that index entry.

8   Click on a topic to read about it in the Help Viewer.

5.21   Logging Out

When you are finished working on the computer, you must "log out." This tells the system that you are finished using it.

1   On the front Panel, press the Exit control.

2   Wait for the login screen to appear. The system is then ready for the next user.

5.22   Command Summary

Each of the commands listed here is entered in a Terminal window at the shell prompt.

Changing Your Password

passwd (RETURN)   change password

Miscellaneous UNIX Commands

date (RETURN)   print current date and time

who (RETURN)   print a list of users currently logged in

who am i (RETURN)   print your login

man cal (RETURN)   show the manual page describing the cal command

5.23 Exercises

1. Be sure you can define the following terms:

Front Panel	screen saver	desktop
Workspace	mouse	click
double-click	drag	menu
pull-down menu	maximize	minimize
pop-up menu	subpanel	icon
keyboard focus	active window	shell prompt

2. You can change workspaces using the appropriate button in the Workspace switch. (Try it.) By default, the buttons are designated One, Two, Three, and Four. You can give a button a more descriptive name using the Rename option on the button's pop-up menu. (Try it.)

3. The Top Level Help Volume provides a good introduction to the Common Desktop Environment. Use Help Manager to open and read through the Top Level Volume.

4. The CDE Style Manager allows you to change the appearance and behavior of the desktop. For example, you can choose a patterned backdrop for the current workspace, and you can select a color palette for the backdrop, window frames, and other components. Open the Style Manager, click on Backdrop, and try out the various patterns. Then click on Colors and try the available color palettes.

5. Using the CDE Style Manager, you can choose between the point-to-focus method and the click-to-focus method. Try it. Open the Style Manager, click on Keyboard, and select the option you want in the window.

6. The Style Manager allows you to change the behavior of the mouse, including the functions of the buttons. Open the Style Manager, click on Mouse, and select the option(s) you want.

7. The CDE normally opens one Terminal Emulator window when you log in. You can have several Terminal windows running simultaneously. To start a Terminal window, open the Hosts subpanel and click on This Host or Terminal.

8. Another way to start a new Terminal is to enter a command in an existing terminal window. Try it:

   Be sure to include the ampersand. ——————

   § dtterm & (RETURN)

PART II:
UNIX FILE SYSTEM

6 UNIX FILE SYSTEM

A UNIX *file* is a collection of related information—anything from a chocolate cake recipe to a computer program. Ordinary UNIX files are organized into special files called *directories*. The distinction between an ordinary file and a directory file is simple: ordinary files hold information; directories hold ordinary files and other directories. In this chapter, you will learn how the UNIX system keeps track of your files and directories.

6.1 Home and Working Directories

When you first log into your UNIX account, you enter what is known as your *home directory*. This is where you will keep any files or directories that you create. The name of your home directory is the same as your login name.

After you have logged into your home directory, you are free to move to other directories in the system. Whichever directory you happen to be working in at the time is called your *current directory* or *working directory*. When you first log in, your working directory is your home directory.

Each user on the system is given a home directory. On a typical large UNIX system, there may be hundreds of these home directories, each containing scores of other files and directories.

6.2 The UNIX File Tree

Figure 6–1 is a simplified diagram of a typical UNIX system. It looks something like an upside-down tree, with its root at the top. In fact, the directory at the very top, the one that contains all of the other directories, is called the *root*. Various other directories reside inside the root directory:

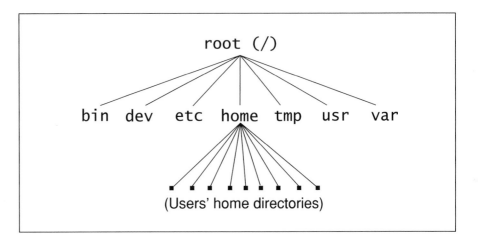

Figure 6–1
Directory structure of a typical UNIX system. Users' home directories are kept in the directory home in this system.

bin   This directory contains the software for the shell and the most commonly used UNIX commands. Although bin is short for "binary," you may want to think of it as a "bin" for holding useful software tools.

dev   The name is short for "devices"; this directory holds the software needed to operate peripheral devices such as terminals and printers.

etc   Various administrative files are kept in this directory, including the list of users that are authorized to use the system, as well as their passwords.

home   Users' home directories are kept here. On some large systems there may be several directories holding user files.

tmp   Temporary files are often kept in this directory.

usr   Some versions of UNIX keep users' home directories in usr; others keep such useful things as the on-line manual pages here.

var   Files containing information that varies frequently are kept in the var directory. An example would be user mailboxes, which are typically found in the /var/mail directory.

Although your particular UNIX system may be set up a bit differently, all UNIX systems have a root directory at the top.

A directory will sometimes be referred to as the "parent" or the "child" of another directory. For example, root is the parent of bin, dev, etc, home, tmp, usr, and var; these directories, in turn, are the children of root. (Child directories are often called *subdirectories*.) Note that every directory except root has exactly one parent, but may have many children.

6.3 File and Directory Names

Every file and directory has a name. The name of your home directory is the same as your login, and you normally cannot rename it. However, you must choose names for any other files and directories you make. UNIX file names may comprise from one to fourteen of the following characters, in any combination:

- Uppercase letters (A to Z)

- Lowercase letters (a to z)

- Numerals (0 to 9)

- Period (.), underscore (_), comma (,)

The file name should not contain spaces or any of the following special characters:

    & * \ | [ ] { } $ < > ( ) # ? ' " / ; ^ ! ~ %

It is a good idea to choose reasonably short names (to save typing) that convey information about the contents of the file. Also, avoid using UNIX command names as file names.

This book follows the convention that ordinary file names are given in lowercase letters, while directory names inside users' home directories are capitalized. This will help you distinguish at a glance directories from ordinary files.

6.4 Absolute Pathnames

To use a file in your current directory, all you need is the file's name. However, if the file is located in another directory, you will need to know the file's *pathname*. A pathname is an address that shows the file's position in the file system.

An absolute pathname shows how to find a file, beginning at the root.

Absolute or *full* pathnames give the location of a file in relation to the top of the file system. The simplest full pathname is for the root directory, which is represented by a slash:

    /

The absolute pathnames for the root's child directories, shown in Figure 6–1, are

/bin	/dev	/etc
/home	/tmp	/usr
/var		

All absolute pathnames begin with a slash.

Note that each of these begins with a slash (/), which tells you that the path starts at the root.

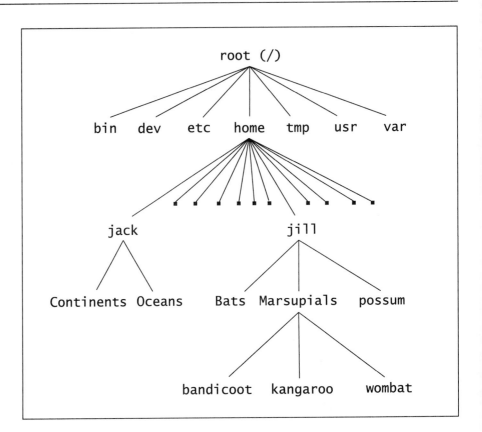

Figure 6–2
The home directories
jack and jill. A
large UNIX system
may contain hundreds
of home directories.

Figure 6–2 shows home and two of the users' home directories it contains (jack and jill). You have already seen that the pathname for home is

/home

The full pathname for the user directory jill is

/home/jill

This is called the pathname of jill because it tells what path to follow to get from the root directory to jill. In this case, the path goes from the root directory, to the directory home, and finally to jill. Continuing further, the subdirectory Marsupials has the absolute pathname

/home/jill/Marsupials

Ordinary files also have absolute pathnames. For example, the pathname of the file wombat is

/home/jill/Marsupials/wombat

This means that wombat may be found by starting at the root, moving down to the directory home, then to the user directory jill, to the directory Marsupials, and finally to the file wombat itself.

You may have noticed that the slash (/) serves two purposes in writing these pathnames. The first slash in the sequence stands for the root; the other slashes serve merely as separators between the file names.

As you can easily imagine by now, full pathnames can become long and unwieldy. There is a shorthand notation that allows you to abbreviate some absolute pathnames. A tilde (~) by itself stands for your home directory's pathname; a tilde preceding a user name stands for that user's home directory. Thus,

~ = absolute pathname of your home directory
~jack = absolute pathname of jack's home directory

6.5 Relative Pathnames

A relative pathname shows how to find a file, beginning at your working directory.

More often than not, you are interested in the position of a file or directory relative to your current working directory. Relative pathnames start from the working directory rather than the root.

When writing out a relative pathname, a single period or dot (.) is the shorthand notation for your current working directory. Similarly, two dots (..) are used to signify the parent of your working directory—the one above it in the directory structure. These are usually called *dot* and *dotdot*. Hence

.   ("dot ") = current working directory
.. ("dotdot") = parent of the working directory

For files in the current directory, the relative pathname is easy: it is simply the name of the file. Suppose you were working in the directory jack shown in Figure 6–2. The relative pathnames of the two directories in jack would be

Continents Oceans

The parent of jack is home. Therefore, the relative pathname of home would be

..

Suppose now that you wanted the relative pathname of the directory that contains home, which is the root directory. From the directory jack this would be

../..

To find the Marsupials directory from the directory jack, you would first move up to home (represented by dotdot), then down to jill, and finally down to Marsupials itself. Putting this altogether, the relative pathname becomes

```
../jill/Marsupials
```

While absolute pathnames always begin with a slash (/), representing the root directory, relative pathnames begin either with dot (.), dotdot (..), or the name of a file or directory in your current working directory.

6.6 Listing Files

You now know how to write absolute pathnames and relative pathnames, but you may reasonably wonder what good this is. To answer that, consider how pathnames may be used with a few UNIX commands. Start with the `ls` ("list") command.

Suppose `jack` is working in his home directory, and he wants to remind himself which files he has in his home directory. He would type the command

§ `ls` (Return)

The response would be

```
Continents  Oceans
```

Now suppose `jack` wants to know what `jill` has in her `Marsupials` directory. From his home directory, he would use the `ls` command with the pathname of `Marsupials`:

§ `ls ../jill/Marsupials` (Return)

The computer's answer would be

```
bandicoot  kangaroo  wombat
```

Thus, without leaving home, `jack` can list files in a distant directory—even a directory belonging to another user—if he knows the directory's pathname.

6.7 Hidden Files and Directories

A *hidden* (or *invisible*) file is one that is not listed when you use the simple `ls` command. A file or directory will be hidden if its name begins with a period. For example,

```
.hidden    .jim    .lost    .profile    .login    .  ..
```

would all be hidden—they would not be listed by the simple `ls` command. To list all of the files in a directory, including the hidden ones, requires the `ls –a` ("list all") command. Suppose, for example, that `jack` is working in his home directory, and he types

§ `ls –a` (Return)

He would see

```
.  ..  Continents  Oceans
```

Similarly, if jack were to use this command with the pathname of jill's Marsupials directory, he would see something like this:

```
§ ls -a ../jill/Marsupials Return
```

```
.  ..  bandicoot  kangaroo  wombat
```

Note that dot (.) and dotdot (..) are both names of hidden directories, and that both appear when jack uses the ls -a command. Remember, dot is just another name for the current directory, while dotdot refers to the parent of the current directory.

6.8   Renaming and Moving Files

The ls command takes one pathname; now consider a command that uses two. The mv ("move") command has the general form

```
mv pathname1 pathname2
```

This can be interpreted to mean "move the file found at pathname1 to the position specified by pathname2." To see how this works, consider how jill might tidy up her home directory using mv.

The file name possum is wrong because the proper name for the animal is "opossum." If jill is still working in her home directory, the pathname of the file possum is just the file name. To change the name of the file without changing its location, she simply uses mv with the new name:

```
§ mv possum opossum Return
```

This tells UNIX "move the contents of possum (in the current directory) into the file opossum (also in the current directory)." Since there is no existing opossum file, one is created, and the old file name disappears.

Next, jill remembers that the opossum is a marsupial, and therefore should be moved to the Marsupials directory. The mv command will do the trick:

```
§ mv opossum Marsupials Return
```

This means "move opossum from the current directory into the Marsupials directory." Thus jill can use the mv command twice, once to rename a file and again to move it to another directory. The end result is shown in Figure 6–3.

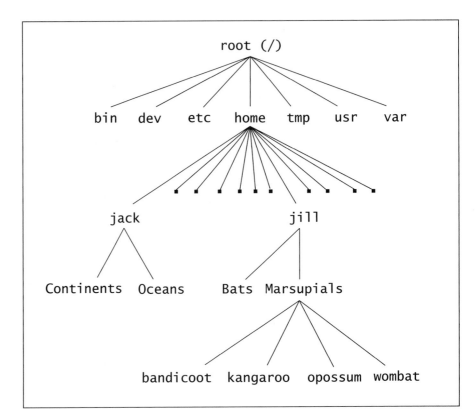

Figure 6–3
The home directory after the file possum was renamed opossum, then moved to the Marsupials directory.

jill could have moved the file and renamed it at the same time using the command

§ mv possum Marsupials/opossum (Return)

This means "move the contents of possum to the Marsupials directory and into a file named opossum."

6.9 Creating a File

There are four common ways to create a UNIX file:

1. Copy an existing file.

2. Redirect the "standard output" from a UNIX utility.

3. Open a new file using a text editor.

4. Write a computer program that opens new files.

Of these, (1) and (2) are considered in this chapter; (3) is covered later in the book.

6.10   Copying Files

The cp ("copy") command has the form

cp pathname1 pathname2

This means "copy the file found at pathname1 and place the copy in the position specified by pathname2." Suppose that jack has developed a sudden interest in wombats and asks jill for a copy of her file on the subject. From her home directory, jill uses the command

§ cp Marsupials/wombat ../jack/Continents ⟨Return⟩

to make a copy of the wombat file and put it in the Continents directory. The result is shown in Figure 6–4.

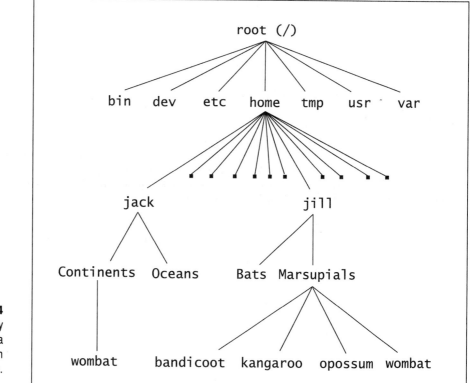

Figure 6–4
The home directory after jill places a copy of wombat in Continents.

6.11 Creating a File by Redirection

Redirection puts the output into a file rather than the terminal screen.

The second method of creating a new file is to redirect the output of a command. In other words, instead of displaying the results of the command on the screen, UNIX puts the results into a file. As an example, consider what happens if jill moves to her Marsupials directory and issues the ls command:

§ ls (Return)

bandicoot kangaroo opossum wombat

Think of the redirection symbol (>) as an arrow pointing to the place where the output should go.

Suppose now that she wants to redirect this list into a file named filelist. She does this using the *output redirection symbol* (>):

§ ls > filelist (Return)

§

Usually, the standard output is the terminal screen, and the standard input is the keyboard.

This time, nothing appears on the screen because the output was rerouted into the file. In UNIX terminology, the information was redirected from the *standard output* (the terminal screen) to the file. If jill lists her files now, she will see that there is a new one named filelist in the directory:

§ ls (Return)

bandicoot filelist kangaroo opossum wombat

Redirection is powerful and convenient, but it can be dangerous. If you redirect the output into a file that already exists, the original contents of the file will be lost. If you want to add something to the end of an existing file without losing the original contents, you can use the *append* operation, which requires two redirection symbols (>>):

The append operation adds the output to the end of the file.

§ ls >> filelist (Return)

§

6.12 Access Privileges

The UNIX operating system is designed to make it easy for users to share files. However, there are times when you do not want others to copy, move, or even examine the contents of your files and directories. You can easily control access to the files in your home directory. To see how this is done, refer to Appendix D, "Access Privileges."

6.13 Exercises

1. What are the rules for naming UNIX files and directories?

2. Which of the following would be valid names for ordinary UNIX files? Explain.

foo	guess?	book.chap1	BOOK.chap2
2good2Btrue	{2bad}	>right>	<left<
name	rank*	serial#	^up^
el_paso	w.lafayette	New York	/slash\
.hideNseek	.357	747	passwd

3. Which of the following would be valid directory names? Explain.

doo_wa	dir1	Dir2	Directory.3
*Hook	|Line|	"Sinker"	Money.$
Game	Set	Match	Sticks
[Groucho]	'Chico'	Harpo.#	Karl?
.hideNseek	.357	747	passwd

Exercises 4 through 11 refer to the hypothetical UNIX file system previously shown in Figure 6–4. (Hint: It may be helpful to sketch the directory structure as you go along.) These exercises should be done in order.

4. What are the absolute pathnames for root, bin, jill, and kangaroo?

5. Suppose that Marsupials is now your working directory. What are the relative pathnames of root, bin, jill, and kangaroo?

6. jack has two subdirectories, Continents and Oceans. (a) What are the absolute pathnames of Continents and Oceans? (b) From Oceans, what are the relative pathnames of root, etc, and bandicoot?

7. Imagine that jack sets up additional subdirectories to hold geographical information. Continents contains Africa, Antarctica, Asia, Australia, Europe, NAmerica, and SAmerica. Each of these directories contains subdirectories for individual countries or regions. For example, NAmerica contains the subdirectories Canada, CentralAm, Mexico, and USA. Assuming every file and directory to be in its proper place, give the absolute pathnames of the directories (a) Norway; (b) India; (c) Egypt; (d) Argentina.

8. Suppose jack's working directory is USA. Show how he could accomplish the following tasks, *using a single command line and relative pathnames in each case*: **(a)** list the contents of the Marsupials directory belonging to jill; **(b)** list the contents of Australia; **(c)** make a copy of jill's file kangaroo, and place it under the name kangaroo in his Australia directory.

9. Repeat the previous problem using absolute pathnames.

10. The directory Canada has twelve subdirectories, one for each of the ten provinces and two territories. Suppose jack's working directory is SAmerica. Show how he could accomplish the following tasks, *using a single command line and relative pathnames in each case*: **(a)** list the contents of BC, the directory for British Columbia, Canada; **(b)** place a copy of the file for Vancouver, British Columbia, in the directory jill.

11. Repeat the previous problem using absolute pathnames.

7 TUTORIAL: WORKING WITH FILES

In this chapter, you will learn how to create, view, copy, rename, and print files. All of your work will take place in your home directory—you'll see how to make subdirectories in the next chapter.

7.1 Printing a Calendar

Many of the examples in this chapter make use of the UNIX utility `cal`, which displays a calendar for any month or any year from AD 1 to AD 9999. To see how this works, try some examples:

1   **Print a calendar for a given month.** For example, to show the calendar for the twelth month of the year 2001, type the command

    § cal 12 2001 ⟨RETURN⟩

The computer will respond with the calendar:

```
   December 2001
 S  M Tu  W Th  F  S
                   1
 2  3  4  5  6  7  8
 9 10 11 12 13 14 15
16 17 18 19 20 21 22
23 24 25 26 27 28 29
30 31
```

2   **Print a calendar for an entire year.** To do this, specify the year but not the month:

    § cal 2001 ⟨RETURN⟩

A calendar for the year 2001 should have appeared on your screen, although it probably scrolled by too fast for you to read it all. Don't worry; in a moment you will see how to save this calendar in a file that you can examine at your leisure.

7.2 Creating a File by Redirection

Many UNIX commands such as the `cal` command print their output on the standard output, which is usually the computer screen. However, the UNIX shell allows you to redirect the output from one of these commands so that it goes to a file instead of the screen.

The rules for naming UNIX files are given in Section 6.3.

1 **Select a name for the file.** Remember to use relatively short, descriptive file names. An appropriate name for a file holding the calendar for the year 2001 might be 2001.

2 **Enter the `cal` command, followed by the redirection operator (>) and the file name.** To put the calendar for the year 2001 into the file 2001, type

Think of > as an arrow pointing where the output will go.

§ `cal 2001 > 2001` (RETURN)

This time, the calendar does not appear on the screen; instead, the standard output from `cal` has been redirected into the file 2001.

The UNIX shell does not tell you when it has successfully created a file by redirection.

3 **List the file names in your current working directory.** How do you know if the new file was created? You can check this by listing the files in your working directory using the `ls` command:

§ `ls` (RETURN)

The name of the new file should appear:

2001

WARNING	Since there was no file named 2001 in your home directory, the redirection operation created one. However, if you already had a file named 2001, the new information would have replaced anything previously in the file.

7.3 Viewing a File with cat

Catenate means "join together," which is one of the functions of `cat`.

Suppose you want to see the *contents* of a file, not just its name. One way to do this is by the use of the `cat` ("catenate") command.

• **Type `cat`, followed by the file name.** Thus, to look at the 2001 file, type

§ `cat 2001` (RETURN)

This displays the file, but it scrolls by so fast that the first few lines cannot be read. Fortunately, UNIX provides a more convenient means of viewing files.

7.4 Viewing with more

The more command allows you to display a file, one screen at a time.

1 **Enter the more command and the file name.** To view the file 2001, type the command line

§ more 2001 (RETURN)

This will display as much of the file as will fit on the screen at one time. If the entire file does not fit, a message will appear in the lower corner of the screen, telling you that more remains to be seen:

--More--

2 **To see more of the file, press the space bar.** This will show you the next screenful.

3 **To exit without viewing the entire file, type q or Q (for quit).** It is not necessary to press (RETURN):

q

You will know that you are out of the more program when you see the UNIX shell prompt:

§

7.5 Viewing with pg

Many UNIX systems offer the pg ("page") command as an alternative to more.

1 **Enter the pg command and the file name.** To view the file 2001, type the command line

§ pg 2001 (RETURN)

This will display as much of the file as will fit on the screen at one time. If the entire file does not fit, a colon (:) appears at the bottom of the screen to indicate that more of the file remains to be seen.

:

2 **To see more, press** (RETURN). This will show you the next screenful of the file.

3 **To exit without viewing the whole file, type q or Q (for quit).** It is not necessary to press (RETURN):

q

You will know that you are out of the pg program when you see the UNIX shell prompt:

§

7.6 Chaining Files Together with cat

You previously used the cat command to view the contents of a file. When given a single file name, cat simply displays the contents of that file; when two or more file names are used together, cat displays all of the files, one after another. This can be used to join together the contents of multiple files.

Your next task is to use cat to make a calendar for the summer months of 2001. First, use the cal utility to make three files:

§ cal 6 2001 > jun.2001 ⦅RETURN⦆
§ cal 7 2001 > jul.2001 ⦅RETURN⦆
§ cal 8 2001 > aug.2001 ⦅RETURN⦆

1 **View the files with** cat. Enter the cat command followed by the file names:

§ cat jun.2001 jul.2001 aug.2001 ⦅RETURN⦆

The contents of the files will be displayed, one right after another:

```
      June 2001
 S  M Tu  W Th  F  S
                1  2
 3  4  5  6  7  8  9
10 11 12 13 14 15 16
17 18 19 20 21 22 23
24 25 26 27 28 29 30
      July 2001
 S  M Tu  W Th  F  S
 1  2  3  4  5  6  7
 8  9 10 11 12 13 14
15 16 17 18 19 20 21
22 23 24 25 26 27 28
29 30 31
     August 2001
 S  M Tu  W Th  F  S
          1  2  3  4
 5  6  7  8  9 10 11
12 13 14 15 16 17 18
19 20 21 22 23 24 25
26 27 28 29 30 31
```

2 **Use cat again, but redirect the output into another file.** For example, to create a file named summer.2001, enter the command

§ cat jun.2001 jul.2001 aug.2001 > summer.2001 (RETURN)

This creates a new file containing a three-month calendar. Note that the redirection operator is required here.

3 **List the files.** The new file should appear:

§ ls (RETURN)

2001 aug.2001 jul.2001 jun.2001 summer.2001

7.7 Appending to a File

The UNIX shell allows you to add information to the end of an existing file, an operation called *appending*.

- **Type the command, the append operator, and the name of the file.** To append the calendar for September 2001 to the file summer.2001, type the following line, making sure to use the append symbol (>>):

§ cal 9 2001 >> summer.2001 (RETURN)

Had you used the regular redirection symbol (>), the calendar for September would have replaced the calendars for June, July, and August that were already in the file. Instead, the September calendar was added to the end of the summer.2001 file.

7.8 Copying a File with cp

The cp ("copy") command is used to copy files. We will use it to make a copy of the file summer.2001.

1 **Think of a name for the copy.** The usual rules for naming UNIX files apply. An appropriate name for a file containing a calendar for the summer of 2001 might be SUMM.2001.

2 **Enter the cp command, followed by the names of the original file and the copy.** To make a copy of summer.2001 named SUMM.2001, type

§ cp summer.2001 SUMM.2001 (RETURN)

This means "copy summer.2001 into SUMM.2001."

In this case, there is no existing file with the name SUMM.2001, so one is created.

3 **Verify that the new file appears.** UNIX does not alert you that a file has been copied, so you will have to check this yourself using the ls command:

§ ls (RETURN)

The computer will list all of the files in the current directory, including the new file:

```
2001  SUMM.2001  aug.2001  jul.2001  jun.2001  summer.2001
```

There is just one small problem with this example: the convention in this book is to use lowercase letters for file names, and to capitalize directory names. (You don't have to do this, but it helps distinguish files from directories.) SUMM.2001 is an ordinary file, not a directory, so in the next section you will give it a different name.

7.9 Renaming a File with mv

The mv ("move") command is used for renaming files. (It is also used for moving files to other directories, as you will see in the next chapter.)

1 Choose a new name for the file. As usual, you should choose names that are short and descriptive. An appropriate name for a file containing a calendar for the summer of 2001 might be vacation.2001.

2 Enter the mv command, followed by the old name and the new name. To rename SUMM.2001 as vacation.2001, type the command line

§ mv SUMM.2001 vacation.2001 (RETURN)

3 Verify that the new file name appears in the directory. Because UNIX does not tell you that the file has been renamed, you will have to check this yourself using the ls command:

§ ls (RETURN)

The computer will list all of the files in the current directory:

```
2001 aug.2001 jul.2001 jun.2001 summer.2001 vacation.2001
```

The difference between cp (copy) and mv (move) is that cp creates a new file, leaving the old file intact, while mv simply renames the old file.

7.10 Printing on the Default Printer

Frequently, you are likely to require hardcopy output from your files. How you produce this depends on the number and type of printers available to you, as well as the type of UNIX you are using.

• Enter the simple line printer command, followed by the file name. If you are using Berkeley UNIX, enter the lpr ("line printer") command:

§ lpr 2001 (RETURN)

On AT&T UNIX, enter the lp command:

§ lp 2001 (RETURN)

7.11 Printing on Other Printers

If your computer system has more than one printer attached to it, the simple line printer command used in the previous section will send your files to the default printer. You can specify another printer with the –P or –d option. To do this, you first have to know the code for the printer you are to use; ask your instructor, consultant, or system administrator.

• **Enter the line printer command and specify the printer and the file to be printed.** On Berkeley UNIX you would type the following command, making sure to insert the proper printer code in place of *code*:

§ lpr -P*code* 2001 (RETURN)

Note that there is a space before the –P and before the file name, but not between the –P and the printer code.

On AT&T UNIX, you would type the following command, inserting the printer code in place of *code*:

§ lp -d*code* 2001 (RETURN)

Here again, there is a space before –d and before the file name, but not between the –d and the printer code.

7.12 Removing Unneeded Files

When a file is no longer useful, you should remove it so that it won't take up valuable storage space. This is done with the rm ("remove") command, which takes the pathname of the file to be removed. Since you probably don't need two copies of the summer 2001 calendar, remove one of them.

1   **Use the ls command to check the file name.** Since on many systems you cannot retrieve a file once it has been removed, it is a good idea to be sure of the file name:

§ ls (RETURN)

2001 aug.2001 jul.2001 jun.2001 summer.2001 vacation.2001

2   **Type rm, followed by the file's pathname.** To remove vacation.2001, type the command line

§ rm vacation.2001 (RETURN)

3   **Verify that the file is gone.** UNIX does not tell you that the file has been removed, so you will have to check this yourself using the ls command:

§ ls (RETURN)

2001 aug.2001 jul.2001 jun.2001 summer.2001

7.13   Command Summary

Each command is typed in after the UNIX shell prompt, and each is terminated by a (RETURN). Note that file, file1, and file2 may be simple file names or pathnames.

Making Calendars

cal m year	show a calendar for the mth month of year
cal year	show a calendar for year
cal year > file	redirect calendar for year into file
cal year >> file	append calendar for year to file

Listing and Viewing Files

ls	list files in working directory
cat file	show contents of file all at once
more file	show contents of file one screen at a time; press space-bar to continue or q to quit
pg file	Like more. Press (RETURN) to see next screen, q to quit

Printing Files

lpr file	send file to default line printer (BSD UNIX)
lp file	send file to default line printer (AT&T UNIX)
lpr -Pcode file	send file to printer designated by code (BSD)
lp -dcode file	send file to printer designated by code (AT&T)

Copying, Renaming, and Removing Files

cp file1 file2	copy file1 into file2; retain both copies of the file
mv file1 file2	move (i.e., rename) file1 to file2; retain only file2
rm file	remove (i.e., delete) file

7.14   Exercises

1. What are the rules for selecting UNIX file names?

2. Because of the need to make certain adjustments to the calendar, the month of September 1752 was a very unusual one. What was different about it?

3. The echo command takes a line that you type in and repeats it back on the screen. Thus if you type

    echo This is fun! (RETURN)

    The computer will respond with

    This is fun!

    Redirect this phrase into a file named fun.

4. Using the commands who, who am i, and date, append to the fun file (see Exercise 3 above) a list of the users currently logged onto the computer, your login, and the current date.

5. A hidden file has a name that begins with a period (.). Use the cal utility and the redirection operator (>) to create a file named .hidden, then use ls to list your files. Do you see the .hidden file? Now try the ls -a command. Does .hidden appear? What other hidden file entries do you see?

6. Many UNIX systems offer a utility named file, which classifies files according to their contents. The utility examines the file and tries to determine what kind of information it may contain. Some of the classifications used by file are

ascii text	c program text	commands
data	directory	empty
English text	executable	

    Try out the file command on the files and directories in your system. Does file always classify files correctly?

8 TUTORIAL: WORKING WITH DIRECTORIES

A directory is a file that contains other files and directories. In this chapter, you will see how to create directories, move files between directories, rename files, and delete directories you no longer need.

8.1 Your Directory Structure Thus Far

If you have carefully followed the examples in the text and worked through all of the end-of-chapter exercises, your file system should resemble the structure shown in Figure 8–1. At this point, your home directory contains no subdirectories. You are now ready to create new subdirectories inside your home directory.

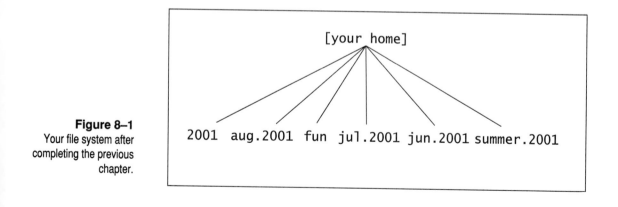

Figure 8–1
Your file system after completing the previous chapter.

8.2 Creating a Subdirectory

It's time to make a directory to hold the calendars you made in the previous chapter. For this we use the mkdir ("make directory") command.

Note that the directory name Cal differs from the cal command—remember, UNIX is case-sensitive.

1 **Select an appropriate name for the new directory.** The rules for naming directories are the same as for files. (However, in this book we will capitalize the names of any new directories we create to distinguish them from ordinary files.) A descriptive name for a directory to hold calendars would be Cal.

2 **Enter mkdir followed by the new directory name.** Remember to capitalize the directory name:

§ mkdir Cal (RETURN)

3 **Use the ls command to see that the new directory exists:**

§ ls (RETURN)

The new directory name should appear, along with the names of the files you made before:

2001 Cal aug.2001 fun jul.2001 jun.2001 summer.2001

(If you have been following the examples in the text, your file system should resemble Figure 8–2.)

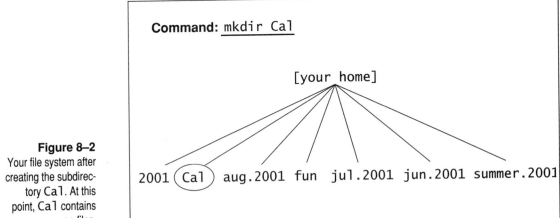

Figure 8–2
Your file system after creating the subdirectory Cal. At this point, Cal contains no files.

Command: mkdir Cal

[your home]

2001 (Cal) aug.2001 fun jul.2001 jun.2001 summer.2001

8.3   Moving Files between Directories

Recall that you used mv before to rename a file.

When a new subdirectory is first created, it contains no files. In this section, you will see how to move a file to a new subdirectory using the mv ("move") command, which you previously used to rename files.

1   **Type the mv command, the file's name, and the destination directory's name.** To put 2001 into the directory Cal, enter the command line

§ mv 2001 Cal (RETURN)

This puts 2001 inside Cal (see Figure 8–3).

2   **List the files in your home directory.** Check to see that 2001 has indeed been moved:

§ ls (RETURN)

The 2001 file will not appear because it is now inside the Cal subdirectory:

Cal aug.2001 fun jul.2001 jun.2001 summer.2001

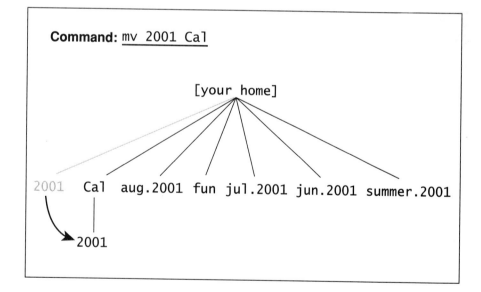

Figure 8–3
Moving the file 2001 into Cal.

8.4   Creating Directories Using Pathnames

Your next task is to create a subdirectory inside Cal to hold monthly calendars. A good, descriptive name for this directory is Months. Since this is to go inside Cal, the pathname of the new directory relative to your home directory will be Cal/Months.

•   **Enter the mkdir command, followed by the pathname of the new directory.**
Thus, to create a directory Months inside the directory Cal, type

§ mkdir Cal/Months (RETURN)

Remember to capitalize Months to emphasize that it is a directory name.

With the creation of Months, your directory structure should resemble the one shown in Figure 8–4.

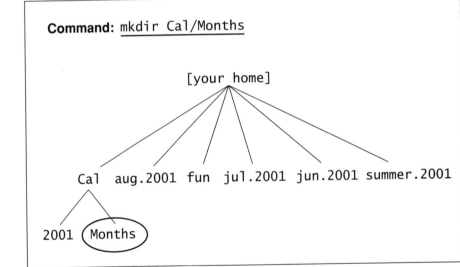

Command: mkdir Cal/Months

[your home]

Cal   aug.2001   fun   jul.2001   jun.2001   summer.2001

2001   Months

Figure 8–4
Directory structure after creation of the subdirectory Months.

8.5 Using Pathnames to Move Files

In this section, you will move a file into the Months directory, using a pathname to specify the file's new location.

1 **Enter the** mv **command, the file name, and the new pathname.** Thus, to move the file jun.2001 into Months, type

§ mv jun.2001 Cal/Months (RETURN)

At this point, your directory structure should look something like Figure 8–5.

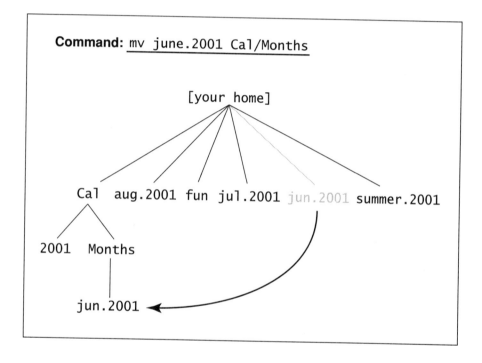

Figure 8–5
Directory structure after moving jun.2001 into the subdirectory Months.

2 **List the files in the current directory.** The ls command should show that jun.2001 is no longer in the current directory:

§ ls (RETURN)
Cal aug.2001 fun jul.2001 summer.2001

8.6   Using Pathnames to Move and Rename Files

In this section, you will move a file and rename it with one command, using a pathname to specify both the file's new location and its new name.

- **Enter the mv command, the file name, and the new pathname.** To move the file aug.2001 into Months, and rename it 08.2001, type

  § mv aug.2001 Cal/Months/08.2001 (RETURN)

  The result of this operation is shown in Figure 8–6.

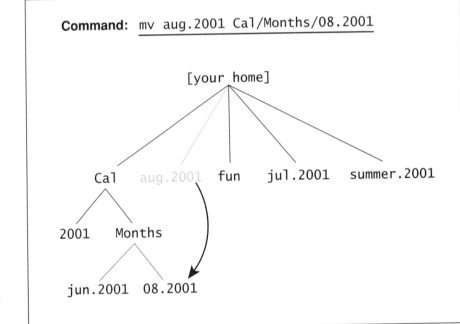

Figure 8–6
Moving and renaming
aug.2001.

8.7   Working in a Distant Directory

As you have seen, the simple ls command only lists files and directories in the current working directory. To list files in another directory, you must give ls that directory's pathname. As you will see in this section, you can work with the files in the directory Months without leaving your home directory.

1   **Enter the list command, followed by the pathname of the directory you wish to examine.** Thus, to see the contents of Months, type:

§ ls Cal/Months (RETURN)

You should see

08.2001   jun.2001

2   Enter the cat command, followed by the pathname of the file you want to view. You can view the contents of the file 08.2001 from your home directory using the cat command with the appropriate pathname:

§ cat Cal/Months/08.2001 (RETURN)

The contents of 08.2001 will appear on the screen:

```
    August 2001
 S  M Tu  W Th  F  S
             1  2  3  4
 5  6  7  8  9 10 11
12 13 14 15 16 17 18
19 20 21 22 23 24 25
26 27 28 29 30 31
```

8.8   Changing Your Working Directory

You can change your current working directory using the cd ("change directory") command with the pathname of the target directory.

•   **Enter the cd command followed by the pathname of the target directory.** Thus, to move to the subdirectory Months, type

§ cd Cal/Months (RETURN)

This makes Months your working directory.

8.9   Returning to Your Home Directory

To return to your home directory, you *could* use cd with either the absolute or the relative pathname of your home directory. However, there is a much easier way.

•   **Enter the cd command without a pathname.** This will always get you back to your home directory, regardless of where you are in the file structure:

§ cd (RETURN)

8.10   Printing Your Working Directory

As you might imagine, it is easy to get lost among the hundreds of directories in a large UNIX system. The pwd ("print working directory") command always displays the absolute pathname of your current working directory.

- **Type pwd.** This will print your location relative to the root:

    § pwd (RETURN)

8.11   Removing Directories

A directory that is no longer needed may be removed using the `rmdir` ("remove directory") command. You cannot remove a directory unless it is first emptied of files and other directories. This is a safety feature, intended to prevent you from accidentally throwing away files that you meant to keep.

1 **Enter the `rmdir` command, followed by the pathname of the directory.** To remove the subdirectory `Cal`, type

    § rmdir Cal (RETURN)

   If the directory contains files, the shell will respond with a message such as

    `rmdir: Cal: Directory not empty`

2 **If necessary, use `rm` to remove any files in the directory.** Then repeat step 1. Because you will need the `Cal` directory to complete the exercises, do not remove it yet.

8.12   Command Summary

Each of these commands is typed in after the UNIX prompt, and each is terminated by a (RETURN). `Dir` and `file` represent the pathnames of a directory and a file, respectively.

mkdir Dir	make a directory having the pathname Dir
mv file Dir	move file into the directory Dir
cd Dir	change to directory having the pathname Dir
cd	change to home directory
rmdir Dir	remove (i.e., delete) the directory Dir
pwd	print working directory's pathname

8.13   Exercises

1. What are the rules for naming UNIX directories?

2. What is the absolute pathname of your home directory?

3. Create a new directory `Misc` and move the file `fun` inside this new directory.

4. Without leaving your home directory, create a directory named `Vacations` inside `Cal`. Then move `summer.2001` into this new directory.

5. Prepare a sketch of your directory structure after completing Exercises 2 through 4 above.

9 TUTORIAL: USING FILE MANAGER

Skip this chapter if your system does not have CDE.

In previous chapters, you have seen how to use traditional UNIX utilities for working with files and directories. File Manager provides alternative file-processing tools that take full advantage of the CDE graphical user interface.

9.1 Your File Structure Thus Far

If you have followed the examples and worked through all of the end-of-chapter exercises in the previous two chapters, your file system should resemble that shown in Figure 9–1.

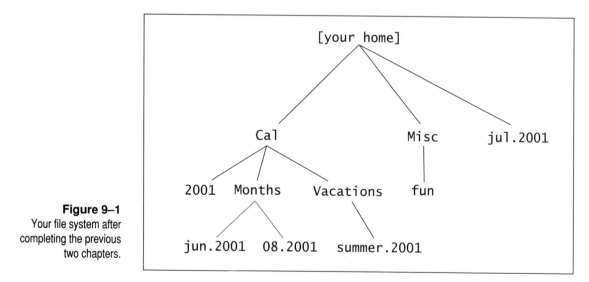

Figure 9–1
Your file system after completing the previous two chapters.

In this chapter, you will use File Manager to do the following:

In CDE, directories are called *folders.*

- Create a new folder (directory) named Years.

- Move the file 2000 into the folder Years.

- Move the file jul.2001 to the Months folder.

- Print the file jun.2001 on your default printer.

- Change the name of the file 08.2001 to aug.2001.

- Delete the file fun and the folder Misc.

9.2 Starting File Manager

Start the File Manager:

- **Click on the File Manager control.** This is usually located on the Front Panel:

If the control is not visible on the Front Panel, look for it on the File subpanel.

The File Manager window (Figure 9–2) will open on your home folder.

Note the various parts of the window:

- *Window Menu button, Minimize button, and Maximize/Restore button.* These perform the usual functions on the window.

- *Menu bar.* Note in particular the menu labeled Selected—it lists actions that can be performed on a selected file or folder.

- *Iconic path.* The pathname of the current folder (in this example, the home folder for jsmith) is depicted graphically as a row of folder icons:

/   home   jsmith

- *Status line.* Here, the current folder's path is shown using traditional UNIX notation:

/home/jsmith

- *View area.* Also called the Object Viewing area, this is where the contents of the folder are shown. (More about this later.)

- *Message line.* This gives the total number of objects (files and folders) and the number of hidden objects contained in the current folder.

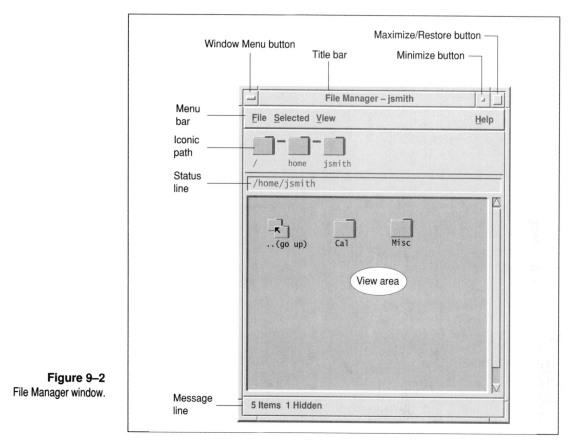

Figure 9–2
File Manager window.

In general, three types of objects may appear in the File Manager's View area:

- **Action icons.** An action icon, also known as an *application icon*, represents a software tool, application, or command. Double-clicking or dropping a file on an action icon will launch the tool, application, or command.

- **File icons.** These icons represent ordinary files. A distinctive icon is used to indicate the type or format of the data in the file. Thus, a different icon will be used for a text file than for a spreadsheet file.

- **Folder icons.** A folder is simply a directory—that is, a file that can contain other files, directories, and action icons.

9.3 Changing Your Working Folder

There are several ways to move through the folder tree:

- **To move to a subfolder, double-click on its icon.** For example, double-clicking on Cal will put you into that folder:

Cal

- **To move to the parent folder, double-click on the .. (go up) icon.** The icon looks like this:

..(go up)

- **Go to any folder in the current path by double-clicking on its icon.** Remember, the current path is shown iconically below the Menu bar:

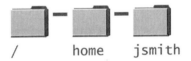

/   home   jsmith

- **To go home, open the File menu and choose the Go Home option.**

Take a moment to try out each of these options.

9.4 Displaying a Pop-up Menu

A pop-up menu is associated with each object (file icon, folder icon, or action icon) in File Manager. This menu provides information on the object's properties, and it allows you to perform various operations on the object. Let's get the pop-up menu for the file jun.2001:

1   **If necessary, move to the folder containing the object.** We want the file jun.2001, which is contained in the Months folder inside the Cal folder.

2   **Point to the object's icon.** Move the pointer to the jun.2001 icon.

3   **Click with the right (#3) mouse button.**

The pop-up menu will appear:

```
┌─────────────────────────┐
│       jun.2001          │
├─────────────────────────┤
│ Properties...           │
│ Put in Workspace        │
│ Put in Trash            │
│ Help                    │
├─────────────────────────┤
│ Open                    │
│ Print                   │
└─────────────────────────┘
```

Note that the file name is listed at the top of the menu. Below this is a list of options:

- **Properties.** This option allows you to find out useful information about a file or folder: who owns it; how large it is; when it was created; when it was last modified; and who has permission to read, write, and execute it.

You can also drag the file to the Workspace.

- **Put in Workspace.** If you select this option, a copy of the object's icon will be placed on the Workspace backdrop. In effect, this gives the object two icons, one in the original folder, the other on the backdrop.

- **Put in Trash.** As you might expect, this option moves the file to the Trash Can. (More about this later.)

- **Help.** This tells you the data type of the file.

The next section of the menu is a list of the actions you can perform on the object. The first item in the list is always the *default action*, which is what occurs when you double-click on the object's icon:

- **Open.** If the object is a folder, this action causes the contents of the folder to appear in the File Manager window. If the object is a file, this typically starts up the application program that created the file, then loads the contents of the file.

- **Print.** This action prints a hard copy of the file on the default printer.

Always keep in mind that any option on the pop-up menu is also available on the Selected menu.

9.5   Printing a File

There are several ways to print a file on the default printer. The simplest is to use the Printer control on the Front Panel:

1   **Drag and drop the file on the Printer control.** The control should be visible on the Front Panel.

The Print dialog box will appear.

2   **Specify the print options.** You can change printers (the default printer is listed), request more than one copy, have page numbers printed, and so on.

3   **Select Print.**

You can also print from the file's pop-up menu:

1   **Open the pop-up menu.** Point to the file icon and press the right (#3) mouse button.

2   **Select Print.**

The Print dialog box will appear, as before.

3   **Specify the print options and select Print.**

Finally, you can print from File Manager's Selected menu:

1   **Select the file to be printed.** Click on the file icon.

2   **Open the Selected menu.** This menu is located on the File Manager menu bar.

3   **Select Print.**

The Print dialog box will appear, as before.

4   **Specify the print options and select Print.**

Try each of these methods to print the file `jun.2001` on the default printer.

9.6   Creating a New Folder

Let's create a new folder in the `Cal` folder:

1   **Move to the parent folder.** The parent folder in this case is `Cal`.

2   **Pull down the File menu and choose New Folder.**

A dialog box will appear.

The rules for naming files and directories are summarized in Section 6.3.

3   **Type a new name into the New Folder field.** Since the new folder will hold yearly calendars, an appropriate name would be `Years`.

4   **Click OK or press** (Return).

The new folder will appear in the View area.

9.7   Moving or Copying to a Nearby Folder

You can move a file from one folder to another simply by dragging and dropping. For this to work, however, you must be able to see both icons—the icon for the file and the icon for the destination folder—in the same File Manager window. For example, let's move the file 2001 into the folder Years, both of which are contained in Cal:

1   **Obtain a File Manager view showing the file and the folder.** In this case, you need to be in the Cal folder.

2   **Drag and drop the file onto the destination folder.** Drag the file 2001 and drop it on the folder Years.

You can also use the Move to... option on the Selected menu.

If you hold down the (Control) key while dragging and dropping, the file will be *copied* to the new location instead of merely being moved.

You can also copy using the Copy To... option on Selected menu.

9.8   Moving or Copying to a Distant Folder

The method used in the previous section for moving a file works only if the file and the destination folder are visible in the File Manager at the same time. This is true if both have the same parent folder. Otherwise, you must open a second File Manager window:

1   **Go to the folder containing the file.** We are going to move the file jul.2001, which should be located in your home folder.

2   **Open a second File Manager window.** We want to put the file in the folder Months, which cannot be seen from your home folder; for this, another File Manager window is needed. Double-click on the File Manager control.

A new File Manager window will appear, showing your home folder.

3   **Make the destination folder visible in the second File Manager window.** By moving down to the Cal folder, you should be able to see the Months folder.

4   **Drag and drop the file onto the destination folder.**

As before, holding down the (Control) key while dragging and dropping causes the file to be *copied* to the new location.

As we shall see in the next section, a folder (including any files or folders it contains) can be moved or copied the same way as a file.

9.9　Deleting an Object

Our next task is to delete the Misc folder and its contents. You can delete an object by putting it in the Trash Can. The easiest way to do this is by dragging and dropping:

You can also use the Put in Trash option on the pop-up or Selected menu.

• **Drag and drop the object on the Trash Can.** To remove the folder Misc, drag and drop it on the Trash Can control.

  Note that the Trash Can changes shape to indicate that it is no longer empty.

An object placed in the Trash Can is not deleted immediately, but remains there until it is either retrieved or shredded. You can retrieve an object by dragging it out of the Trash Can; on some systems, shredding occurs automatically when you log out. If you do not want to wait until then, you can shred the trash yourself:

1　**Double-click on the Trash Can icon.** This opens a view of the objects in the trash.

2　**Select the object(s) to be shredded.** To select several objects, drag the pointer across them, or hold down the ⟨Control⟩ key while you click on the icons individually. To select all of the objects in the Trash Can, pull down the File menu and choose Select All.

To shred all objects in the Trash can, you can open the Trash subpanel and double-click on the Empty Trash control.

3　**Select Shred.** This option is available on the File menu and the object's pop-up menu; either may be used.

  A dialog box will appear, asking you to confirm whether you really want to shred the trash. Keep in mind that on many systems, a shredded object cannot be recovered.

4　**Click OK.** The selected objects will be shredded and removed from the Trash Can.

5　**Close the Trash Can window.**

9.10　Renaming an Object

You can also use the Rename option on the Selected menu.

If you have been carefully following the examples and exercises thus far, you should have a folder named Months that contains three files: 08.2001, jul.2001, and jun.2001. A better name for the first file would be aug.2001. Let's rename the file:

1　**If necessary, select a File Manager window to be active.**

2　**Go to the folder containing the file.** Move to the folder Months, which is inside the folder Cal.

3　**Click on the file name.** Do not click on the icon itself, but on the name below the icon. In this case, click on 08.2001.

4 **Type the new file name.** Type the new name `aug.2001`. You can backspace to delete erroneous characters.

5 **Press the** (**Return**) **key.** If you decide not to change the name, either press (**Esc**) or click outside the name.

Keep in mind that you cannot have two objects sharing the same name in the same folder.

9.11 Selecting a Tree View

File Manager gives you the choice of several ways to view your files and folders. We have been using the Single Folder view, which is the default view.

You can also choose a *tree view*, which resembles in concept the kind of upside-down tree structures we have been drawing (such as in Figure 9–1). The main difference is that File Manager draws "squared-off" trees in which the branches grow down and to the right (Figure 9–3).

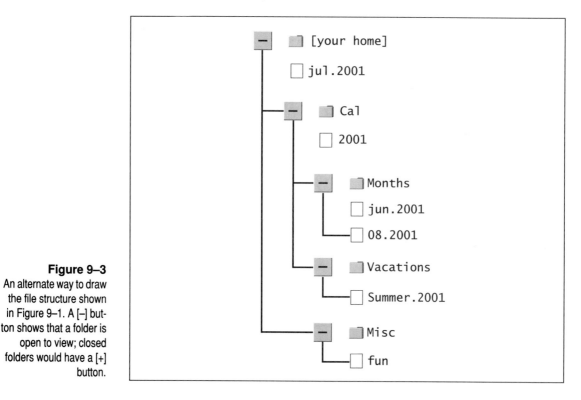

Figure 9–3
An alternate way to draw the file structure shown in Figure 9–1. A [–] button shows that a folder is open to view; closed folders would have a [+] button.

There are three different tree view options:

- *Folders only.* This is the default tree view. It shows just the folders in the tree. To see any files in a particular folder, you must double-click on that folder.

- *Folders, then Files.* This option shows the folders in the tree. To see any subfolders, you simply click on the [+] button next to the folder. Click again to show files inside the subfolders.

- *Folders and Files.* This option shows all folders and files, as in Figure 9–3.

Try a tree view:

1 **Move to the folder that will appear at the top of the tree.** For now, go to your home folder.

2 **Pull down the View menu and choose Set View Options.**

   A dialog box will appear.

3 **Select the By Tree option.**

4 **Select one of the tree view options.**

5 **Click OK.**

9.12 Exercises

1. Prepare a sketch of your file structure after completing this chapter.

2. File Manager offers several ways to represent files and folders:

    Names shows the names of all objects, but not their icons. Folders have a slash (/) appended to their names; executable files have an asterisk (*) appended.

    Large icons shows names and large icons. (This is the default representation.)

    Small icons shows names and small icons.

    Name, date, size ... shows additional information about the file or folder.

    To try out these representations, pull down the View menu and select Set View Options. Then select the appropriate button in the dialog box.

3. By default, File Manager lists files and folders alphabetically by name. However, you can choose a different sorting order:

    File type sorts by the object type.

    Date sorts by the date the files were last modified, either in ascending order (oldest files first) or descending order (newest first).

    Size sorts according to size, either in ascending order (smallest files first) or descending order (largest first).

To try out these options, pull down the View menu and select Set View Options. Then select the appropriate buttons in the dialog box.

4. When you accumulate a large number of files and folders, you may occasionally have trouble finding the particular one you want. File Manager can search for a file or folder according to its name or contents. To search by name, pull down the File menu and select Find. A dialog box will appear. Enter the file or folder name, specify a search folder, and press Start. Try it. (For searching by a file's contents, see the next exercise.)

5. Refer to the CDE Help volumes to learn how to search for a file by its contents. Then try this procedure on one of your files.

6. Using the Properties option on the Selected or pop-up menu, you can control who is permitted to read, write, or execute a file. Try it on one of your files. (You may want to review Appendix D, "File Permissions.")

Part III:
UNIX Shell

10 UNIX Shell

The *shell* is the UNIX command processor. When you type a command and press (Return), it is the shell that interprets the command and takes the appropriate action. In this chapter, you will see how the shell works, and how you can make it work better for you.

10.1 Your Login Shell

There are three common UNIX shells available on most systems: the Bourne Shell (abbreviated sh), the C Shell (csh), and the Korn Shell (ksh). When your UNIX account was created, the system administrator selected a shell for you. This is called your *login shell*, because this is the shell you use each time you log in.

Once you have worked with the various shells available on your system, you may decide to change your login shell. On some systems, you can do this yourself using the chsh ("change shell") command; on others, the system administrator must make the change for you.

10.2 How the Shell Processes Commands

The entire process can be summarized this way:

1. **The shell displays a prompt symbol on the screen.** The prompt tells you the shell is ready to receive your commands.

2. **You type in a command.** As you type, the shell stores the characters and also echoes them back to the terminal screen.

3. **You type (Return).** This is the signal for the shell to interpret the command and start working on it.

4. **The shell looks for the appropriate software to run your command.** In

most cases, it looks for a file having the same name as the command. If the shell can't find the right software, it gives you an error message; otherwise, the shell asks the kernel to run it.

5. **The kernel runs the requested software**. While the command is running, the shell "goes to sleep." When the kernel finishes, it "wakes up" the shell.

6. **The shell again displays a prompt symbol**. This indicates that the shell is once again ready to receive your commands.

This is a good place to point out the difference between a program and a process in UNIX jargon. A *program* is a set of coded instructions contained in a file. An example of a program is the `ls` command: it is just a sequence of computer instructions contained in the file `/bin/ls`. Similarly, your login shell is also just another program residing in the directory `/bin`.

A process is a running program.

A *process* is what you get whenever you tell the computer to run a program. Thus, when you issue the `ls` command, the computer creates an `ls` process by running the program in the file `/bin/ls`. Likewise, when you log in, the computer looks in the file containing the shell program and creates a shell process for you.

The important thing to remember is that there is only one copy of the `ls` program, but there may be many active `ls` processes. In the same way, there is only one copy of each shell program, but there may be many active shell processes.

10.3   Options and Arguments

The typical UNIX command can take one or more options, which modify what the command does. For example, the `ls` command takes numerous options:

Command	Effect
`ls`	List files in the current directory (except hidden files)
`ls -a`	List all files in the current directory, including hidden files
`ls -F`	Flag the files: show a slash (/) after each directory, an asterisk (*) after each executable file
`ls -l`	Print "long" list of files (except hidden files)
`ls -r`	List in reverse order
`ls -s`	List files by size
`ls -t`	List files by time of last modification
`ls -u`	List files by time of last access

Most commands allow you to specify multiple options. Thus, to prepare a reversed long listing of all files in the directory `Dir`, flagging directories and executable files, you could type

§ `ls -a -l -r -F Dir`(**Return**)

Note that each option is preceded by a hyphen.

Or you could combine the options:

§ `ls -alrF Dir`(**Return**)

Incidentally, anything that follows the command name—including the options and file names—is generally referred to as an *argument*.

10.4   The Standard Input, Output, and Error

Whenever you run a UNIX command, the operating system opens up three standard channels for input and output:

- *Standard input.* The standard input (or `stdin`) is the place the program normally looks for input.

- *Standard output.* The standard output (or `stdout`) is where the program sends its output.

- *Standard error.* The standard error (or `stderr`) is used by the program to display error messages.

10.5   Redirection

Most of the time we use the terms "standard input" and "standard output" as synonyms for the keyboard and terminal screen, respectively. However, the shell allows you to redirect the standard output so that output goes into a file instead. For example, you have already seen how to use the output redirection operator (>) to create a file containing a calendar:

§ `cal 2001 > calendar.file`(**Return**)

You can add output to a file using the append operator (>>):

§ `cal 2002 >> calendar.file`(**Return**)

It is also possible to redirect the standard input so that a process takes its input from a file rather than the keyboard. For example, the `mail` command allows you to send and read electronic mail. To send the contents of the file `my.message` to the user `jones`, you could enter the command line

§ `mail jones < my.message`(**Return**)

You can combine input and output redirection in the same command line. For example, the following command line invokes the wc utility to count the lines, words, and characters in the file input, then redirects the results into the file output:

§ wc < input > output (Return)

10.6 Grouping Commands

Normally you type one command at a time, following each command by a (Return), which is the signal for the shell to begin its work. However, it is possible to put multiple commands on the same line, if you separate the commands with semicolons. Thus the command line

§ who; ls; cal (Return)

has the same effect as the three separate command lines

§ who (Return)
§ ls (Return)
§ cal (Return)

Grouping commands can be especially useful when you want to redirect the output into a file. You could make a calendar for the summer of 2001 in three steps:

§ cal 6 2001 > summer.2001 (Return)
§ cal 7 2001 >> summer.2001 (Return)
§ cal 8 2001 >> summer.2001 (Return)

You could accomplish the same thing with just one line:

§ (cal 6 2001; cal 7 2001; cal 8 2001) > summer.2001 (Return)

Note the parentheses; these are necessary to make sure the calendars for June, July, and August are all redirected into the same file. Suppose you were to omit the parentheses, like this:

§ cal 6 2001; cal 7 2001; cal 8 2001 > summer.2001 (Return)

In this case, the calendars for June and July would appear on the screen, and only the August calendar would be redirected into the file.

10.7 Pipes

Suppose you wanted to display the calendars for the years 2001, 2002, and 2003, one right after the other. You could type the command line

§ cal 2001; cal 2002; cal 2003 (Return)

This will print the calendars on the standard output, but they will scroll by so fast that you cannot read them. One way around this problem is to redirect the output into a file:

§ (cal 2001; cal 2002; cal 2003) > temp (Return)

Now you can view the contents of temp using the more or pg utility:

§ more temp (Return)

or

§ pg temp (Return)

This will work, but it requires that you create a temporary file just to look at the output from the commands. You can avoid creating a file by using what is called a *pipe* which connects the output from one utility to the input of another. A vertical bar (|) is the pipe symbol. You would pipe the output from command1 to command2 like this:

command1 | command2

Thus, to view the calendars for 2001, 2002, and 2003, we can pipe the output of the cal utility to either more or pg:

§ (cal 2001; cal 2002; cal 2003) | more (Return)

or

§ (cal 2001; cal 2002; cal 2003) | pg (Return)

Note how this differs from redirection with > or >>. Redirection places the output from a utility into a file; the piping operation directs the output to another utility.

10.8 Tees

A *tee* allows you to save the output from a command in a file at the same time the output is piped to another command. We could take the output from command1 and send it to the file outfile and to command2 like this:

command1 | tee outfile | command2

Thus the command line

§ (cal 2002; cal 2003) | tee calfile | more (Return)

places copies of the calendars for 2002 and 2003 into the file calfile as they are also displayed on the terminal screen by more.

10.9　Filters

A *filter* takes a stream of data from its standard input, transforms the data in some way, and sends the results to the standard output. Here are some of the filters commonly found on UNIX systems.

Filter	Function
cat	Concatenate and display text
comm	Compare sorted files, selecting or rejecting lines common to both
crypt	Encode or decode text
cut	Cut out selected fields from input lines
diff	Display line-by-line differences between two files
egrep	Search text for a pattern using full regular expressions
fgrep	Search text for a character string
fmt	Format text
grep	Search a file for a pattern
head	Display the beginning (head) of a file
more	Show text, one screenful at a time
nl	Number lines
paste	Merge lines of text
pg	Show text, one screenful at a time
pr	Format and print text
sort	Sort and/or merge text
spell	Check for spelling errors
tail	Display last part of a file
tr	Translate characters
uniq	Display lines in a file that are unique
wc	Count number of lines, words, and characters in text

Filters are often used with pipes and tees. Consider the sort utility, which, as you might expect, sorts its input. Suppose you wanted to list, alphabetically by their login names, the users currently logged onto your machine. You could do this by piping the output from who into sort:

§ who | sort (Return)

You can also give sort the name of a file to sort:

sort is discussed in
Chapter 11.

§ `sort poems` (Return)

This would sort the lines of the file `poems` alphabetically by the first character of the line.

10.10 Wildcards

Wildcards are also called
metacharacters.

Typing and retyping file names can be a nuisance, especially if the names are long or there are very many of them. You can abbreviate file names using *wildcards,* which are characters that can stand for other characters (just as a joker in a pack of cards can stand for other cards in the pack). The wildcard symbols are the asterisk (*), the question mark (?), and the square brackets [ ]. To see how these symbols are used, suppose that you had a directory named Fun containing the following files:

backgammon	backpacking	baseball	basketball
biking	blackjack	boxing	bridge
camping	canoeing	checkers	chess
crossword	dancing	eating	fencing
fishing	football	golf	hearts
hiking	karate	poker	rugby
sailing	skiing	softball	swimming
team1	team2	team3	team4
teamA	teamB	teamC	teamD
teamM	teamW	teamX	teamY
teamZ	track	wrestling	

The asterisk matches one
or more characters.

The asterisk (*) is by far the most commonly used wildcard. It matches any character or string of characters, including blanks. As you can see, the directory Fun contains a large number of files. Using wildcards you can avoid having to list all of them when you are interested in just a few. For example, the command

§ `ls f*` (Return)

will cause the shell to list only those files beginning in *f*:

`fencing fishing football`

The command

§ `ls *ball` (Return)

will cause the shell to list the files that end in *ball*:

`baseball basketball football softball`

You are not limited to using a single asterisk. For instance, the command

§ ls *ack* (Return)

will list file names that contain the sequence of letters *ack*:

backgammon backpacking blackjack track

WARNING	The asterisk wildcard is very powerful, and must be used with care. The following command, for example, can erase all of the files in the current directory: § rm * (Return)

The question mark matches a single character.

The question mark (?) wildcard matches just one character at a time. For example,

§ ls ?iking (Return)
biking hiking

The brackets specify the character(s) to match.

The square brackets [ ] are used to instruct the shell to match any characters that appear inside the brackets. For example

§ ls team[ABXYZ] (Return)
teamA teamB teamX teamY teamZ

You can also indicate a range of characters, rather than list each character:

§ ls team[1-4] (Return)
team1 team2 team3 team4

You can combine the wildcards *, ?, and [ ]. Suppose you wanted to list all of the files in the directory Fun that begin with the letters *a*, *b*, or *c*. This command will do the trick:

§ ls [abc]* (Return)

The bracketed letters tell the shell to look for any file names that have *a*, *b*, or *c* at the beginning. The asterisk matches any other sequence of letters. The result is the list

backgammon backpacking baseball basketball biking blackjack
boxing bridge camping canoeing checkers chess crossword

Likewise, to list all of the files having names that end with any letter from *m* through *z*, you could use the command

§ ls *[m-z] (Return)

The asterisk matches any sequence of characters; the brackets match only letters from *m* through *z* that appear at the end of the file name.

backgammon checkers chess hearts

10.11   Quoting Special Characters

You will recall that UNIX file names should not contain any of the following special characters:

```
& * \ | [ ] { } $ < > ( ) # ? ' " / ; ^ ! ~ %
```

By now it should be clear why: each of these characters has a special meaning to the shell. But sometimes this can be a problem. You may want to use a special character in its usual, everyday meaning. Consider, for example, the command line

```
§ echo What time is it? (Return)
```

The shell will interpret the question mark as a wildcard, and it will try to find a file name to match it. Unless you happen to have a file with a three-character name beginning with *it*, the shell will not be able to find a match, and it will complain:

```
§ echo: No match.
```

If you want the shell to treat a question mark as a question mark, not as a special character, you must quote it. One way to do this is to write a backslash (\) immediately before the question mark:

Without the backslash, ? is treated as a wildcard.

```
§ echo What time is it\? (Return)
```

This produces the output

```
What time is it?
```

Note that the backslash does not appear in the output; its only purpose is to cancel the special meaning of the question mark.

The backslash only works on a single character. Thus, to produce the output

```
**** STARS ****
```

you would have to place a backslash in front of each of the special characters:

```
§ echo \*\*\*\* STARS \*\*\*\* (Return)
```

Having to quote each special character individually like this can be tedious. As an alternative, you can quote the entire string of characters all at once using single quotes:

Without the single quotes, the asterisks would be treated as wildcards.

```
§ echo '**** STARS ****' (Return)
```

The single quotes ('...') used here should not be confused with the backquotes (`...`). Backquotes, which are also called *grave* accent marks, are used to enclose commands that you want the shell to run. Thus, the command line

The backquotes run the date command.

```
§ echo It is now `date`. (Return)
```

will produce output that looks something like this

```
It is now Mon Aug 13 16:04:41 EST 2001.
```

where the shell has run the `date` utility and included the result in the output from `echo`. In contrast, this is what would happen if you left off the backquotes:

```
§ echo It is now date. (Return)
It is now date.
```

Double quotes are less powerful than single quotes.

Double quotes ("...") are like single quotes but less powerful. Putting double quotes around a string of characters cancels the special meaning of any of the characters except the dollar sign ($), backquotes (` ... `), or backslash (\).

The different ways of quoting special characters are summarized below, where `string` represents a string of characters:

Quote	Effect
\	Cancel the special meaning of the next character
'string'	Cancel the special meaning of any characters in `string`
"string"	Cancel the special meaning of any characters except $, ` `, and \
`string`	Run any commands in `string`; output replaces `string`

10.12   Background Processing

Processes that can run unattended are often put in the background.

As we said before, UNIX is a multitasking operating system, which means that it can run more than one program for you at the same time. You can start a command and put it in the "background," to continue running while you work on another task in the foreground.

Running a background process is simple: Type an ampersand (&) at the end of the command line before pressing (Return). Consider a hypothetical long-running program called `longrun`. You could run this program in background with the command

```
§ longrun & (Return)
```

If you were running the Bourne Shell, you would then see something like this:

3216 is the process identification number (PID).

```
3216
§
```

Running either the C Shell or the Korn Shell, you would see something like this:

[1] is the job number; 3216 is the PID.

```
[1]     3216
§
```

Whichever shell you are using, it assigns a *process identification number* or PID to every process running in the background. The C Shell and Korn Shell also assign a *job number,* which is the number in brackets. A prompt then lets you know that the shell is ready to process another command line, even if `longrun` is not yet finished:

§

The PID is important if you want to terminate a background job before it finishes. This is done with the `kill` command. To kill background process number 3216, for example, you would use the command

§ `kill 3216` (Return)

Incidentally, some hard-to-kill processes require stronger medicine. Using `kill` with the −9 option will usually deal with them:

§ `kill -9 3216` (Return)

10.13 Job Control

Job Control is discussed in
Section 11.12.

All of the three common shells allow you to run processes in the background with the ampersand (&) and eliminate them with the `kill` command. In addition, the C Shell and Korn Shell have a capability called *job control,* which allows you to stop processes temporarily, move background processes to the foreground, and move foreground processes to the background.

10.14 Exercises

1. Be sure you can define each of the following terms:

shell	program	process
option	argument	standard input
standard output	grave accent	redirection
pipe	tee	filter
metacharacter	wildcard	quote
background process	foreground process	process id number
PID	job number	job control

2. What would each of the following commands do?

```
echo *
echo /*
echo \*
echo "*"
```

```
echo
echo */*
rm *        [Careful—do not try this!]
```

For Exercises 3–6, suppose your working directory contained the following files:

backgammon	backpacking	baseball	basketball
biking	blackjack	boxing	bridge
camping	canoeing	checkers	chess
crossword	dancing	eating	fencing
fishing	football	golf	hearts
hiking	karate	poker	rugby
sailing	skiing	softball	swimming
team1	team2	team3	team4
teamA	teamB	teamC	teamD
teamM	teamW	teamX	teamY
teamZ	track	wrestling	

3. How would you use `cat` to show the contents of the files ending in *ing*?

4. How would you list any files containing *x* or *X* (in this case, `boxing` and `teamX`)?

5. How would you show the contents of files with names containing *o*?

6. How would you show the contents of the files `backgammon`, `backpacking`, and `blackjack` using just one command?

11 TUTORIAL: WORKING WITH THE SHELL

In this chapter, you will gain experience using the shell as a command interpreter. You will practice grouping commands; working with wildcards, filters, pipes, and tees; and running commands in the background.

11.1 Grouping Commands

First you should try grouping several commands on the same command line, using semicolons as separators between commands. Then repeat this, but redirect the output into a file:

1 **Enter the commands on one line, separated by semicolons.** You can print your working directory, the calendar for September 2001, and the current date and time with this command line:

§ pwd; cal 9 2001; date (Return)

2 **Run the same commands again, but redirect the output into a file.** Be sure to put parentheses around the commands:

§ (pwd; cal 9 2001; date) > out1.tmp (Return)
§

Without the parentheses, only the output from date *would go into the file.*

Nothing appears on the screen except the prompt because the output was redirected into out1.tmp instead of going to the standard output.

3 **Use the** cat **command to check on the contents of the file.**

§ cat out1.tmp (Return)

You should see something like this:

```
/home/yourlogin
    September 2001
 S  M Tu  W Th  F  S
                   1
 2  3  4  5  6  7  8
 9 10 11 12 13 14 15
16 17 18 19 20 21 22
23 24 25 26 27 28 29
30
Sun  May 6   13:21:46  EST   2001
```

11.2 Creating a File with cat

cat prints on the standard
output the contents of any
file(s) specified as
arguments.

The cat command is one of the simplest—and most useful—of the UNIX utilities. You have already used cat to view and to combine ("concatenate") files. As you will see in this section, cat can also serve as a "quick and dirty" alternative to a text editor.

1 **Invoke cat without an input file, redirecting the output into the file you want to create.** If cat is not given an input file to read, it reads from the standard input. Thus, to create a file named out2.tmp, type

§ cat > out2.tmp (Return)

At this point, you should see nothing happening on the screen, because cat is waiting for you to enter text.

2 **Type the text you want to put into the file.** For example,

My Bonnie looked into the gas tank, (Return)
  The contents she wanted to see. (Return)
I lit a match to assist her: (Return)
  Oh, bring back my Bonnie to me! (Return)

3 **Generate an end-of-file (EOF) signal.** This is done by typing

(Control) - (D)
§

The prompt tells you that cat has finished and you are back in the shell.

4 **Check the file.** The cat command will show that the text has been stored in the file:

§ cat out2.tmp (Return)

You should see something like this:

```
My Bonnie looked into the gas tank,
   The contents she wanted to see.
I lit a match to assist her:
   Oh, bring back my Bonnie to me!
```

You can also indicate explicitly that you want cat to read the standard input by typing a hyphen (–) instead of a file name. Try it:

1   Invoke cat with a hyphen instead of an input file, redirecting the output into the file you want to create. Thus, to create a file named out3.tmp, type

> The hyphen tells cat to read from the standard input.

```
§ cat - > out3.tmp (Return)
```

At this point, you should see nothing happening on the screen, because cat is waiting for you to enter text.

2   Type the text you want to put into the file. For example,

```
There once was a fellow named Frank, (Return)
   Who drove around town in a tank. (Return)
It was noisy and dark, (Return)
   And quite hard to park, (Return)
But it got him good rates at the bank. (Return)
```

3   Generate an end-of-file (EOF) signal. This is done by typing

```
(Control) - (D)
§
```

4   Check the file. The cat command will show that the text has been stored in the file:

```
§ cat out3.tmp  (Return)
```

You should see something like this:

> Retain out1.tmp, out2.tmp, and out3.tmp—you will use them later in the chapter.

```
There once was a fellow named Frank,
   who drove around town in a tank.
It was noisy and dark,
   and quite hard to park.
But it got him good rates at the bank.
```

The cat utility is not a replacement for a text editor—cat does not allow you to change or delete text from a file—but it can be useful in creating short text files.

11.3   Using Wildcards

If you worked through the previous sections carefully, you should now have three new files in your directory named out1.tmp, out2.tmp, and out3.tmp.

- **Examine the files using the** `cat` **command and the asterisk wildcard (*).** Thus, to view the files that begin in *out*, type

  § cat out* (Return)

  To view all of the files ending in *.tmp,* type the command line

  § cat *.tmp (Return)

- **Examine the files using the** `cat` **command and the question mark (?).** Recall that the question mark matches any single character. Thus, to view the files `out1.tmp`, `out2.tmp`, and `out3.tmp`, type

  § cat out?.tmp (Return)

  The file names `out1.tmp`, `out2.tmp`, and `out3.tmp` differ only by one character—a number in the fourth position—and the question mark can stand for any of the numbers.

- **Examine the files using the** `cat` **command and the brackets.** The brackets can be used to indicate a range of letters or numerals. To view the files `out1.tmp`, `out2.tmp`, and `out3.tmp`, type

  § cat out[1-3].tmp (Return)

11.4 Using wc

The `wc` ("word count") filter counts the lines, words, and characters in a file or collection of files. It has the following general form:

Items in square brackets are optional.

    wc [-lcw] filelist

where `filelist` is a list of one or more file pathnames. You can apply various options so that `wc` prints only the number of lines (`-l`), or the number of words (`-w`), or the number of characters (`-c`). The `wc` command is very simple to use:

- **Enter the** `wc` **command and the file name.** Try it on the `out2.tmp` file:

  § wc *2.tmp (Return)

  This produces the output

      4   27   133   out2.tmp

  showing that there are 4 lines, 27 words, and 133 characters in the `out2.tmp` file. (To `wc`, a "word" is simply any group of characters followed by blanks, tabs, or newlines.)

- **Run the** `wc` **command on multiple files.** Try this command line:

  § wc *[2-3].tmp (Return)

This runs wc on `out2.tmp` and `out3.tmp`, producing the output

```
4        27        133   out2.tmp
5        33        160   out3.tmp
9        60        293   total
```

Note that wc shows the line, word, and character counts for the files individually, as well as the totals for both files.

11.5   Using grep

The grep filter searches line by line through its standard input for a pattern of characters. Any line containing the desired pattern is printed on the standard output. The format of grep is

Items in square brackets are optional.

```
grep [-cilnv] pattern [filelist]
```

The `pattern` may be a simple word or string of characters, or it may be a *regular expression*. A regular expression is a compact notation that specifies a general string of characters, in much the same way that a wildcard represents a set of file names. We will not use regular expressions in this book.

- **Search for a particular word in a set of files.** Thus, to search the files `out1.tmp`, `out2.tmp`, and `out3.tmp` for lines containing the word *tank*, you would use the command

  § grep tank *tmp (Return)

  Any lines containing the pattern *tank* are listed on the screen:

  ```
  out2.tmp:My Bonnie looked into the gas tank,
  out3.tmp:who drove around town in a tank.
  ```

- **Search using the line-number option.** The –n option causes grep to print the number of any line containing the pattern:

  § grep -n tank *tmp (Return)

  The word *tank* occurs on the first line of `out2.tmp` and on the second line of `out3.tmp`. Hence, grep prints

  ```
  out2.tmp:1:My Bonnie looked into the gas tank,
  out3.tmp:2:who drove around town in a tank.
  ```

- **Search using the list-only option.** This causes grep to list only the names of the files containing the pattern. For example,

  § grep -l Bonnie *tmp (Return)
  ```
  out2.tmp
  ```

- **Reverse the sense of the test.** The -v option causes grep to list the lines that do *not* contain the pattern. For example,

```
§ grep -v dark out3.tmp (Return)
```

```
There once was a fellow named Frank,
    who drove around town in a tank.
    and quite hard to park.
But it got him good rates at the bank.
```

11.6   Using sort

As you might expect, sort sorts the lines in a file or collection of files. It can also merge two or more files without sorting them. The sort command has the general format

Items in square brackets are optional.

```
sort [-bcdfimMnortuyz] [±field] [filelist]
```

As you can see, sort takes quite a large number of options, only a few of which will be discussed in this section. A *field* is a sequence of characters bounded by white space. (The individual words in a line of text might be considered as fields, for example.) Sorting is normally done according to the first field in each line, but you can specify that other fields be examined instead.

- **Perform a simple sort on the first field of the files.** The following command line will list the contents of out1.tmp, out2.tmp, and out3.tmp:

```
§ sort *.tmp (Return)
                    1
    September 2001
    Oh, bring back my Bonnie to me!
    The contents she wanted to see.
    and quite hard to park.
    who drove around town in a tank.
    2  3  4  5  6  7  8
    9 10 11 12 13 14 15
    S  M Tu  W Th  F  S
/home/yourlogin
16 17 18 19 20 21 22
23 24 25 26 27 28 29
30 31
But it got him good rates at the bank.
I lit a match to assist her:
It was noisy and dark,
My Bonnie looked into the gas tank,
Sun May 6   13:21:46  EST   2000
There once was a fellow named Frank,
```

The sorting order is also called the *collating sequence*.

This may appear strange until you understand the sorting order that the sort utility employs. This varies from system to system, but the following is typical:

1. Control characters

2. White space (i.e., blanks and tabs)

3. Numerals

4. Uppercase letters

5. Lowercase letters

You can apply various options to modify the sorting order. Here are just a few possibilities:

sort -b   Ignore leading blanks

sort -f   Fold upper- and lowercase letters together (ignore case)

sort -n   Numeric sort

sort -r   Reverse usual order (e.g., Z precedes *a*)

- **Sort on the first field, ignoring leading blanks and case.** Specifying a field offset of +0 will cause sort to examine the first field of each line:

```
§ sort -bf +0 *.tmp (Return)
```

```
/home/yourlogin
                      1
16 17 18 19 20 21 22
 2  3  4  5  6  7  8
23 24 25 26 27 28 29
30 31
 9 10 11 12 13 14 15
   and quite hard to park.
But it got him good rates at the bank.
I lit a match to assist her:
It was noisy and dark,
My Bonnie looked into the gas tank,
   Oh, bring back my Bonnie to me!
 S  M Tu  W Th  F  S
     September 2001
Sun  May 6   13:21:46  EST    2001
   The contents she wanted to see.
There once was a fellow named Frank,
   who drove around town in a tank.
```

- **Sort on the second field of the files.** Specifying a field offset of +1 will cause sort to skip the first field of each line and examine the second field. Try this on the file out3.tmp:

```
§ sort -bf +1 out3.tmp Return
```

```
  who drove around town in a tank.
But it got him good rates at the bank.
There once was a fellow named Frank,
  and quite hard to park.
It was noisy and dark,
```

There is much more to the sort utility than we can detail here. If you want to know more, refer to the UNIX manual.

11.7 Pipes and Tees

A pipe connects the standard output from one utility to the standard input of another utility. A tee allows you to take the output from a command and direct it into a file and to another command. In this section, you will practice using pipes and tees.

- **View the calendars for 2001 and 2002, one page at a time.** One of the following command lines will do:

```
§ (cal 2001; cal 2002) | more Return
```

or

```
§ (cal 2001; cal 2002) | pg Return
```

- **View the calendars for 2001 and 2002, and create a file containing these calendars.** This requires a tee and two pipes:

```
§ (cal 2001; cal 2002) | tee calfile | more Return
```

- **List the files in the root's subdirectories, one page at a time.** Either of the following commands will work to pipe the output from ls to the more or pg utility:

```
§ ls -a /* | more Return
```

or

```
§ ls -a /* | pg Return
```

- **List the files in the root's subdirectories and create a file containing this listing.** This can be done using two pipes and a tee:

```
§ ls -a /* | tee root.list | more Return
```

This places a list of the root and its subdirectories into the file `root.list` as this list is also displayed on the terminal screen.

- **Count the files in the root's subdirectories.** This can be done with the command line

  § `ls -a /* | wc -l` (Return)

- **Print a long listing of the root's subdirectories, sorted by size.** The fifth field in a long file listing normally shows the size of the file. To sort on the fifth field, skip the first four fields (+4):

  § `ls -al /* | sort -nr +4 | more` (Return)

- **Prepare a long listing of the root's subdirectories; sort it by size; and send it to the standard output and to a file.** The fifth field in a long file listing normally shows the size of the file. To sort on the fifth field, skip the first four fields (+4):

  § `ls -al /* | sort -nr +4 | tee list.by.size | more` (Return)

- **Find a file among the root's subdirectories.** Thus, to find the file `passwd`, enter the command line

  § `ls -a /* | grep passwd` (Return)

11.8   Sleeping

sleep is not a filter.

The `sleep` command creates a process that "sleeps" for a specified period of time. In other words, `sleep` waits the specified number of seconds before returning to the shell. It has the general format

`sleep n`

where `n` is a nonnegative integer that indicates the number of seconds the process is to sleep.

1   **Run the `sleep` command.** To sleep for 15 seconds, enter

   § `sleep 15` (Return)

2   **Use `sleep` to delay execution of another command.** This is a common application of the sleep utility. For example,

   § `(sleep 60; echo I am awake now)` (Return)

3   **Wait for the process to finish.** When `sleep` finishes, `echo` will print a message:

   `I am awake now`

11.9   Interrupting a Foreground Process

If you start a long-running process such as sleep the usual way (that is, in the foreground), you cannot work on any other commands until it finishes. If for some reason you do not wish to wait that long, you must interrupt the process. This is done with the (Control) - (C) key combination.

1   Start the process. For example,

§ (sleep 120; echo I am awake now) (Return)

2   Interrupt the process. Type

(Control) - (C)

This will interrupt sleep and invoke the **echo** command:

^CI am awake now
§

11.10   Running a Background Process

As we said before, UNIX allows you to run a process in the "background" while you work on another task in the foreground. This is useful for long-running processes, especially those that do not require your attention. As an example of such a long-running process, we will once again use the sleep command.

1   Start a long-running process in the background. For example,

§ (sleep 60; echo I am awake now)& (Return)

If you are running the Bourne shell, you should see something like this:

The number you see will likely be different.

3271

In this example, the shell assigned a process identification (PID) number of 3271. (The actual PID on your system may be different.)

If you are running C Shell or Korn Shell, you should see something like this:

The numbers you see will likely be different.

[1]   3271

Here, [1] is the job number and 3271 is the PID.

The shell will display a prompt to let you know it is ready for more commands:

§

2   Check status of the process. Enter the ps ("process status") command to check on what is happening:

§ ps (Return)

You might see something like this (the PIDs will be different):

```
PID  TTY  TIME   COMMAND
3140 p0   0:01   sh
3271 p0   0:00   sleep 60
3290 p0   0:00   ps
§
```

Note that there are three processes: the shell (`sh` in this example); `sleep`; and the `ps` command itself.

3 Wait for the process to finish. After about 60 seconds, you should get the message:

```
I am awake now
```

```
§
```

11.11 Killing a Background Process

Sometimes it is necessary to terminate a background process. This is done with the `kill` command. To see how this works, try the same background process you used in the previous section.

1 Start the background process. Be sure to note the PID:

```
§ (sleep 60; echo Stop this command) & (Return)
3310
§
```

2 Kill the process. Type `kill`, a space, and the PID number:

```
§ kill 3310 (Return)
```

Some systems will tell you when a background job has been killed:

```
Terminated  (sleep 60; echo Stop this command)
§
```

11.12 Using Job Control (C Shell and Korn Shell)

The Bourne shell does not have job control.

The job control feature of the C Shell and Korn Shell provides additional flexibility in dealing with background processes. In this section you will see how to use job control to suspend a job, move it to the background, and (if necessary) kill it.

1 Start the process in the foreground. To practice, use the `sleep` utility as before:

§ (sleep 120; echo I am awake now) (Return)

2   **Stop (suspend) the job.** This is done with the key combination

(Control) - (Z)

The shell will tell you that the job has been stopped:

^Z
Stopped (user)

3   **Check the status of the job.** Enter the jobs command:

§ jobs (Return)

This will list, by job number, each job and its status. In this case, there is just one job:

[1] + Stopped (user)   (sleep 120; echo I am awake now)

4   **Move the stopped job to the background.** Use the bg ("background") command and the job number. Note the percent sign (%) preceding the job number:

§ bg %1 (Return)

The shell will indicate that the process is now running in the background (note the &):

[1]   (sleep 120; echo I am awake now) &

5   **Kill the job or allow it to finish.** To kill job number 1, enter

§ kill %1 (Return)

The shell will display a prompt:

§

6   **Check the status of the job.** If you killed the job, the jobs command will show that it has been terminated:

§ jobs (Return)
[1]   Terminated   (sleep 120; echo I am awake now)
§

11.13   Command Summary

Counting Lines, Words, and Characters

`wc file(s)`	count lines, words, and characters in `file(s)`
`wc -l file(s)`	count the lines in `file(s)`

Searching

`grep pattern file(s)`	print line(s) in `file(s)` containing `pattern`
`grep -n pattern files(s)`	as before, but print line numbers as well
`grep -l pattern files(s)`	print the name of any file containing `pattern`.
`grep -v pattern file(s)`	print line(s) *not* containing `pattern`

Sorting

`sort file(s)`	sort file(s) observing usual collating sequence
`sort -b file(s)`	sort, ignoring leading blanks
`sort -f file(s)`	sort, converting lowercase to uppercase
`sort -n file(s)`	sort numerically
`sort -r file(s)`	reverse sort (*9* before *0*, *Z* before *A,* etc.)
`sort +n file(s)`	sort on field $n + 1$ (skip n fields)

Sleeping

`sleep n`	sleep n seconds

Foreground and Background Processing

`^C`	interrupt (kill) a foreground process
`^D`	generate end-of-file signal
`^Z`	stop (suspend) a foreground process
`command &`	run command in background
`ps`	obtain process status
`kill n`	terminate background process n

Job Control

`bg %n`	move job n to background
`fg %n`	move job n to foreground
`jobs`	list status of all jobs
`kill %n`	kill job n

11.14   Exercises

1. How accurately does the sleep command count seconds? Try the following command to find out:

    (date; sleep 60; date)

2. Refer to the man entry for cat to determine what each of the following commands is supposed to do:

    ```
    cat -e file
    cat -s file
    cat -t file
    cat -u file
    cat -v file
    cat -vet file
    ```

3. Refer to the man entry for grep to determine what each of the following commands is supposed to do:

    ```
    grep -c pattern file
    grep -i pattern file
    grep -l pattern file
    grep -n pattern file
    grep -v pattern file
    ```

4. Refer to the man entry for sort to determine what each of the following commands is supposed to do:

    ```
    sort -d
    sort -m
    sort -M
    sort -n
    sort -o
    sort -r
    sort -t
    sort -u
    sort -y
    sort -z
    sort -nr
    ```

5. The -R ("recursive") option causes ls to list not only the files in the specified directory, but also the files inside any subdirectories. How could you use this with an appropriate pipe-and-filter arrangement to determine whether a file exists in your account?

PART IV:
TEXT EDITORS

12 TEXT EDITORS

A *text editor* is a program that you can use to create and modify files. UNIX systems typically offer a choice of text editors. In this chapter, you will learn about UNIX text editors in general.

12.1 Text Editors versus Word Processors

Before learning what a text editor is, you should understand what it is not. *A text editor is not a word processor.* True, both text editors and word processors are used to create and edit text files, but that is where the similarity ends.

A word processor typically does more than a text editor. Besides adding text to a file, most word processing programs allow you to control the appearance of the text—the page layout, paragraph styles, typefaces, and so on—when it is printed. With some word processor programs, you can create tables, enter mathematical equations, and insert graphics.

In contrast, a text editor does just that: edit text. Most text editors have limited text formatting capabilities. Generally speaking, a text editor is not intended to format text for printing.

12.2 UNIX Text Editors

There are a number of different text editors available on most UNIX systems. The following are perhaps the most widely used:

The name of this editor is pronounced "vee-eye".

- vi. This editor was written by Bill Joy, a graduate student at the University of California at Berkeley (who later became one of the founders of Sun Microsystems). Although originally found only on Berkeley UNIX, vi is now the standard editor on most UNIX systems.

- emacs. Originally written by Richard Stallman at MIT, emacs is a powerful, feature-rich editor known for its flexibility: emacs can be personalized to fit the tastes of the user. Some versions of emacs supported windowing before windowing systems became common on UNIX.

- pico. This editor was developed at the University of Washington for composing messages in the pine mail program. The menu structure of pico makes it especially easy for beginners to learn.

- xedit. This X client is a simple window-based text editor. It is available on most systems that run X. (We will not cover xedit in this book.)

- CDE Text Editor. The Common Desktop Environment (CDE) includes a simple, yet powerful, text editor.

We will examine vi, emacs, pico, and Text Editor in this and subsequent chapters.

12.3   How a Text Editor Works

Regardless of the text editor you choose, the process of editing a text file can be summarized as follows:

1. You start the editor and give it the name of a file to edit.

2. If you specified an existing file, the editor makes a copy of it and places the copy in a temporary workspace called the *work buffer*. If you are creating a new file, the editor simply opens up an empty work buffer.

3. You use editor commands to add, delete, and/or change the text in the work buffer. When you are satisfied with the changes you have made, you tell the editor to save or write into the file.

4. The editor saves in a file the contents of the work buffer. If you are editing an existing file, the editor replaces the original file with the updated version in the buffer.

Note that you do not work directly on the file, but only on the copy that is in the buffer. This means that if you leave the editor without writing your changes into the file, the changes are lost, and the original file is not altered.

12.4   Line, Screen, and GUI Editors

All editors do much the same things, but some are decidedly easier to use than others. The original UNIX editor ed is called a *line editor* because it makes changes in the buffer line by line. To make a change using a line editor, you must first specify the line where you want the change to be made, and then you must specify the change itself. This can be a lot of work for even minor changes. Furthermore, it can be difficult to keep in mind the way the changes fit into the text as a whole because you are working with just one line at a time.

Screen editors are sometimes called *visual editors*; vi is short for "visual."

A *full-screen editor*, on the other hand, allows you to view and to work with as much of the work buffer as will fit on your screen. You can easily move the cursor around the screen, making changes to characters, words, and paragraphs as well as lines. Any changes you make are always apparent because the screen is updated immediately. And you can see clearly how the changes affect the rest of the text because you can view many lines at the same time. vi, emacs, and pico are full-screen editors.

The proliferation of graphical user interfaces (GUIs) has led to the development of a new class of text editors that allow you to use the pointer and mouse. The CDE Text Editor is an example of this class of editor.

12.5   Spell and Look

Text Editor and pico have built-in spell-checkers; vi and emacs do not.

For the benefit of people who occasionally misspell words, UNIX offers the spell utility. spell goes through a file and checks every word against the UNIX word list (sometimes called a "dictionary"). When spell encounters words or groups of characters that are not on the word list, it displays them on the screen.

Although spell is very useful, it has its limitations. It cannot detect grammatical errors or words used incorrectly. (Few spelling checkers can.) Thus if you wrote "up" when you meant "down," or "wait" instead of "weight," spell cannot help you.

A related utility named look allows you to look up words on the word list that is used by spell. You will learn how to use both look and spell in the chapters on vi and emacs.

12.6   Which Editor Is Right for Me?

The choice of an editor depends on availability and personal preference. Here are some considerations:

- vi. Because the POSIX standard specifies vi as the standard editor, it is likely to be found on every UNIX system. It works well on dumb terminals, and can be used if you are using a personal computer and modem to log in remotely. Some users prefer it to emacs.

- emacs. Although not officially a standard editor, emacs is widely available. It can be used on a dumb terminal or over the telephone lines. Some users prefer it to vi.

- pico. If you intend to use pine as your mail program, you may want to learn pico as well. It can be used on a dumb terminal, or remotely over the telephone lines. In general, pico is easier to learn than either vi or emacs. However, it may not be available on all systems.

- CDE Text Editor. Arguably the most powerful editor—and the easiest to learn—Text Editor will naturally be the first choice of anyone using the Common Desktop Environment. However, you cannot use Text Editor remotely over the telephone lines.

Thus, if your concern is to learn one editor that will be universally available, you should consider vi. For ease of use, choose pico or Text Editor. (If you learn Text Editor, it makes sense to learn one of the others as well.)

12.7   Exercises

1.   Be sure you can define the following terms:

text editor	word processor	work buffer
cursor	line editor	screen editor
GUI editor	word list	dictionary

2.   Which text editors are available on your system?

13 TUTORIAL: EDITING WITH VI

In this chapter, you will see how to use the vi editor to create and edit text files.

13.1 vi Modes

To use vi, you have to know something about its operating modes (Figure 13–1). When you first enter the vi editor, it is set to the *command mode*. This means that vi will treat all keystrokes as editing commands, and not as text to be entered into the file. Pressing (Return), (Backspace), or the space bar while in the command mode moves the cursor without introducing new lines or spaces into the text.

To add text to the file, you must switch to the *insert mode*, which you can do using any of the following commands:

i   insert text to the left of the current cursor location

I   Insert text to the left of the current line

a   append text to the right of the cursor

A   Append text to the end of the current line

R   Replace (type over) existing text

o   open a new line below the current line and move the cursor there

O   Open a new line above the current line and move the cursor there

None of these insert-mode commands appears on the screen, but everything typed in afterward does. Pressing the (Esc) key returns vi to the command mode.

In general, you use the insert mode when adding text to the file, and the command mode for everything else (moving around the file, deleting text, etc.).

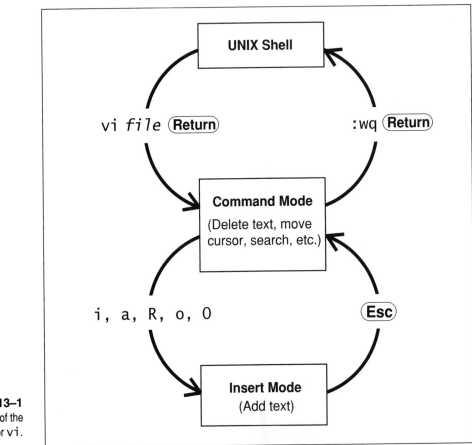

Figure 13–1
Operating modes of the
visual editor vi.

Perhaps the most common difficulty that beginning vi users have is remembering which mode they are working in. When in doubt, hit the (Esc) key a couple of times to get back to the command mode. (If the terminal beeps or the screen flashes when you press (Esc), that is a signal that you are already in the command mode.)

13.2 Opening a New File

If you haven't already done so, log in and set your terminal. Then follow the examples.

1 **Select a name for the new file.** The name should be descriptive. Thus, a good name for a file that will contain poetry might be poems.

2 **Enter the vi command, followed by the name of the new file.** To create a file named poems, type the command line

§ vi poems (Return)

If your terminal is set properly, you should see something like this:

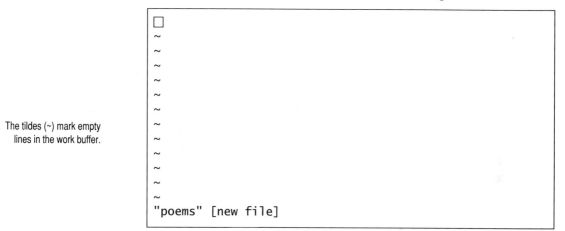

The tildes (~) mark empty lines in the work buffer.

```
□
~
~
~
~
~
~
~
~
~
~
~
~
"poems" [new file]
```

The box on the first line represents the *cursor*, which shows the point at which any new text would be entered. (The actual appearance of the cursor depends on the particular type of terminal you are using.)

13.3 Inserting Text

1 **Switch to insert mode.** This is done using the i ("insert") command. Type

The *i* does not appear on screen.

i

This command does not appear on the screen, but everything you type subsequently will.

2 **Enter text into the work buffer.** Try typing in the following lines of verse (ignore any mistakes for now—you'll see how to correct them later):

```
Mary had a little lamb, (Return)
A little cheese, (Return)
A little ham. (Return)
Burp!□
```

Although these lines appear on the terminal screen, they are not yet saved in the file. Remember, you must "write" these lines from the buffer into the file to save them.

13.4   Writing Text to the File

1   **Press** (Esc) **to get back into the command mode:**

(Esc)

2   **Enter the Write command.** Type a colon (:), a *w*, and a (Return). Note that the cursor jumps to the bottom of the screen when you type the colon:

This command appears at the bottom of the screen as you type.

:w (Return)

The computer will respond with a message that shows the number of lines and characters that were saved in the file:

```
"poems" [New file] 4 lines, 61 characters
```

3   **Leave the** vi **editor.** This is done using the Quit command.

:q (Return)

The computer will answer with the shell prompt to let you know you are out of vi and back in the UNIX shell:

§

13.5   Moving the Cursor

When editing a file, you will often need to move the cursor around the file. Moving the vi cursor is always done in the command mode.

1   **Reopen the file using** vi. To open the file named poems, type the command

§ vi poems (Return)

This will cause vi to copy the contents of the file into the work buffer, then display this on the screen:

```
Mary had a little lamb,
A little cheese,
A little ham.
Burp!
~
~
~
~
~
"poems" 4 lines, 61 characters
```

Note that the cursor is positioned over the first character in the work buffer.

2   **Switch** vi **to the command mode.** If you are unsure which mode you're working in, simply press the (Esc) key to get into the command mode.

3   **Use the arrow keys to move the cursor.** Many computer keyboards have arrow keys—also called *cursor-control keys*—that move the cursor one space at a time in the direction indicated:

These may not work on your machine.

←   ↓   ↑   →

4   **Use the alternative cursor-control keys to move the cursor.** In the command mode, the h, j, k, l, (Space), (Backspace), – (hyphen), and (Return) keys may be used in place of the arrow keys:

On many terminals, holding a key down causes its function to be repeated rapidly. This can be useful when you want to move quickly through the file.

h	move one space left
j	move one space down
k	move one space up
l	move one space right
(Space)	move one space right
(Backspace)	move one space left
(Return)	move to beginning of next line down
–	move to beginning of previous line

Practice using the various cursor-control keys until you get a feel for how they work.

13.6   Replacing Text

You have seen how to create a new text file using the vi editor. Now you will see how to edit existing text by typing over it with new text.

1   **If the file is closed, open it using the** vi **editor.** To edit the file poems, type

§ vi poems (Return)

This will put a copy of the file poems into the work buffer and display it for you on the screen.

2 **If necessary, put** vi **into the command mode.** When you invoke the vi editor, it should start up in the command mode. You can always make sure vi is in the command mode by pressing (Esc):

(Esc)

3 **Move the cursor to the text you intend to replace.** Use the arrow and/or alternative cursor-control keys discussed in the previous section. In the file poems you might want to replace *Burp!* with something more suitable. (Mary is very polite and would never burp at the dinner table.) Move the cursor down to the fourth line and position it over the *B* in *Burp*.

4 **Type the Replace command.** In the command mode, type an *R* (for "Replace"). The *R* does not appear on the screen, but it does take vi from the command mode into the insert mode.

This command does not
appear on the screen.

R

5 **Enter the new text.** Whatever you type now will be written over the old text. To replace *Burp!* with *Delicious!*, type

Delicious!

Note how *Delicious!* is written right over the offending *Burp!*.

6 **Return to the command mode.** Pressing the (Esc) key puts vi back into the command mode:

(Esc)

At this point, you have made changes to the text in the work buffer, but these changes have not yet been saved in the file.

13.7 Writing the File and Quitting the Editor

If you want to save the changes you have made to the work buffer, you must "write" these changes into the file. (Remember, the editor always works on a copy of the file.)

1 **Put** vi **into the command mode.** Press the (Esc) key.

2 **To save your work, write the changes into the file.** From the command mode, press the colon (:) key, then the *w* key. Note that when you press the colon, the cursor jumps to the bottom of the screen:

This appears at the bottom
of the screen.

:w (Return)

The editor will show you how many lines and characters were written to the file:

```
"poems" 4 lines, 66 characters
```

Note that the cursor returned to the last character you typed. This will allow you to continue editing the file, if you wish.

3   **If you are finished with the file, quit the editor.** This is done using the Quit command.

:q (Return)

The computer will answer with the shell prompt to let you know you are out of vi and back in the UNIX shell:

§

If you try to quit the file without saving your changes, the computer will respond with the message

```
No write since last change (:q! overrides)
```

At times, you may decide not to save the changes you have made. In that case, do not write the changes into the file, but enter the command

:q! (Return)

13.8   Appending Text

In this section, you will see how to add text to the file using the a ("append") command.

1   **If the file is not already open, reopen it.** To edit the file poems, type

§ vi poems (Return)

This will put a copy of the file poems into the work buffer and display it for you on the screen.

2   **If necessary, put vi into the command mode.** Remember, you can always make sure vi is in the command mode by pressing (Esc):

(Esc)

3   **Position the cursor.** Keep in mind that the Append command adds the text to the right of the cursor position. Move the cursor to the bottom of the file.

4   **Enter the Append command.** Just type the letter *a*:

This command does not appear on the screen.

a

Now type the following lines (hit (Return) at the end of each line to start a new line):

(Return)
Mary had a polar bear (Return)
Whose fur was white as snow, (Return)
And everywhere that big bear went (Return)
The people (Return)
let it go. (Return)

5   Return to the command mode. Hit (Esc):

(Esc)

6   If you are finished editing, write to the file and quit the editor. You can do this in one step by typing:

This appears at the bottom of the screen.

:wq (Return)

The computer will respond with a message telling you how many lines and characters were written into the file:

"poems" 9 lines, 175 characters

The prompt (§) indicates that you are back in the UNIX shell:

§

13.9   Joining Two Lines

In vi, the J ("join") command allows you to join two lines together.

1   If the file is not already open, open it. To edit the file poems, type

§ vi poems (Return)

This will put a copy of the file poems into the work buffer and display it for you on the screen. Note that in this example, the last two lines of the poem are the ones that should be joined together:

The people
let it go.

2   If necessary, press (Esc) to put vi into the command mode.

3   Move the cursor to the first of the two lines you want to join. The cursor can be put anywhere on that line:

Put the cursor on the first of the two lines.

The people
let it go.

This command does not
appear on the screen.

4   **Enter the Join command.** Just type the capital letter *J*:

J

The computer will join the lines:

The people let it go.

5   **If you are finished, write the changes to the file and quit the editor.**

This appears at the bottom
of the screen.

:wq (Return)

The computer will tell you how many lines and characters were written into the file:

"poems" 8 lines, 174 characters

The prompt (§) indicates that you are back in the UNIX shell:

§

13.10   More Ways to Insert Text

Four more insert-mode commands are frequently useful:

A   Append text to the end of the current line

I   Insert text at the beginning of the current line

o   open a new line below the current line and move the cursor there

O   Open a new line above the current line and move the cursor there

The exercises at the end of this chapter will give you the opportunity to try out these commands.

13.11   Correcting Mistakes

Everyone makes an occasional error, so vi thoughtfully provides several means of correcting mistakes. These commands work only in the command mode. (When in doubt, hit (Esc) to get into the command mode.)

x   delete one character

dd   delete entire line

u   undo most recent change

U   Undo any changes made to current line

:q! quit without saving changes

To delete a single character, move the cursor over that character and press the *x* key. To delete an entire line, type *dd*. To delete *n* lines (where *n* is any positive integer), move the cursor to the first of the lines to be deleted and type *ndd*.

If you make a change and then think better of it, you can undo the most recent change by the u ("undo") command

(Esc) u (Return)

If you want to undo several changes to the line you are currently working on, you can restore the current line to its previous condition with the U ("Undo") command:

(Esc) U (Return)

Note, however, that U works only so long as you remain on the line; if you go to another line, you cannot go back and use the U command to undo the changes.

If you make too many changes to undo with the u or U commands, you can always use the command

(Esc) :q! (Return)

which quits the text editor without saving any changes.

13.12   Writing to a Different File

Sometimes, it is convenient to make changes to a file and save those changes under a different file name. Because we plan to try out the spell utility later in this chapter, let's create a file to contain misspelled words:

1   **If the file is not already open, open it.** To edit the file poems, type

§ vi poems (Return)

2   **Make changes.** Use the R ("Replace") command to introduce a few misspelled words into the file poems:

Marye had a wittle wamb,
A wittle cheese,
A wittle ham.
Delisious!

Mary had a polar beer
Whose fir was white as snow,
And everywhere that big bare went
The people let it go.

3   **Write the changes to a different file.** Use the :w ("write") command, as before, but this time specify a new file name. Since the new file is to contain misspelled words, call it misspelled. Type the command

(Esc):w misspelled (Return)

vi will tell you that the text has been saved in a new file:

"misspelled" [New file] 9 lines, 176 characters

4   Quit without saving changes. You have saved the misspellings into the file misspelled; you do not want to save them in the file poems as well. Use the command

:q! (Return)

13.13   Using spell

spell is a UNIX utility that checks your spelling. Unlike many spell-checkers that are supplied as part of a word processor or text editor, spell is an entirely separate program. Consequently, you will not use spell at the same time you are editing a file with vi.

1   If you are still working in vi, write the file and quit the editor. Type

(Esc):wq (Return)

2   At the shell prompt, enter the spell command and the file name.

§ spell misspelled (Return)

The spell utility searches through the file and prints any words that are not found on the UNIX word list:

Delisious
Marye
wamb
wittle

Note that although wittle appears three times in the file, it is listed only once by spell. Note too that spell caught the unusual spelling of Mary; the word list includes many proper names. But spell missed some words: beer, fir, and bare. The reason is simple: these are legitimate words in spell's word list. Remember, spell does not really check for spelling errors; rather, it looks for groups of characters that do not match those in its word list. Consequently, it will not detect words that are used out of context.

13.14   Finding Text

The vi editor can locate particular words or groupings of characters anywhere in the file. This is useful when correcting spelling errors. For example, spell identified the misspelled word Delisious in the file misspelled.

1 Open the file if it is not already open. Suppose you want to correct the mis-spelled words in the file `misspelled`. Type

§ vi misspelled (Return)

2 If necessary, put vi into the command mode.

3 Type a slash (/) followed by the word or characters you want to find. Note that when you type the slash, the cursor jumps to the bottom of the screen:

This appears at the bottom of the screen.

/Delisious (Return)

When you press (Return), the cursor will move to the place where the word is located. You may then use vi's editing commands to edit the text.

4 To search for further occurrences of the same word or characters, return to the command mode and type a slash. There is no need to enter the word again:

(Esc)/(Return)

When vi can find no other instances of this word, it will tell you so:

Pattern not found

5 To search backward through a file from the current cursor location, use a question mark (?):

(Esc)?wittle (Return)

This will find one of the occurrences of the word `wittle`. To check for the next occurrence, type

(Esc)? (Return)

13.15 Global Substitution

"Global" means "comprehensive."

The forward search (/) and backward search (?) commands provide a quick way to find an error in a file. Once you have found the error, you can use the vi editor commands to make the necessary change. Although this approach works well if there are only one or two such changes to make, it is even faster to make the changes using the Global Substitution command.

1 If necessary, put vi into the command mode.

2 Enter the Global Substitution command, the text you wish to replace, and the new text. Thus, to replace all occurrences of *wittle* with *little*, type

This line appears at the bottom of the screen.

:%s/wittle/little/g (Return)

3 Write the changes into the file.

See Exercise 15 for a variation on the Global Substitution command.

If you have not already done so, you may wish to take a moment now to correct the errors in your `misspelled` file.

13.16   Jumping around the File

The `vi` editor provides a convenient way to move the cursor rapidly to a specific line in the file.

1   If necessary, open the file with vi.

2   In the command mode, type the line number and the Go command. Thus, to go to the seventh line of the file, type

This command does not appear on screen.

    7G

in which the G stands for "Go."

3   To go to the bottom of the file, type G. No line number is necessary:

This command does not appear on screen.

    G

You can also jump a certain number of lines above or below your current position:

•   **To jump backward, enter the number of lines you wish to jump, followed by a minus sign (–).** Thus, to jump back 9 lines from your current position, type

This command does not appear on screen.

    9–

•   **To jump forward, enter the number of lines you wish to jump, followed by a plus sign (+).** Thus, to jump forward 5 lines from your current position, type

    5+

13.17   Setting Line Numbers

Of course, if you are to be jumping forward or backward to specific lines, it would be helpful to be able to number the lines.

1   Put vi into the command mode.

2   Enter the Set Numbers command. Type the line

This command appears at the bottom of the screen.

    :set nu (Return)

This causes line numbers to be placed down the left-hand margin:

```
1   Mary had a little lamb,
2   A little cheese,
3   A little ham.
4   Delicious!
5
6   Mary had a polar bear
7   Whose fur was white as snow,
8   And everywhere that big bear went
9   The people let it go.
```

The line numbers appear on the screen but are not written into the work buffer or the file.

3   To remove the line numbers, enter the Set No Numbers command. This must be done in the command mode:

```
:set nonu (Return)
```

13.18   Buffers and More Buffers

Recall that vi actually works on a copy of the file in the work buffer. While using vi, you have access to other buffers as well. There are 36 of these:

- unnamed buffer

- named buffers "a, "b, "c, . . . ,"z

- numbered buffers "1, "2, "3, . . . ,"9

The unnamed buffer is sometimes called the *general-purpose buffer.* When you change or delete text, the old text is not thrown away immediately. Instead, vi moves the old material into the unnamed buffer, and holds it there until you change or delete more material. The advantage of this is that it allows you to change your mind and restore the deleted text using the "undo" command:

u

This puts the old text back where it came from. Since vi has only one unnamed buffer, the undo command can only restore the most recent change you made; previous changes are lost.

The named buffers and numbered buffers are useful for moving blocks of text around a file or between different files. In the next section, for example, you will move four lines of text from one place in a file to another. You will do this by positioning the cursor at the beginning of the block of text and issuing the command

"a4yy

This is best understood when read backwards: yy stands for "yank," which means in this case "copy"; the 4 refers to four lines of text; and "a (double quote-a) specifies a particular named buffer. Therefore, this command tells vi to copy four lines of text and place them in the named buffer "a.

To retrieve the text from the named buffer, place the cursor where you want the text to go and type the command

`"ap`

which tells vi to "put" a copy of the contents of the named buffer "a into the work buffer.

Remember that buffers are only temporary storage locations; their contents are lost once you leave vi.

13.19   Yanking Text

Let's use a named buffer to move blocks of text around in the file:

1   **Use vi to open the file.** If you have been following the examples thus far, open the file poems.

2   **In the command mode, move the cursor to the first of the lines you wish to copy.** To copy the second poem, move the cursor to the first line of the poem:

`Mary had a polar bear`

3   **Yank the lines into a named buffer.** Thus, to copy four lines into named buffer "a, type the following line (no (Return) is required):

This does not appear on screen.

`"a4yy`

Although the command itself does not appear on the screen, the computer usually puts a message at the bottom of the screen:

On some systems, this message does not appear.

`4 lines yanked`

13.20   Putting Text

Once you have yanked text into a buffer, the text will remain in that buffer until you either put more text in its place or you leave the editor. You can put (copy) the text from the buffer to the file:

1   **Move the cursor to the place you want to put the text.** In the current example, move the cursor down to the last line in the file.

2   **Put the lines of the named buffer into the work buffer.** The following command will put a copy of the contents of the named buffer "a below the current cursor location.

This does not appear on screen.

```
"ap
```

The four lines of the second poem should appear. The computer will also tell you how many lines were placed:

```
4 lines
```

If you try the Put command on a buffer that has nothing in it, the computer will respond with an error message such as

Buffers are also called *registers.*

```
Nothing in register a
```

The contents of the named buffer are not changed by the Put operation; you could put the same four lines into the text again if you wanted to.

3   **Write the changes into the file.**

WARNING	It is important to remember that buffers are only temporary storage locations; their contents are lost once you quit vi.

13.21   Moving Text between Files

The named and numbered buffers are used to transfer text from one file to another.

1   **If necessary, put vi into the command mode.**

2   **Move the cursor to the first of the lines you want to transfer.** Suppose you want to copy the first four lines of poems into a new file. Make sure the cursor is on the first line of the lines that you wish to transfer.

3   **Yank the lines into a named buffer.** To yank four lines into the buffer "m, type

This does not appear on screen.

```
"m4yy
```

The computer will print the number of lines that were yanked:

```
4 lines yanked
```

4   **Enter the Edit File command, followed by the name of the file that is to receive the yanked text.** Thus, to put the text into the file stuff, type

```
:e stuff (Return)
```

This tells the editor that you want to work on the file stuff. The editor will close the file poems and attempt to open a file named stuff. If there is no file named stuff in your current directory, the editor opens an empty work buffer:

□
~
~
~
~
~
~
```
"stuff" No such file or directory
```

5   **Put the lines.** To put the contents of "m into the newly opened work buffer, type

```
"mp
```

You should see something like this appear on the screen:

```
Mary had a little lamb,
A little cheese,
A little ham.
Delicious!
4 lines
```

6   **Write these lines into the file.** This is done the usual way:

(Esc) :w (Return)

The editor will tell you the size of the new file that you just created:

```
"stuff" [New file] 5 lines, 109 characters
```

Note that the new lines were entered below the original cursor position, leaving a blank line at the top of the file. As a result, the new file contains five lines, not four.

7   **Edit the file as necessary, then quit the editor.**

13.22   Command Summary

You must press (Return) after a UNIX shell command (such as vi or spell) or a vi command that begins with a slash (/), question mark (?), or colon (:). Press (Esc) to obtain the vi command mode. Note that vi commands beginning with a colon (:) or slash (/) appear at the bottom of the screen, but none of the other vi commands appear on-screen.

Opening, Writing, and Closing Files (use (Return))

vi file	open file named file (UNIX shell command)
:w	write changes into default file
:w file	write changes into file named file
:q	quit vi
:wq	write changes into file and quit vi
:q!	quit without writing changes into file

Inserting Text (vi command mode)

a	add text to the right of the current cursor location
i	insert text to the left of the cursor
O	Open up a new line above the current line
o	open up a new line below the current line
R	Replace (type over) text
(Esc)	return to command mode

Moving the Cursor (vi command mode)

← ↓ ↑ →	move one space in direction indicated
h	move one space left
j	move one space down
k	move one space up
l	move one space right
(Spacebar)	move one space right
(Backspace)	move one space left
(Return)	move to beginning of next line down
–	move to beginning of previous line

Correcting Mistakes (vi command mode)

x	delete one character
dd	delete entire line
$n$dd	delete n lines
u	"undo" most recent change
U	"undo" all changes on current line

Checking Spelling (UNIX shell command)

`spell file`   list misspelled words found in `file`

Searching (vi command mode)

`/word`   search forward through the file for the first occurrence of `word`

`/`   continue search for the next occurrence of `word`

`?word`   search backward for the first occurrence of `word`

`?`   continue search backward for the next occurrence of `word`

Jumping to a Line (vi command mode)

n+   jump forward (down) *n* lines

n−   jump backward (up) *n* lines

*n*G   Go to line number *n*

G   Go to the bottom of the file

Setting Line Numbers (vi command mode)

`:set nu`   set line numbers on the screen

`:set nonu`   remove line numbers

Yanking and Putting (vi command mode)

`"k`*n*`yy`   yank (copy) *n* lines into buffer `"k`

`"kp`   put the contents of buffer `"k` below the current line

Substituting (vi command mode)

`:%s/old/new/g`   replace `old` by `new` everywhere in the file

Editing Another File (vi command mode)

`:e file`   edit `file`

13.23 Exercises

1. If there are any typos in your file `poems`, use the `vi` editor to correct them.

2. Specify which `vi` mode you would use to **(a)** delete a line; **(b)** yank a line; **(c)** write over old text; **(d)** move the cursor; **(e)** add text to a new line above the current cursor position.

3. How do you get from the `vi` command mode to the insert mode? How do you get back again?

4. Describe what happens when the following `vi` commands are given:

   ```
   "z10yy
   "kp
   u
   ```

5. You have already seen how the `vi` command `a` allows you to insert text to the right of the current cursor position. The command `A` is also used to insert text, but at the end of the current line. Using the `vi` editor, open the file `poems`, type an `A`, and enter the following line:

   ```
   This demonstrates the A command.
   ```

6. The `vi` command `I` ("Insert") allows you to insert text. How does it differ from the `i` ("insert") command?

7. The `vi` command `o` ("open") opens an empty line below the current cursor position. Try out this command.

8. The `vi` command `O` ("Open") opens an empty line above the current cursor position. Try out this command.

9. Using the `vi` editor, create a new file named `747art` and type in the following quote, making sure that you press (Return) each time the cursor nears the right edge of the screen:

   It is hard to deny, yet rarely said, that the creative impulse was redirected at some point early in this century, or perhaps in the 19th, away from some of its normal artistic channels and into new ones associated with engineering and technology. Quite apart from being useful, a Boeing 747 is a far more impressive aesthetic object than what passes for "art" in our contemporary museums.

   --Tom Bethell

   Make sure to write this into the file before you quit the `vi` editor. (Bonus question: Do you agree with Mr. Bethell?)

10. Most computer terminals have a useful feature called *wraparound*. Try an experiment to find out whether your terminal does:

    a. Open a new file named `wrap` and begin typing in the quote by Tom Bethell, only this time do not press (Return) when the cursor reaches the end of the screen. Instead, keep typing and observe what happens. If the cursor automatically moves down to the next line as you type, your terminal has wraparound—it wraps a long line around to the next line to fit it on the screen. If, on the other hand, the cursor remains at the end of the line as you type, your terminal lacks wraparound.

    b. Continue typing in the entire Bethell quote without pressing the (Return) key. (This may be a bit difficult if your terminal does not have the wraparound feature, but do the best you can.) Write the quote into the file and quit the vi editor.

    c. Reopen the file `wrap`. How many lines and characters do you see on the screen? How many lines and characters does the editor say are in the file? (Moral #1: What you see on the screen is not necessarily what you get in the file. Moral #2: If you want to start a new line, press (Return)—don't rely on the wraparound.)

11. If you are unsure of the spelling of a word, you can use the `look` utility to check its spelling in the UNIX word list. Suppose you wanted to know how to spell *relief*. Is it "*i* before *e*" or "*e* before *i*"? At the UNIX shell prompt, type `look`, followed by the word in question:

    § `look relief`(Return)

    If the word appears on the UNIX word list, `look` will print it on the screen:

    `relief`

    Try a misspelled word (e.g., "releif").

    If the word is not on the list, `look` will print nothing. Instead, you will see the UNIX shell prompt:

    §

    You can also use `look` to examine all of the words on the UNIX word list that begin with a particular sequence of letters. To see the words that begin with *rel*, type

    § `look rel` (Return)

    Use `look` to determine whether the following are found in the UNIX word list: **(a)** your first name; **(b)** your last name; **(c)** the last name of the vice president; **(d)** Kabul, the capital of Afghanistan; **(e)** herpetologist; **(f)** ornithology.

12. One of the requirements for a good UNIX password is that it not be a common word or name. Some UNIX installations will not accept any word in the internal word list. Use look to see whether any of the following passwords is listed: **(a)** Hi54Luck; **(b)** 4Tune8; **(c)** 1DayMayB; **(d)** Much2Gr8; **(e)** 14DRoad; **(f)** FOR@ward; **(g)** gin/GER; **(h)** hydro.GEN.

13. Use spell on the files that you created in the previous chapters. If spell reports an error in a file, open that file and use the Search command to find the misspelled words. Make the necessary corrections.

14. In a previous exercise, you created a file named 747art. Open this file and use the search commands to locate the sentence beginning with the word Quite. Yank the lines that contain this entire sentence. (You may have to take a few words from the preceding sentence as well.) Use the edit command to transfer these lines to a new file art.

15. There is a modification of the previous Global Substitution command that you might find useful:

:%s/wittle/little/gc (Return)

The c at the end of the command line stands for "confirm." Under this option, the editor will show you each change and ask you for confirmation before actually making the change:

Marye had a wittle wamb
              ^^^^^^
If you want to make the change, type y (for *yes*); otherwise, type n (for *no*).

14 TUTORIAL: EDITING WITH EMACS

In this chapter, you will see how to use emacs to create and edit a text file. If you haven't already done so, log in and set your terminal. Then follow the examples.

14.1 Starting emacs

- **Start emacs.** Enter the emacs command at the UNIX shell prompt

  § emacs (Return)

  In a moment, you should see the emacs screen, as shown in Figure 14–1.

14.2 The emacs Screen

Take a moment to identify the various parts of the emacs screen:

- *Buffer window.* This is the place where you enter text or modify text. It shows the contents of the work buffer.

- *Cursor.* The cursor is a small box that marks your current location in the buffer. Any character you type is inserted to the left of the cursor.

- *Echo Area.* Also called the *minibuffer*, this is an area at the bottom of the screen in which messages and one-line commands appear.

- *Mode Line.* Located above the Echo Area, the Mode Line is a contrasting (reverse-video) band that provides useful information about the status of the buffer and the editor.

Let's examine the Mode Line in greater detail. The Mode Line in Figure 14–1 includes the following information:

- *Modification status.* Dashes (--) in this position show that no changes have been made to the text. When you make changes, asterisks (**) appear instead.

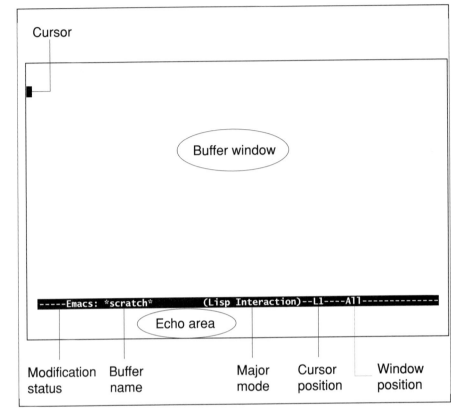

Figure 14–1
The emacs screen.
The dark band near the
bottom of the screen is
the Mode Line.

- *Buffer name.* Every buffer has a name. If the contents of the buffer were obtained from a file, the file name will appear in the Mode Line. "Scratch" is used for a new buffer that has not yet been saved to a file.

- *Major mode.* An emacs *mode* is a set of features that can speed specialized tasks, such as editing C, Lisp, or Fortran programs. Some commands behave slightly differently in different modes. (We will not discuss emacs modes in this book.)

- *Cursor position.* "L1" shows that the cursor is currently positioned on Line 1.

- *Window position.* "All" means that the current buffer fits entirely in the emacs window. For longer buffers, "Top" indicates that the window is positioned to show the top of the buffer, and "Bot" means the window is positioned at the bottom of the buffer. A percentage (e.g., "15%") indicates that 15% of the buffer is above the top of the window.

14.3   Command Notation

Many emacs commands require that you use the (Control) key in combination with other keys. In traditional emacs notation, (Control) is indicated by C-. For example, the command sequence to save changes in a file is

(Control)-(X)   (Control)-(S)

In emacs notation, this command sequence is written as C-x C-s.

Other emacs commands require that you use the (Meta) key, denoted M-. Thus, the command to move to the top of the buffer is the combination

(Meta)-(V)

In emacs notation, this command sequence is written as M-v. If your keyboard does not have a (Meta) key, you can use the (Alt) key instead:

(Alt)-(V)

Alternatively, you can press *and release* the (Escape) or (Esc) key, then press the (V) key:

(Esc) (V)

This would be written in emacs notation as <ESC>v.

Other common abbreviations used in the emacs manual are <Return> or <RET> for the (Return) key; <Delete> or <Del> for the (Delete) key; and <SPC> for the (Spacebar).

14.4   Entering Text

Let's put some text into the buffer:

- **Enter the text.** Type the following lines of verse:

      Poem #1 (Return)
      Mary had a little lamb, (Return)
      A little cheese, (Return)
      A little ham. (Return)
      Burp! ☐

Although these lines appear in the emacs buffer window, they are not yet saved in the file. That is the next step.

14.5   Saving Text to a File

1   **Use the Save command.** This is the key combination C-x C-s. First hold down

the (Control) key while pressing the (X) key; then hold down the (Control) key while pressing the (S) key:

(Control)-(X)   (Control)-(S)

A prompt will appear in the Echo Area:

```
File to save: ~/
```

The rules for naming files and directories are summarized in Section 6.3.

2   **Enter a valid file name.** It is a good idea to select a descriptive name for the file. Try the name poems:

```
File to save: ~/poems
```

3   **Press** (Return). Note that a message appears in the Echo Area, telling you what just happened:

```
Wrote /home/yourlogin/poems
```

14.6   Ending the Editing Session

We have created a new file; now let's exit the emacs editor.

1   **Use the Exit command.** This is the combination C-x C-c:

(Control)-(X)   (Control)-(C)

This puts you back into the UNIX shell. You should see the UNIX prompt:

§

2   **Check that the new file exists.** The ls command should list the file:

§ ls (Return)

3   **Check the contents of the file.** The cat command will show the contents:

§ cat poems (Return)

14.7   Finding a File

Let's reopen the file you just created:

1   **Restart** emacs.

§ emacs (Return)

2   **Select the Find File command.** The command is C-x C-f:

(Control)-(X)   (Control)-(F)

A prompt will appear in the echo area:

```
Find file: ~/
```

3 **Enter a valid file name.** Thus, to open the file poems, enter

```
Find file: ~/poems
```

4 **Press** (Return). Note that the file name appears in the Mode Line.

14.8 Moving the Cursor

When editing a file, you will often need to move the cursor around the file. There are a number of commands for doing this:

- **Use the arrow keys to move the cursor.** Many computer keyboards have arrow keys—also called *cursor-control keys*—that move the cursor one space at a time in the direction indicated:

  These may not work on your machine.

  ← ↓ ↑ →

- **Use the alternative cursor-control keys to move the cursor.** A number of commands may be used in place of the arrow keys:

  On many terminals, holding a key down causes its function to be repeated rapidly. This can be useful when you want to move quickly through the file.

  C-f   move one space forward (right)

  C-b   move one space back (left)

  C-p   move to previous line (one line up)

  C-n   move to next line (one line down)

  C-a   move to the beginning of the current line

  C-e   move to the end of the current line

14.9 Correcting Text

Of course, you need to be able to correct errors and make changes to text. There are a number of commands that can be used to delete characters from the buffer:

<Del>   ((Delete) key) delete the character to the left of the cursor

C-d   delete the character under the cursor

Let's make changes to the current buffer.

1 **Move the cursor to the right of the text to be deleted.** In the buffer poems you might want to replace *Burp!* with something more suitable. (Mary is very polite and would never burp at the dinner table.) Position the cursor to the right of *Burp!*.

2   **Delete the unwanted text.** Use the (Delete) key (<Del>) to remove the characters. Note that the cursor moves back one space each time you press (Delete).

3   **Enter the new text.** Whatever you type now will be entered into the work buffer. Try Delicious!:

Delicious! (Return)

4   **Continue entering text.** Let's add another poem to the buffer:

(Return)
    Poem #2 (Return)
Mary had a polar bear (Return)
Whose fur was white as snow, (Return)
And everywhere that big bear went (Return)
The people let it go. (Return)

5   **Quit emacs.** As before, use the Quit (C-x C-c) command:

(Control)-(X)   (Control)-(C)

Because you have not saved the most recent changes, emacs will prompt you to save the file:

Save file ~/poems? (y, n, !, q, C-r, or C-h)

6   **Answer Yes.** Press the *y* key:

y

This will save the changes in the file poems. Something else happens as well: The previous contents of the file poems are placed in a new file named poems~. That way, you do not lose the original file.

14.10   Opening a File from the Command Line

You can start emacs and open a file at the same time:

•   **Restart emacs and reopen the file.** To open the file named poems, type the command line

§ emacs poems (Return)

This causes emacs to copy the contents of the file into the buffer and position the cursor in the upper left corner of the screen.

14.11   Searching for Text

You can move through a file to find a specified word, character, or string of characters using an *incremental search* (I-search). In an incremental search, emacs does not wait until you have completely specified the string of characters you want; instead, it begins searching while you are typing the string.

1   **Enter the Search command.** The command is C-s:

(Control)-(S)

In response, a prompt appears in the Echo Area:

```
I-search:
```

2   **Enter the character or string of characters you want to find.** Suppose you want to find the word *ham* in the buffer. Type the letter *h* at the prompt:

```
I-search: h
```

Note that when you typed the *h*, emacs positioned the cursor to the right of the *h* in *had*. Now add the letter *a*:

```
I-search: ha
```

This time, emacs moved the cursor to the right of the *a* in *had*. Finally, type *m*:

```
I-search: ham
```

Obviously, *had* does not contain the letters *h* and *a* followed by *m*, so emacs searches forward through the file until it finds a string of characters that matches this pattern. In this case, *ham* is the next string that works. The editor repositions the cursor at the end of this word.

3   **If necessary, modify the search string.** Suppose you were really interested in finding all the strings containing the characters *ha*. You can modify the search string by pressing the (Delete) key to remove the last letter of the previous search string:

```
I-search: ha
```

Note that the cursor jumped back to the word *had*.

4   **Find the next occurrence of the search string.** In this example, *had*, *ham*, and *that* will match the search string; emacs has found the first word. To find *ham*, type the search command C-s:

(Control)-(S)

Note that the cursor jumped to the right of the word *ham*.

5   **Repeat search for string.** Type the search command C-s again:

(Control)-(S)

The cursor jumps down to the word *had* in the second poem. Use the search command C-s again:

(Control)-(S)

The cursor jumps to the word *that*. Repeat the search command C-s one more time:

(Control)-(S)

Since there are no more occurrences of the pattern *ha*, emacs gives you a message:

```
Failing I-Search
```

6　**Terminate the search.** Once you are finished searching the file, you can end the search and leave the cursor at its new position by pressing (Return).

The C-s command searches forward through the buffer, starting at the current location of the cursor. Any text above the cursor will not be searched. The C-r command searches backwards from the current cursor location.

14.12　Killing and Yanking

Killing and yanking are often called cutting and pasting.

You may sometimes need to move a block of text—also called a *region* of text—from one place to another within a buffer. To do this, you must first put the text into a temporary storage location called a *Kill Ring*. In emacs terminology, this is called *killing* the text. Then you can move the cursor to another point in the buffer and retrieve the text from the Kill Ring. This is called *yanking* the text.

1　**Move the cursor to the beginning of the text to be moved.** In the poems file, move the cursor to the start of the first poem.

2　**Mark the beginning of the text region.** Use the C-@ ("Set Mark") command:

On some keyboards, the C-<SPC> command may be used instead.

(Control)-(@)

You should see a message that the mark has been set:

```
Mark Set
```

3　**Move the cursor to the end of the text region.** Move the cursor to the end of the first poem.

4　**Kill the text.** The C-w ("Kill Region") command causes the text region to be removed from the work buffer into the Kill Ring:

(Control)-(W)

5　**Move the cursor to the new location.** Move to the end of the poems file.

6 **Yank the text.** The C-y ("Yank") command copies text from the temporary buffer into the work buffer:

(Control)-(Y)

You can paste the text again, if you wish. Try it:

(Control)-(Y)

14.13 Undoing Changes

You probably would not want to save the most recent changes made in the poems buffer. (There is no need for two copies of Poem #1, nor should Poem #1 come after Poem #2.) The emacs editor allows you to "undo" recent changes:

1 **Give the Undo command.** Type C-x u:

(Control)-(X) (U)

This will undo the effect of the most recent command.

2 **Repeat the Undo command.** Try the alternate Undo command C-_ (which may or may not work on your keyboard):

Here, _ is the underscore.

(Control)-(__)

This should undo the next most recent command. (If this does not work, try the C-x u command instead.)

3 **Repeat as needed.** When you finish, the first poem should be back in its original position.

14.14 Saving to a Different File

1 **Make changes in the buffer.** Because we will want to try out the spell-checker, first use emacs to introduce misspelled words (underlined below) into the file poems:

```
    Poem #1
Marye had a wittle wamb,
A wittle cheese,
A wittle ham.
Delisious!

    Poem #2
Mary had a polar beer
Whose fir was white as snow,
And everywhere that big bare went
The people let it go.
```

2 **Save the changes.** Use the Write (C-x C-w) command:

(Control)–(X)   (Control)–(W)

emacs will tell you the current file name in the Echo Area:

File to save: ~/poems

3 **Replace the file name.** Delete the current file name, and replace it with another. In this case, try misspelled:

File to save: ~/misspelled

4 **Press** (Return). The changes will be saved in the file misspelled.

14.15   Using spell

spell is a UNIX utility that checks your spelling. Unlike many spell-checkers that are supplied as part of a word processor or text editor, spell is an entirely separate program. Consequently, you will not use spell while you are editing a file with emacs.

1 **If you are working in** emacs, **write the file and quit the editor.** Recall that the command sequence to do this is C-x C-s followed by C-x C-c.

2 **At the shell prompt, enter the** spell **command and the file name.**

§ spell misspelled(Return)

The spell utility searches through the file and prints any words that are not found on the UNIX word list:

Delisious
Marye
wamb
wittle

Note that although *wittle* appears three times in the file, it is listed only once by spell. Note too that spell caught the unusual spelling of *Mary*; the word list includes many proper names. But spell missed some words: *beer*, *fir*, and *bare*. The reason is simple: these are legitimate words in spell's word list. Remember, spell does not really check for spelling errors; rather, it looks for groups of characters that do not match those in its word list. It will not detect words used out of context.

14.16   Reading the emacs Tutorial

We have barely scratched the surface of emacs; an entire book could be written on the subject. To learn more, you can refer to the emacs on-line tutorial:

1 **If necessary, start emacs.** Enter the emacs command at the UNIX shell prompt

   § emacs (Return)

2 **Start the emacs tutorial.** The command is C-m t:

   (Control)-(M) (T)

   This will open a new window containing the tutorial.

3 **Work through tutorial.**

4 **Cancel the tutorial.** The emacs Cancel command is C-g:

   (Control)-(G)

14.17 Command Summary

Opening, Writing, and Closing Files

emacs file	open file (UNIX shell command)
C-x C-s	save buffer in current file
C-x C-w	write buffer to a file specified by user
C-x C-f	find a file and copy it into the buffer.
C-x C-c	Exit emacs session

Moving the Cursor

← ↓ ↑ →	move one space in direction indicated
C-f	move one space forward (right)
C-b	move one space back (left)
C-p	move to previous line (one line up)
C-n	move to next line (one line down)
C-a	move to the beginning of the current line
C-e	move to the end of the current line

Deleting Text

<Del>	((Delete) key) delete the character to the left of the cursor
C-d	delete the character under the cursor

Searching for Text

C-s	search forward through the buffer for string of characters
C-r	search backward through the buffer for string of characters

Killing and Yanking Text

C-@	mark start of text block
C-w	kill (cut) text from buffer into Kill Ring
C-y	yank (paste) the text from Kill Ring into buffer

Undoing Changes

C-x u	undo most recent command
C-_	alternate undo command

Miscellaneous Commands

`spell file`	check `file` for spelling errors (UNIX command)
`C-M t`	run tutorial
`C-g`	cancel or stop a command

14.18   Exercises

1. If there are any typos in your file `poems`, use the `emacs` editor to correct them.

2. Using the `emacs` editor, create a new file named `747art` and type in the following quote:

    It is hard to deny, yet rarely said, that the creative impulse was redirected at some point early in this century, or perhaps in the 19th, away from some of its normal artistic channels and into new ones associated with engineering and technology. Quite apart from being useful, a Boeing 747 is a far more impressive aesthetic object than what passes for "art" in our contemporary museums.

    --Tom Bethell

    Make sure to write this into the file before you quit the editor.

3. Use `spell` on the files that you created in the previous chapters. If `spell` reports an error in a file, open that file and use the Search command to find the misspelled words. Make the necessary corrections.

4. If you are unsure of the spelling of a word, you can use the `look` utility to check its spelling in the UNIX word list. Suppose you wanted to know how to spell *relief*. Is it "*i* before *e*" or "*e* before *i*"? At the UNIX shell prompt, type `look`, followed by the word in question:

    § `look relief` (Return)

    If the word appears on the UNIX word list, `look` will print it on the screen:

    `relief`

    Try a misspelled word (e.g., "releif").

    If the word is not on the list, `look` will print nothing. Instead, you will see the UNIX shell prompt:

    §

    You can also use `look` to examine all of the words on the UNIX word list that begin with a particular sequence of letters. To see the words that begin with *rel*, type

§ look rel (Return)

Use look to determine whether the following are found in the UNIX word list:
(a) your first name; (b) your last name; (c) the last name of the vice president;
(d) Kabul, the capital of Afghanistan; (e) herpetologist; (f) ornithology.

5. One of the requirements for a good UNIX password is that it not be a common
   word or name. Some UNIX installations will not accept any word in the internal
   word list. Use look to see whether any of the following passwords is listed: (a)
   Hi54Luck; (b) 4Tune8; (c) 1DayMayB; (d) Much2Gr8; (e) 14DRoad; (f)
   FOR@ward; (g) gin/GER; (h) hydro.GEN.

15 TUTORIAL: EDITING WITH PICO

In this chapter, you will see how to use pico to create and edit a text file. If you haven't already done so, log in and set your terminal. Then follow the examples.

15.1   Starting pico

- **Start pico.** Enter the pico command at the UNIX shell prompt

  § pico (Return)

If all goes well, you should see the pico window, as shown in Figure 15–1. Take a moment to identify the various parts of the window.

- *Status line.* The dark bar at the top of the window shows the current version of pico, the name of the file being edited, and other information concerning the status of the file.

- *Content area.* This is the place where you enter text or modify text. It shows the contents of the work buffer.

- *Cursor.* This is a small black box that marks your current location in the content area.

- *Message line.* Located below the content area and above the menu bar, the message line is the place where pico displays messages and prompts.

- *Menu bar.* The menu bar or command list occupies the last two rows of the window. It lists frequently used pico commands. You can enter one of these commands by holding down the (Control) key—represented by a caret (^)— while pressing another key.

Twelve commands are listed on the Menu bar:

^G   Get Help. Provides more information regarding the various functions.

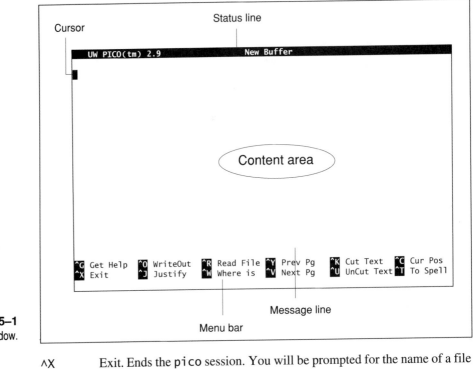

Figure 15–1
The pico window.

^X   Exit. Ends the pico session. You will be prompted for the name of a file into which your work may be saved.

^O   Write Out. Saves your work in a file without ending the editing session.

^J   Justify. Adjusts the appearance of the paragraph where the cursor is sitting.

^R   Read File. Allows you to copy a file into the buffer. You will be prompted for the name of the file.

^W   Where Is. Searches the buffer for characters or words that you specify.

^Y   Previous Page. Scrolls back (up) one page.

^V   Next Page. Scrolls forward (down) one page.

^K   Cut Text. Cuts text from the buffer and saves it temporarily. The text can be pasted back into the buffer.

^U   UnCut Text. Pastes cut text into the buffer.

^C   Current Position. Shows the line number of the current cursor location, and lists the total number of lines and characters in the file.

^T   To Spell. Starts the spell-checker.

15.2   Entering Text

The cursor shows where text is to be entered into the Content Area.

- **Enter the text.** Try typing in the following lines of verse:

```
Mary had a little lamb, (Return)
A little cheese, (Return)
A little ham. (Return)
Burp!□
```

These lines appear in the content area of the pico window, they are not yet saved in the file. Remember, you must "write out" these lines from the buffer into a file to save them.

15.3   Writing Out to a File

1   **Select the Write Out command.** On the menu bar, the Write Out command appears as ^O. Hold down the (Control) key while pressing the (O) key:

(Control)-(O)

A prompt will appear in the message line:

`File Name to write:`

2   **Enter a valid file name.** It is a good idea to select a descriptive name for the file. Try the name poems:

`File Name to write: poems`

3   **Press** (Return). Note that a message will appear in the message line, telling you what just happened:

`[Wrote 4 lines]`

Also, the current file name will appear in the status line at the top of the pico window.

15.4   Ending the Editing Session

We have created a new file; now let's exit the pico editor.

1   **Use the exit command.** The command is ^X:

(Control)-(X)

This puts you back into the UNIX shell. You should see the UNIX prompt:

§

2 **Check that the new file exists.** The `ls` command should list the file:

§ `ls` (Return)

3 **Check the contents of the file.** The `cat` command will show the contents:

§ `cat poems` (Return)

15.5 Reopening a File

Let's reopen the file you just created. There are two ways to do this. You can start `pico`, then read from the file:

1 **Restart `pico`.**

§ `pico`(Return)

2 **Select the Read File command.** The command is ^R:

(Control)–(R)

A prompt will appear in the message line:

`File to insert from home directory:`

3 **Enter a valid file name.** Thus, to open the file `poems`, enter

`File to insert from home directory: poems`

4 **Press** (Return). Note that a message will appear in the message line, telling you what just happened:

`[Inserted 4 lines]`

Alternatively, you can start `pico` and open a file at the same time:

• **Restart `pico` and reopen the file.** To open the file named `poems`, type the command

§ `pico poems`(Return)

This will cause `pico` to copy the contents of the file into the work buffer, then display this on the screen. The cursor will be positioned over the first character in the work buffer. Also, the current file name will appear in the status line at the top of the `pico` window.

15.6 Moving the Cursor

When editing a file, you will often need to move the cursor around the file.

- **Use the arrow keys to move the cursor.** Many computer keyboards have arrow keys—also called *cursor-control keys*—that move the cursor one space at a time in the direction indicated:

These may not work on your machine.

    ← ↓ ↑ →

- **Use the alternative cursor-control keys to move the cursor.** A number of commands may be used in place of the arrow keys:

On many terminals, holding a key down causes its function to be repeated rapidly. This can be useful when you want to move quickly through the file.

^F	move one space forward (right)
^B	move one space back (left)
^P	move to previous line (one line up)
^N	move to next line (one line down)

There are some other commands that can be used to move around the file:

^A	move to the beginning of the current line
^E	move to the end of the current line
^Y	move back (up) one page
^V	move forward (down) one page

15.7 Searching for Text

You can move through a file to a specified word, character, or group of characters using the Where Is command.

1   **Select the Where Is command.** The command is ^W:

    (Control)–(W)

Note that a prompt appears in the message line:

Search:

2   **Enter the character or group of characters you want to find.** If you are working in the file poems, enter the word *Burp*:

Search: Burp

The cursor will move to the *B* in *Burp*. (If the word or characters are not found in the file, you will be given a message to that effect.)

15.8   Replacing Text

You have seen how to create a new text file using the pico editor. Now you will see how to edit existing text by typing over it with new text.

1   **Move the cursor to the right of the text you intend to replace.** In the file poems you might want to replace *Burp!* with something more suitable. (Mary is very polite and would never burp at the dinner table.) Position the cursor to the right of *Burp!*.

The ^D command deletes the character at the cursor position.

2   **Delete the unwanted text.** Use either the (Backspace) or (Delete) key to remove the character to the left of the cursor. Note that the cursor moves back one space each time you delete a character.

3   **Enter the new text.** Whatever you type now will be entered into the work buffer. Try *Delicious!*:

```
Delicious!
```

4   **Continue entering text.**

```
(Return)
Mary had a polar bear (Return)
Whose fur was white as snow, (Return)
And everywhere that big bear went (Return)
The people let it go. (Return)
```

5   **Write the changes to the file.** As before, use the Write Out command, ^O. Since this is an existing file, pico will tell you the file name in the message line:

```
File Name to write: poems
```

You can save the new changes in a different file, if you wish, by entering a different file name. Otherwise, simply press (Return) to save the changes in the file poems.

15.9   Spell-Checking

To test the pico spell-checker, let's introduce some misspelled words (underlined below) into the file poems:

```
Marye had a wittle wamb,
A wittle cheese,
A wittle ham.
Delisious!

Mary had a polar beer
Whose fir was white as snow,
```

```
And everywhere that big bare went
The people let it go.
```

Be sure to write out these changes into the file. Next, check the spelling:

1   Select the To Spell command. The command is ^T:

Control – T

The spell-checker will search through the file and highlight a word that may be misspelled. At the same time, a prompt will appear in the message line:

`Edit a replacement: Marye`

Note that the cursor is positioned to the right of the *e* in *Marye*.

2   Correct the misspelling. Backspace over the *e* in *Marye*, then press Return:

`Edit a replacement: Mary`

The spell-checker will find the next misspelled word:

`Edit a replacement: wittle`

3   Correct the next misspelling. Convert *wittle* to *little* and press Return:

`Edit a replacement: little`

The spell-checker will find the next occurrence of *wittle* and ask whether you want to replace it with *little*:

`Replace "wittle" with "little"?`

4   Enter *y* for yes. The correction will be made and the next error will be found:

`Replace "wittle" with "little"?`

5   Continue correcting the misspellings.

Note that the spell-checker misses some words: `beer`, `fir`, and `bare`. The reason is simple: these are legitimate words in the UNIX word list. Remember, the spell-checker does not really check for spelling errors; rather, it looks for groups of characters that do not match those in its word list. Consequently, it will not detect words that are used out of context.

15.10   Cutting and Pasting

You may occasionally need to move large blocks of text around within a file. This is done by storing the text in a temporary buffer.

1   **Move the cursor to the beginning of the text block.** In the poems file, move the cursor to the start of the first poem.

2   **Mark the beginning of the text block.** Use the ^^ command:

    ⌐Control⌐−⌐^⌐

You should see a message that the mark has been set:

[Mark Set]

3   **Move the cursor to the end of the text block.** Move the cursor to the end of the first poem. Note that the text is highlighted:

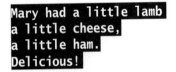

4   **Cut the text.** The ^K ("Cut") command causes the text to be removed from the work buffer into a temporary storage buffer:

    ⌐Control⌐−⌐K⌐

5   **Move the cursor to the new location.** Move to the end of the poems file.

6   **Paste the text.** The ^U ("Uncut") command copies text from the temporary buffer into the work buffer:

    ⌐Control⌐−⌐U⌐

You can paste the text multiple times, if you wish:

    ⌐Control⌐−⌐U⌐

15.11   Exiting without Saving Changes

There is no reason to save the most recent changes in the file poems. You can discard the changes by exiting pico without writing out the changes.

1   **Select the Exit command.** Type ^X.

You will be asked whether you want to save the modified buffer:

Save modified buffer (ANSWERING "No" WILL DESTROY CH/

2   **Answer *n* for no at the prompt.**

The buffer will not be written out to the file.

15.12   Command Summary

Opening, Writing, and Closing Files

`pico file`	open `file` (UNIX shell command)
^O	write out to a file without ending the editing session
^R	read file into the buffer
^X	exit `pico` session

Searching for Text

^W	search the buffer for characters or words

Moving the Cursor

← ↓ ↑ →	move one space in direction indicated
^F	move one space forward (right)
^B	move one space back (left)
^P	move to previous line (one line up)
^N	move to next line (one line down)
^A	move to beginning of the current line
^E	move to end of the current line
^Y	scroll back (up) one page
^V	scroll forward (down) one page

Cutting, Pasting, and Deleting Text

^^	mark start of text block
^K	cut text from work buffer and save temporarily
^U	uncut (paste) cut text into the work buffer
^D	delete text
(Backspace)	delete text
(Delete)	delete text

Miscellaneous Commands

^C	show line number of the current cursor location
^G	get help
^J	justify paragraph where the cursor is sitting
^T	start spell-checker

15.13   Exercises

1.   If there are any typos in your file `poems`, use the `pico` editor to correct them.

2.   Using the `pico` editor, create a new file named `747art` and type in the following quote:

It is hard to deny, yet rarely said, that the creative impulse was redirected at some point early in this century, or perhaps in the 19th, away from some of its normal artistic channels and into new ones associated with engineering and technology. Quite apart from being useful, a Boeing 747 is a far more impressive aesthetic object than what passes for "art" in our contemporary museums.

--Tom Bethell

Make sure to write this into the file before you quit the editor.

3.   The Get Help (^G) command provides useful information on the various `pico` commands. Use it to determine how the Current Position (^C) command works, then try out this command in one of your files.

4.   Use the Get Help command to determine how the Justify (^J) command works. Then try out the Justify (^J) command on one of your files.

16 TUTORIAL: EDITING WITH TEXT EDITOR

Skip this chapter if you are not using CDE.

Text Editor is a tool provided by the Common Desktop Environment for creating and editing text files. If you have previously used a word processor, you should have no trouble learning to use Text Editor.

16.1 Starting Text Editor

1 **Open the Applications subpanel.**

2 **Click on the Text Editor icon.**

An Editor window will appear (Figure 16–1), with the cursor positioned at the top of the window.

16.2 Entering Text

Putting text into the window is easy:

1 **If necessary, select the Editor window.**

2 **Type the text.** Errors can be deleted by backspacing. Enter the following lines of verse:

```
    Poem #1 (Return)
Mary had a little lamb, (Return)
A little cheese, (Return)
A little ham. (Return)
Burp!
(Return)
```

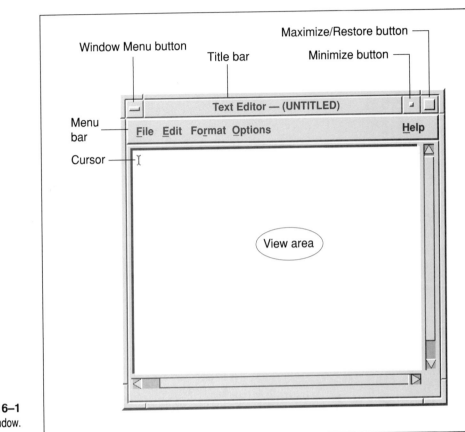

Maximize/Restore button

Window Menu button

Minimize button

Title bar

Text Editor — (UNTITLED)

Menu bar

File Edit Format Options   Help

Cursor

View area

Figure 16–1
The Text Editor window.

Poem #2 (Return)
Mary had a polar bear, (Return)
whose fur was white as snow. (Return)
And everywhere that big bear went, (Return)
The people let it go.

16.3   Saving to a File

The next step is to save in a file the lines you just entered:

The menu remains open if you use the right (#3) mouse button.

1   **Pull down the File menu.** You can use either the mouse or the alternate key combination (Alt)-(F).

2   **Choose Save (needed).** Either click on the Save option or press the *S* key.

A Save As dialog box will appear.

3   **If necessary, type a path or folder name.** By default, your current directory path will appear in the window. If that is acceptable, there is no need to change this.

4   **Enter a valid file name.** By default, UNTITLED appears in the box. It is a good idea to select a descriptive name for the file. Try the name poems.

5   **Press OK.** This will cause the lines to be copied from the screen to the file.

If you entered the name of an existing file, you will be asked whether you want to replace the existing file with the contents of the Editor window.

16.4   Ending the Editing Session

1   **Pull down the File menu.**

2   **Click on Close.** Alternatively, you can press the *C* key.

The Editor window will disappear.

16.5   Re-opening a File

Let's re-open the file you just created. First, restart the Editor:

1   **Open the Applications subpanel.**

2   **Click on the Text Editor icon.** Wait for the Editor window to reappear.

At this point, the editor is open to an empty buffer.

Next open the file:

1   **Pull down the File menu.**

2   **Choose Open....**

A dialog box will appear.

3   **Enter a file name.** To open the file poems, type this name into the box.

4   **Press OK.**

The contents of the file poems will appear in the Editor window.

Keep in mind that it is a *copy* of poems that you see in the window; the file itself is not changed until you save the changes.

16.6   Overstriking Text

In most cases, you will operate the Editor in the *insert* mode. That is, characters you type are inserted to the left of the cursor, and any existing text moves over to make room. However, at times you may want to replace the existing text by typing over it. For this, put the editor into *overstrike* mode:

1   **Position the cursor.** In the file poems you might want to replace *Burp!* with something more suitable. (Mary is very polite and would never burp at the dinner table.) Position the cursor to the left of the *B* in *Burp*.

2   **Pull down the Options menu.** Use the mouse or the alternate key combination (Alt)-(O).

3   **Select Overstrike.** Click on Overstrike or press the *O* key.

Note that a check mark appears next to the option to show it has been selected.

4   **Type the new text over the old text.** Enter *Delicious!* over the offensive *Burp!*.

5   **Return to insert mode.** Pull down the Options menu and select Overstrike.

The check mark will disappear, showing that the overstrike option is no longer in effect.

16.7   Copying, Cutting and Pasting

You can move blocks of text around within a file or between two different files using a temporary buffer called a *clipboard*. Open the file poems and follow these steps:

1   **Select the text.** Position the cursor at the beginning of Poem #1, then hold down the left (#1) mouse button while dragging the cursor over the entire poem. The selected text will be highlighted.

2   **Pull down the Edit menu and choose Copy.** The selected text will be copied from the window into the clipboard. (Alternatively, you can use the Cut command, which copies the text into the clipboard and removes it from the window.)

3   **Move the cursor to the new location.** Position it below Poem #2.

4   **Pull down the Edit menu and choose Paste.**

The text will be copied from the clipboard into the window.

The Paste operation *copies text from the clipboard to the window.*

5   **Repeat pasting as needed.** Since the Paste operation leaves the text in the clipboard unchanged, it is available for pasting as many times as you wish. Try it—paste another copy of the text at the bottom of the file. When you are finished, the window should look something like this:

```
        Poem #1
Mary had a little lamb,
A little cheese,
A little ham.
Delicious!

      Poem #2
Mary had a polar bear,
whose fur was white as snow.
And everywhere that big bear went,
The people let it go.
      Poem #1
Mary had a little lamb,
A little cheese,
A little ham.
Delicious!
      Poem #1
Mary had a little lamb,
A little cheese,
A little ham.
Delicious!
```

16.8   Undoing a Change

There is no reason to have three copies of Poem #1 in the poems file—one is quite enough. The Undo command will reverse the effect of the most recent Cut, Paste, Clear, Replace, Include, Format or Undo. Try it:

- **Pull down the Edit menu and choose Undo.** If the last operation was a Paste, the pasted text should disappear from the Editor window.

If you select Undo again, the text is pasted back into the file—remember, Undo can "undo" itself.

16.9   Deleting Text

We still have a redundant copy of Poem #1 in the file poems. You can either clear it or delete it. Clearing replaces the text with spaces; deleting removes it entirely. Let's delete it:

1   **Select the text to be deleted.** Drag the cursor over the second copy of Poem #1.

2   **Pull down the Edit menu and choose Delete.** The selected text disappears.

3   **Pull down the File menu and choose Save.** The changed text will be saved in the current file, which is poems.

16.10   Saving to a Different File

Later in this chapter we will try out the Editor's spell-checker. For this, we will need a copy of the file `poems`.

1   Pull down the File menu and select the Save As... option.

The Save As window will appear.

2   Enter the new file name. Since the new file will contained misspelled words, name it `misspelled`.

3   Press OK.

Note that the title of the Editor window changes to show the new file name.

Any changes you save now will go into the new file `misspelled`; the original file `poems` will remain unchanged.

16.11   Finding and Changing Text

You can quickly search through a file to find—and replace—a specified string of characters using the Find/Change command. Because we plan to test the spell-checker later in this chapter, let's use this command to introduce some misspellings into the file `misspelled`:

1   Pull down the Edit menu and select Find/Change.... The Find/Change window will appear.

2   Enter the search string in the Find line. Enter the word *little*.

3   Enter the replacement string in the Change line. Enter the misspelling *wittle*. (If all you want is to find a word rather than change it, press (Return).)

4   Press Find. The first occurrence of *little* is highlighted.

5   To change the string, press Change. The highlighted search string *little* will be replaced by *wittle*. (The Change All command replaces every occurrence of *little*.)

If for some reason you do not want to make the change, go on to the next step.

6   Continue finding and changing. When you have changed all instances of the search string *little* in the file, you will see a message:

`Unable to find the string little in the current document.`

Use the Find/Change command to misspell more words (underlined below):

```
Poem #1
Marye had a wittle wamb,
A wittle cheese,
A wittle ham.
Delisious!
```

17 UNIX NETWORKING

A *network* is a group of computers that are interconnected to share information and resources. In this chapter, you will learn about networking of computers. You will also learn about various programs that allow you to communicate with other computer users.

17.1 Local Area Networks (LANs)

Computer networks are often classified according to size and geographical coverage. A *Local Area Network* or LAN consists of computers that are close to one another—often in the same building.

As shown in Figure 17–1, local area networks can be laid out in a variety of configurations, which are often called *topologies*. Each of these arrangements has it advantages and drawbacks; however, from the standpoint of the average computer user, they all appear to be very similar.

There is no generally accepted definition of how "local" a network must be to qualify as a local area network. Some LANs may be large enough to span a university campus or an entire city—although you may occasionally hear the terms *Campus Area Network* (CAN) or *Metropolitan Area Network* (MAN) used to describe these networks. Any network larger than this is generally called a *Wide Area Network* or WAN.

The most common way to create a WAN is by linking together two or more LANs, as shown in Figure 17–2. The LANs may be located at widely separated sites, perhaps in different cities or even on different continents. Each LAN is equipped with a special-purpose computer called a *gateway* to handle communications with the other LANs making up the network. In many cases, the gateways communicate over a high-speed data channel called a *backbone*.

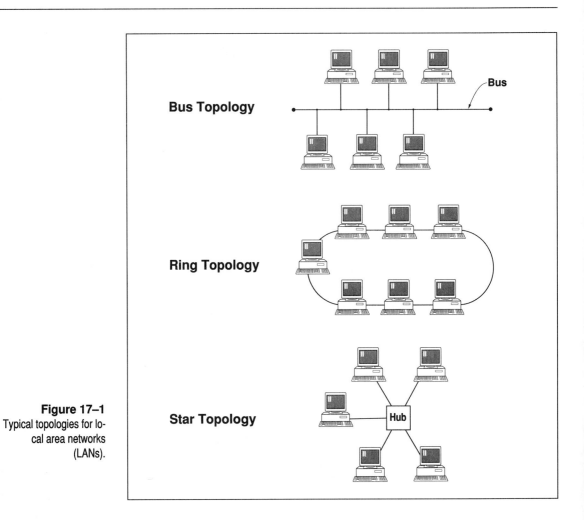

Figure 17–1
Typical topologies for lo-
cal area networks
(LANs).

17.2 **The Internet**

An internet is a network of
networks.

The linking together of networks to form larger networks is called *internetworking*.
Networks created this way can themselves be linked together to form still larger networks. The end result of this process, repeated many times, has been the creation of
a super-internetwork called the *Internet*. It is now connected to thousands of other
networks around the world. The Internet permits users to exchange electronic mail,
to transfer files, and to log in and work on remote machines almost anywhere on
earth.

The Internet grew out of a government research project. (See "A Brief History of the
Internet.") But the government does not own the Internet. In fact, no one "owns" any
more of the Internet than their particular LAN or WAN. Nor is there a president,

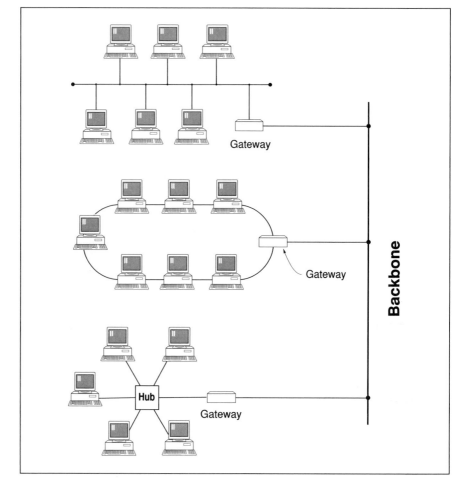

Figure 17-2
A wide area network (WAN) consisting of several LANs connected to a high-speed backbone.

CEO, or board of directors for the entire Internet. (However, many of the networks making up the Internet are governed by presidents, CEOs, and/or boards of directors.) The closest thing to a central governing authority for the Internet is a voluntary international organization called the Internet Society (ISOC). Various advisory boards and task forces operating under the aegis of ISOC periodically issue whatever rules and standards that are needed to keep the Internet humming along.

17.3 Internet Protocols

A protocol is a set of rules that computers must follow to communicate.

Nearly every type of computer system can communicate over the Internet. This is possible only because everyone using the Internet has agreed to observe certain communications rules, or *protocols*, which govern how messages are sent, received, and

A Brief History of the Internet

What is now known as the Internet originated in work sponsored by the Advanced Research Projects Agency (ARPA), an agency of the U.S. Department of Defense. In the late 1960s, ARPA became interested in creating a long-distance network that could function even when some of its nodes were disabled (such as might happen in a war or other national emergency). The proposed network would use a communication method called *packet-switching*, in which messages are broken into units called *packets* and sent over the network, to be reassembled at their destinations. If part of the network fails, the packets are automatically rerouted to a working part of the system.

ARPA awarded a contract to Bolt Baranek and Newman, a Massachusetts consulting firm, to develop software for a new packet-switching network. ARPANET, as it was called, began operations in 1969. It initially linked four computers located at UCLA, Stanford, UC Santa Barbara, and the University of Utah. Other hosts were soon added, at a rate of about twenty per year throughout the 1970s.

A vital step in the development of the Internet occurred in 1974. Vinton Cerf and Robert Kahn described how computers could communicate using TCP/IP (Transmission Control Protocol/Internet Protocol). These protocols were tested on the ARPANET, and would in time become the basis for the worldwide Internet.

Although funded by the Defense Department, ARPANET remained essentially a civilian research project. As such, it was not really suited for the day-to-day requirements of the armed forces. A separate military network named MILNET was formed in 1983. Three years later, in 1986, the National Science Foundation (NSF) created the NSFNET to provide access to five national supercomputing centers. NSFNET featured a high-speed, transcontinental backbone.

ARPANET, MILNET, and NSFNET were funded and administered by different agencies; however, they were also interconnected, and it became common to think of them as a single entity. In 1991, Congress made it official by passing the High-Performance Computing Act, which combined all of the government-sponsored networks into one National Research and Education Network, or NREN.

The National Information Infrastructure Act was passed in 1993 to promote private-sector development of the Internet. Government funding was reduced, and the cost of maintaining the Internet backbone was shifted to commercial operators such as MCI, Sprint, and America Online.

The recent growth of the Internet has been phenomenal. It took twenty years to reach 100,000 hosts, but less than three more years to exceed a million hosts. Since then, the number of hosts has been doubling every year or so, with no end in sight.

interpreted. The most important of these are the *Transmission Control Protocol* (TCP) and the *Internet Protocol* (IP), which are usually lumped together and referred to by their acronyms: TCP/IP.

TCP and IP are designed for communication over dedicated, high-speed transmission lines. Two alternative protocols, which are intended to be used over conventional telephone lines, are the *Serial Line Internet Protocol* (SLIP) and the *Point-to-Point Protocol* (PPP). Many commercial Internet providers offer SLIP connections to users who do not need (or cannot afford) a full TCP/IP connection.

Other Notable Networks

ARPANET was not open to the general public; most of its host computers belonged to defense contractors or universities doing government-funded research. But the researchers at ARPANET were not the only ones interested in networks. The 1970s and 1980s saw the development of a number of other WANs, some of which are still in existence:

- **Telenet.** Not to be confused with the `telnet` program, Telenet was a commercial version of ARPANET created in 1974.

- **Usenet**. Begun in 1979 as an "electronic bulletin board" for sharing information between Duke University and the University of North Carolina, Usenet grew into a decentralized network connecting more than 200,000 UNIX users worldwide. Usenet is best known for its electronic news groups.

- **BITNET**. The name is short for "Because It's Time Network." BITNET was started at the City University of New York (CUNY) in 1981. It has since expanded to include more than 2,000 computers around the world. BITNET handles electronic mail, terminal-to-terminal messages, and file transfers.

- **uucp**. The abbreviation uucp is short for "UNIX to UNIX copy." This is not really a network, but rather a set of programs designed for distributing UNIX software updates and electronic mail over ordinary long-distance telephone lines. However, some people do talk of the "uucp network."

17.4   IP Addresses and Domain Names

Every host on the Internet has a unique address. An Internet or IP address consists of four numbers separated by periods (usually called "dots"):

`128.46.126.96`

This particular address belongs to a workstation named `fairway`, which is part of the Engineering Computing Network (ECN) at Purdue University. That same host also has a unique name, called a *domain name*:

`fairway.ecn.purdue.edu`

This name has four parts:

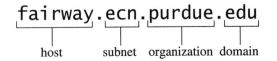

The *domain* indicates the type of organization that owns the host and subnet. The common domains used in the United States are

`com`	commercial organization	`mil`	military agency
`edu`	educational institution	`net`	network support organization
`gov`	government agency	`org`	nonprofit organization
`int`	international organization		

Domain names for hosts outside the United States usually indicate the country or region where the hosts are located. Some of the geographical domains are listed below:

AR	Argentina	DE	Germany	PK	Pakistan
AU	Australia	IN	India	PH	Philippines
AT	Austria	ID	Indonesia	RU	Russia
BR	Brazil	IL	Israel	SA	Saudi Arabia
CA	Canada	IT	Italy	ES	Spain
CL	Chile	JP	Japan	SE	Sweden
CN	China	MX	Mexico	CH	Switzerland
DK	Denmark	NL	Netherlands	TW	Taiwan
FI	Finland	NZ	New Zealand	GB	United Kingdom
FR	France	NO	Norway	US	United States

17.5   Electronic Mail

One of the most popular features of the UNIX operating system is electronic mail (e-mail or E-mail), which allows you to exchange text messages with other users. There are three standard UNIX mail programs:

- *Original UNIX mailer* `mail`. Although superseded by more powerful mail programs, `mail` is still available on most UNIX systems.

- *Berkeley mail program* `Mail`. This program has more features and is easier to use than the original `mail` program.

You will see how to use Mail and mailx in the next chapter.

- *System V mailer* `mailx`. The *x* stands for "extended." The `mailx` program is based on Berkeley `Mail`.

Of these, the original `mail` program is not often used. (In fact, some systems are set up so that the `mail` command calls up one of the other mailers.) In addition to these standard mail programs, your system may offer a choice of other mailers:

- `elm`. Written by Dave Taylor in 1986, the `elm` mailer is a powerful, menu-driven alternative to the standard UNIX mail programs.

You will learn about pine in Chapter 19.

- `pine`. From the same people who wrote the `pico` text editor, `pine` is intended to be an easy-to-use alternative to `elm`. (The name `pine` stands for "`pine` is not `elm`.")

- `RMAIL`. The `RMAIL` program is built into some versions of the `emacs` text editor.

- `mh`. Unlike the other mailers listed here, `mh` is actually a collection of programs rather than a single program. It originated at the Rand Corporation, and is especially useful for handling high volumes of mail. A related program called `xmh` provides a graphical interface to `mh` that runs under the X Window System.

Mailer is discussed in Chapter 20.

- Mailer. The Common Desktop Environment (CDE) includes a powerful mail-handling program called Mailer.

In this book, we will concentrate on the standard mailers `Mail` and `mailx`, the `pine` mail program, and Mailer.

17.6   Internet Mail Addresses

Whichever mail program you prefer, you need to know how to address mail to other users. An Internet mail address consists of the recipient's login name, followed by the "at" symbol (@), and the domain name of the recipient's host computer:

`obadiah@fairway.ecn.purdue.edu`

Table 1: Addressing mail to obadiah@fairway.ecn.purdue.edu

Sender	Address Used	Comments
dinah@host1.podunkst.edu	obadiah@fairway.ecn.purdue.edu	Sender is outside Purdue
micah@merlin.cc.purdue.edu	obadiah@fairway.ecn	Sender is at Purdue, but not on the ecn subnet.
joel@atoms.ecn.purdue.edu	obadiah@fairway	Sender is on the ecn network, but on a different host.
eve@fairway.ecn.purdue.edu	obadiah	Both sender and recipient are on the fairway machine.

Here, the login name is obadiah, and the complete domain name for the host computer is fairway.ecn.purdue.edu. This is the address that someone outside Purdue University would use to send mail to obadiah. However, a user at Purdue University would not need the entire address. Table 1 shows some of the variations in mailing addresses. The general rule of thumb is this:

You may omit those parts of the address that are identical to your own.

17.7   Obtaining an Address

Before you can send mail to someone, you must know his or her login. If you cannot ask the person directly for his or her login, you may have to make an intelligent guess and then use the finger command to confirm your guess. finger tells you the real name of the person who uses a particular login name. Thus, the command

When used without an argument, finger lists everyone who is currently logged into the system.

§ finger jsmith (Return)

may produce information about the user:

```
Login name: jsmith
In real life: John E. Smith
Office: 1313 Mockingbird Hall
Phone: 555-5555
```

Many systems do not allow finger inquiries.

However, if the finger command is not available, the system will say so:

```
finger: Command not found
```

Some versions of finger can tell you the login name, given the user's last name.

Useful—and Quaint—Mail Conventions

Although convenient, electronic mail lacks the expressive power of printed text or the spoken word. E-mail does not allow you to use bold or italic type for emphasis, or to indicate irony or sarcasm by vocal inflection.

It is common practice to USE CAPS FOR EMPHASIS. (But be careful—EXCLUSIVE OR INDISCRIMINANT USE OF CAPS MAKES THE TEXT HARD TO READ.) Another way to emphasize text is to put it between asterisks *like this*.

Many people use *smileys* or *emoticons,* groups of characters that are meant to suggest a face when viewed from a 90° angle. For example, :-) represents a smiling face, and is often used as a way to say "just kidding." Several of the more common smileys—there are hundreds of others—are listed below:

:-)   Smile (indicates humor or irony)

;-)   Wink (sly humor or irony)

:-(Frown (sadness)

Smileys should be used with caution (if at all) because some recipients may find them annoying.

Finally, people in a hurry often abbreviate certain phrases to save typing. Here is a sampling of common e-mail abbreviations:

BTW   By the way

FAQ   Frequently Asked Questions

FAQL   Frequently Asked Questions List

FOAF   Friend of a friend

FYA   For your amusement

FYI   For your information

IMHO   In my humble opinion

IMO   In my opinion

MOTAS   Member of the appropriate sex

MOTOS   Member of the opposite sex

WRT   With respect to

As with smileys, these abbreviations should be used with care. They are acceptable for informal messages, but should be avoided otherwise.

17.8   write and talk

`write` and `talk` are
discussed in Appendix E.

The `write` and `talk` utilities allow two users who are logged into the system to send typed messages to each other. If someone tries to communicate with you this way, you will receive a message like this:

```
Message from george on tty10
```

To learn how to respond using `write` or `talk`, refer to Appendix E.

17.9   Other Traditional Network Services

Some of the most common services provided over the networks are listed below:

- *Remote computing.* `rlogin` ("remote login") and `telnet` allow you to log into a remote computer. `rlogin` works between two UNIX hosts; `telnet` can be used to communicate with either UNIX or non-UNIX hosts. Both of these programs are described in Chapter 21.

- *File transfer.* The `rcp` ("remote copy") and `ftp` ("File-Transfer Protocol") programs are designed for transferring files from one computer to another over the Internet. These programs are discussed in Chapter 22.

- *Network news.* One of the most entertaining—and informative—features of the Usenet is the electronic news service. The Usenet news reader `rn` ("read news") is discussed in Chapter 23.

17.10   The World Wide Web

The World Wide Web (WWW) is not a separate network but rather a way of presenting information on the Internet in the form of *hypertext documents.* A hypertext document may contain links to other documents. A WWW document can present information in textual, graphical, video, or audio form.

A Web server provides
information to Web clients.

The Web operates on a client-server model. The Web client is a program—called a *browser*—that runs on your local host. To obtain information, your browser communicates with the server program, which typically is running on a remote computer called the *Web site.* This is a five-step process:

1.   You instruct the client program on your local host to get a Web document.

2.   The client locates the remote Web site.

3.   The client sends a request over the Internet for the document you specified.

4.   The server on the Web site sends a copy of the document over the Internet.

5.   Your client program formats the document and displays it for you to view.

ASCII, HTML, HTTP, GIF, JPEG, MPEG, and MIME

It seems that every advance in technology unleashes a flood of new acronyms. Here is a selection of important acronyms related to the Internet and World Wide Web:

ASCII. Computers represent all data in terms of numbers—specifically, binary numbers. A standard scheme for representing text numerically is the *American Standard Code for Information Interchange*, more popularly known as ASCII (pronounced "ask-key"). This code represents uppercase and lowercase letters, numerals, and the common punctuation marks as 7-bit binary numbers. Although most users never actually see the ASCII representation, you may hear someone talk about "ASCII files." This simply means a file containing text only—no graphics, video, or audio, for instance.

HTML. Many WWW documents are based on the *Hypertext Markup Language* (HTML). HTML documents contain instructions on how the pages are to be interpreted and displayed by a Web browser. Various versions of HTML have been developed, including SHTML, or the *Secure Hypertext Markup Language*, which is designed for providing security for financial transactions over the Web.

HTTP. To communicate with each other, Web clients and servers observe a set of rules called the *Hypertext Transport Protocol*, or HTTP. You need not know anything about HTTP yourself—your browser will take care of the details—but you will often use this acronym when requesting documents over the Web.

GIF. Graphics—drawings, diagrams, and photographs—are stored and transmitted differently from text. The *Graphic Interchange Format* or GIF (pronounced "jiff") was developed in the 1980s by CompuServe for efficiently transmitting images over networks. GIF employs a file-compression technique to minimize the size of the graphics files. (Unfortunately, the GIF compression algorithm limits the number of colors that may be used in the images.) GIF files are commonly identified by the *.gif* suffix.

JPEG. Although GIF is the most widely used graphics format on the Web, it is not the only one. An industry organization, the *Joint Photographic Experts Group* (JPEG), has defined an alternative file format that is optimized for compressing color photographs. JPEG file names typically carry a *.jpeg* or *.jpg* suffix.

MPEG. This MPEG file format, defined by the *Motion Picture Experts Group*, is commonly used to transmit compressed video and audio data. MPEG files are identified by a *.mpeg* suffix.

MIME. Originally, UNIX mail programs were limited to text (ASCII) messages. Some of the newer mailers also handle MIME (*Multi-Purpose Internet Mail Extensions*), which is a standard for including multimedia objects in electronic mail.

Numerous Web browsers are available, with more appearing all the time. Perhaps the most popular—at least for now—is Netscape. You will learn how to use Netscape in Chapter 24.

17.11 Universal Resource Locators

Every page of information on the World Wide Web has its own unique identifier, called a *Universal Resource Locator* (URL), that tells the browser where to find the page and how to read it. For example, the Library of Congress in Washington, DC, has a WWW server. Its URL is

`http://lcweb.loc.gov/homepage/lchp.html`

gopher was an early, text-based Internet navigator that has been superseded by Web browsers such as Nestcape.

The abbreviation `http`, short for "Hypertext Transport Protocol," indicates that this page of information contains hypertext. A URL that begins with `ftp:` refers to a document that is accessible by `ftp`. Likewise, the prefix `gopher:` indicates a document that is accessible by `gopher`. Most Web browsers can handle `http`, `ftp`, and `gopher` documents.

Double slashes (`//`) precede the domain name of the *Web site* (or host computer), which in this case is `lcweb.loc.gov`.

A single slash (`/`) begins the absolute pathname of the file containing the document. In this example, the pathname is `/homepage/lchp.html`. This pathname is interpreted exactly as the UNIX pathnames you have seen before.

17.12 Exercises

1. Be sure you can define the following terms:

network	LAN	CAN	MAN
WAN	gateway	backbone	topology
internetwork	Internet	packet	protocol
TCP/IP	SLIP	PPP	IP address
domain	e-mail	browser	hypertext
URL	ASCII	HTML	HTTP
GIF	JPEG	MPEG	MIME

2. Is your computer part of a local area network? If so, how many other machines are connected to the same network? Where are they located?

3. Does your system have access to the Internet? If so, what is the Internet address of your host? What is its domain name?

4. What is your e-mail address?

18 TUTORIAL: USING MAIL AND MAILX

In this chapter, you will see how to use the standard UNIX mail programs `Mail` and `mailx` to send and receive text messages.

One source of confusion is that on some systems, the `mail` command calls up either `Mail` or `mailx`; on other systems, the `mail` command calls up the older UNIX mail program.

18.1 Sending Electronic Mail

If you are just getting started with a new UNIX account, it is unlikely that anyone has sent you e-mail yet. However, you can start by sending messages to yourself.

1 **Enter the Mail command, followed by the mail address of the recipient.** If you are using AT&T UNIX, try the `mailx` program:

Enter the recipient's mail address here. ——————

    § mailx address (RETURN)

If you are using BSD UNIX, type

Enter the recipient's mail address here. ——————

    § Mail address (RETURN)

The computer will prompt you for the subject of the message:

    Subject:

2 **Specify a subject.** Enter a short description or title for your message:

    Subject: Test Message #1 (Return)

3 **Enter the body of the message.** The mail program has only limited editing capabilities: you can edit only one line at a time, and you cannot go back to edit a

previous line. Therefore, make sure each line is correct before starting a new line:

```
Don't be alarmed. (Return)
This is only a test. (Return)
```

4   **When you finish the message, send it.** This is done by starting a new line, then pressing (Control)-(D) (for "done"):

```
(Return)
(Control)-(D)
```

On some systems, the computer will ask if you want to send carbon copies (Cc) to anyone:

```
Cc:
```

5   **Send carbon copies, if any.** Enter the login name of anyone who should receive a copy of your message. If you do not intend to send carbon copies to anyone, just press (Return).

```
Cc: (Return)
```

The UNIX prompt tells you that you are back in the UNIX shell:

§

18.2   Mailing a File

Because the mail program has only limited editing capabilities, it is often more convenient to use a text editor to create a file containing your message, then mail the file. In this section, you will see how to use e-mail to send a copy of a file.

1   **Create a file using the text editor.**

2   **Redirect the file to the e-mail program.** To send the file poems to the account login, type

```
§ mailx login < poems (Return)
```

or

```
§ Mail login < poems (Return)
```

The input redirection arrow (<) tells the mail program to take its input from the contents of the file poems.

WARNING	Be sure to use the input redirection arrow (<), not the output redirection arrow (>). Using the wrong arrow can destroy the contents of the file.

18.3 Using vi in the Mailer

One way you can edit a message before you send it is to call up the vi editor from the mail program. You can then use the vi commands to edit the message.

1 **Start the mail program and enter the recipient's address.** To practice, you might specify yourself as recipient:

§ mailx yourlogin (Return)

or

§ Mail yourlogin (Return)

You will be asked for a subject:

Subject:

2 **Specify a subject.**

Subject: Test Message #3 (Return)

3 **Enter your message.** For example,

```
There once was a fellow named Lester,
Whose knowledge grew lesser and lesser.
It at last grew so small,
He knew nothing at all;
So they hired him as a professor.
```

4 **Start the vi editor.** Begin a new line, then type a tilde (~), followed by a v (for vi), then RETURN:

(Return)
~v (Return)
(Return)

This will bring up the vi editor and place your message in the buffer:

On some systems, the Subject line will also appear in the buffer.

```
There once was a fellow named Lester,
Whose knowledge grew lesser and lesser.
It at last grew so small,
He knew nothing at all;
So they hired him as a professor.


~
~
~
/tmp/Re24223 6 lines, 163 characters
```

5 **Use the vi commands to edit the message.** If you are following along with the example, you might try changing "Lester" to "Chester.")

6 **When you finish editing, save the changes into the file and quit the editor.** Do this with the usual commands:

(Esc) :wq (Return)

This will put you back in the mail program. You may see a prompt of some sort:

(continue)

7 **Send the message.** This is done the usual way:

(Return)
(Control)-(D)

You may be asked to specify carbon copies.

Cc:

8 **Send the carbon copies, if any.** Press (Return) if you do not wish to send any copies:

Cc: (Return)

This will get you out of the mail program and back into the UNIX shell:

§

18.4 Your Mailboxes

The mail program uses two kinds of mailboxes. Your *system mailbox* is a file that holds mail you have received but have not read, deleted, or saved to another file. On many systems, this file is located in the /var/spool/mail directory, and has the same name as your user ID. For example, if your user ID is jdoe, then your system mailbox is the file /var/spool/mail/jdoe.

In addition to the system mailbox, you may have a *personal mailbox*. This is a file named mbox in your home directory. Any mail messages you have read but not deleted or saved in another file are automatically put into your mbox file when you quit the mail program.

If you use either the Bourne Shell or Korn Shell, your shell checks your system mailbox periodically and notifies you of any new messages:

New mail has arrived.

You can also use the biff or xbiff program to alert you when new mail arrives. These programs are discussed in the exercises.

18.5 Reading Your Mail

You can read the messages in your system mailbox with the same electronic mail program that you used to send messages:

1 Start the mail program without specifying a recipient. How you do this depends on whether your system uses `Mail` or `mailx`:

§ Mail (Return)

or

§ mailx (Return)

The mail program will list the messages in your system mailbox:

```
>U 1 yourlogin Thu Nov 22 15:27 15/433 "Test Message #1"
 N 2 yourlogin Thu Nov 22 15:35 27/573
 N 3 yourlogin Thu Nov 22 15:42 19/559 "Test Message #3"
 &
```

The > in the first column points to the current message. A U indicates a previously unread message; N indicates a new message. The messages are numbered (1 through 3 in this case). The login name and address of the sender is shown, along with the date and time the message was received and the number of lines and characters the message contains (lines/characters). The subject of the message is given in quotes.

The ampersand (&) on the last line is the *mail prompt*. It tells you that the mail program is awaiting your instructions. Some systems use a question mark (?) as a prompt.

2 If necessary, list the next screenful of messages. If there are too many messages in your mailbox to list on one screen (perhaps because you have many admirers or have not been keeping up with your mail), you can list the next screenful by typing a z at the mail prompt:

&z (Return)

You can list the previous screenful of messages again by typing z- (z hyphen):

&z- (Return)

To list the current screenful of messages, enter h at the mail prompt:

&h (Return)

3 Select a message to read. To do this, simply type in the message number at the prompt and press (Return). To see the first message, for example, type

&1 (Return)

This will cause the first message to appear:

```
Message 1:
From yourlogin Day Month Time Year
Date: Day Month Time Year
From: yourlogin (Your name)
To: (Your login name)

Subject: Test Message #1

Don't be alarmed.
This is only a test.
&
```

The mail program places some additional lines at the top of a message before sending it on. These lines make up the *mail header*, which contains such information as the name, the login, and the address of the person who sent the message. Note that the mail header makes it difficult to send an anonymous mail message!

Once you have read the message, there are a number of things you can do with it. Without leaving the mail program, you can reply to the message, save it in a file, or delete it.

18.6 Replying to a Message

It is a good idea to respond promptly to any e-mail that you receive. While you are still in the mail program, use the R ("Reply") command.

1 Enter the Reply command and specify a message number. Thus, to reply to the second message, type

```
&R1 (Return)
```

This tells the mail program that you want to reply to the user who sent the first message. The mail program will take care of addressing your reply; it even fills in the Subject field for you.

```
Subject: Re: Test Message #1
```

2 Enter your message. This is done as you did before:

```
What a relief.
```

3 Send the message. Press (Return), then (Control)-(D):

```
(Return)
(Control)-(D)
```

18.7 Saving Messages

You may decide to keep some messages for future reference. You can save a message in a file with the s ("save") command.

- **Enter the Save command, followed by the message number.** Thus, to save the message 1 in a file named message1.file1, type

  &s1 message1.file1 (Return)

  This creates a new file in your home directory named message1.file1, and places in it the text of the message, including the mail header. (If you already have a file named message1.file1 in your home directory, the message is appended to the file.) The original message is deleted from your system mailbox. The mail program will tell you that the message has been saved.

18.8 Deleting Messages

Some messages are not worth saving. You should delete these with the d ("delete") command.

1   **Enter the Delete command, followed by the message number.** For example, to delete the third message, type

   &d3 (Return)

   Normally, the mail program does not tell you that it has deleted a message. Instead, it will simply show you a mail prompt:

   &

2   **Check that the message has been deleted.** The h ("headers") command will list the messages remaining in the mailbox:

   &h (Return)

   A deleted message will no longer appear in the list of mail headers.

18.9 Restoring Deleted Messages

What if you delete a message by accident and want to get it back? If you have not exited the mail program, you can retrieve deleted messages using the Undelete command.

- **Enter the Undelete command, followed by the message number.** For example, to restore the third message, type

  &u3 (Return)

18.10 Quitting the Mail Program

The x command is useful when you accidentally deleted a message you want to keep.

There are two common ways you can quit the e-mail program after reading your mail, which differ in what is done to the messages in your mailbox. The q ("quit") command puts any messages that you read, but did not delete, into a file named mbox in your home directory. Unread messages are left in the system mailbox. The x ("exit") command quits the mail program without changing the mailbox, restoring any deleted messages.

Of these, the q command is more commonly used:

- **Type q, then** (Return)**:**

  &q (Return)

  Some versions of the mail program will tell how many messages were saved in the mailbox and how many were placed in your mbox file:

  Saved 3 messages....

18.11 Reading Your mbox File

Your mbox file receives messages that you have read but not deleted or saved in another file. The -f ("file") option allows you to read and process the messages in your mbox file just as you did with the messages in your system mailbox.

1 **Start the mail program with the** -f **option.**

  § Mail -f (Return)

  or

  § mailx -f (Return)

  The mail program will list the messages in your mbox.

2 **Process the messages.** Use the usual mail commands.

3 **Quit the mail program.** Either the q or x command will do this.

18.12 Using finger

The finger utility tells you the real name of the person who has a particular login name. It can be useful when you are trying to guess a person's e-mail address.

- **Enter the** finger **command, giving the person's login as an argument.** The first time, try it on your own login:

  § finger yourlogin (Return)

When entered without an argument, finger lists everyone who is currently logged in.

You should see information about the user—in this case, yourself. However, if the finger command is not available, the system will say so:

```
finger: Command not found
```

Some versions of finger can tell you the login name, given the user's last name.

- **Enter the finger command, giving the person's last name as an argument.** Try it on your own name:

    § finger yourname (Return)

    This will produce either a list of users having your last name or an error message.

18.13   Getting Help

Any time you forget what commands are used by mailx or Mail, type the ? ("help") command after the mail prompt. This will display a list of commands.

```
h                        print out active message headers
m [user list]            mail to specific users
n                        goto and type next message
p [message list]         print messages
pre [message list]       send messages back to system mailbox
q                        quit (unresolved messages in mbox)
R [message list]         reply to sender (only) of messages
r [message list]         reply to sender and recipients
s [message list] file    append messages to file
t [message list]         type messages (same as print)
top [message list]       show top lines of messages
u [message list]         undelete messages
v [message list]         edit messages with display editor
w [message list] file    append to file, without from line
x                        quit, do not change system mailbox
z                        display next page of headers
z-                       display previous page of headers
!                        shell escape
```

A [message list] consists of integers, ranges of same, or user names separated by spaces. If omitted, Mail uses the current message.

18.14   Command Summary

Some of the commands discussed in this chapter are UNIX shell commands, others work only within `mailx` or `mail`. All of these commands must be terminated by a (Return).

Reading Mail in Your Mailbox (UNIX shell commands)

`Mail`	list e-mail messages received (BSD UNIX)
`mailx`	list e-mail messages received (AT&T System V UNIX)

Reading Mail in Your mbox File (UNIX shell commands)

`Mail -f`	list messages stored in `mbox` file (BSD UNIX)
`mailx -f`	list messages stored in `mbox` file (System V UNIX)

Deleting, Saving and Replying (Mail or mailx command)

d*n*	delete message number *n*
s*n* `file`	save message number *n* in `file`
R*n*	Reply to the sender of message number *n*
r*n*	same as R*n*, but also sends reply to everyone who received the original message

Note that R and r may have the reverse effects on some systems.

Sending Mail (UNIX shell commands)

`Mail jdoe`	send message to user `jdoe` (BSD UNIX)
`mailx jdoe`	send message to user `jdoe` (AT&T System V UNIX)

Mailing a File (UNIX shell commands)

`Mail jdoe < file`	mail `file` to user `jdoe` (BSD UNIX)
`mailx jdoe < file`	mail `file` to user `jdoe` (AT&T System V UNIX)

Editing a Message Using vi (Mail or mailx tilde escapes)

`~v`	call up `vi` program to edit current message

Identifying a User

`finger user`	get the real name of the user with login `user`

18.15   Exercises

1. Find someone with an account on your computer (or on the same network) and
    practice using `mailx` or `Mail` to exchange messages.

2. As you have seen, the `s` ("save") command is used inside the mail program to
    append a message to a file. The `w` ("write") command also appends messages to
    files. Mail yourself a message, then use the `w` command to put it into a file. Exit
    the mail program and examine the contents of the new file. What is the differ-
    ence between `w` and `s`?

3. The mail `S` ("save") command will save a mail message in a file that has the
    same name as the sender's login. (If such a file already exists, the message will
    be appended to the file.) Try out the `S` command.

4. The mail programs `mailx` and `Mail` make use of so-called *tilde escapes*. These
    are mail commands that begin with a tilde (~). You have seen how to use the
    tilde escape sequence `~v` to edit a message using the `vi` editor. Find out about
    other tilde escapes. Start up the mail program as if you were going to send a
    message. However, instead of typing a message, enter the tilde escape sequence

    `~?` (Return)

    to display a list of the tilde escapes. What do the following tilde escapes do?

    `~p`

    `~h`

    `~q`

    `~r`

    `~s`

    `~x`

5. You have seen how to mail a file using the redirection operator on the command
    line. Thus, to send the file `myfile` to the user `fred@host`, you would type

    § `Mail fred@host < myfile` (Return)

    or

    § `mailx fred@host < myfile` (Return)

    When `fred` receives the message, it will not have a subject. You can remedy
    this using the `-s` ("subject") option, like this:

    § `Mail -s "This is the subject" fred@host < myfile` (Return)

    or

§ `mailx -s "This is the subject" fred@host < myfile` (Return)

Try out the −s option by mailing a file to yourself.

6. An electronic mail message may pass through a number of intermediate stops before reaching its destination. The −v ("verbose") option allows you to track the progress of your message as it is delivered:

§ `Mail -v fred@host` (Return)

or

§ `mailx -v fred@host` (Return)

Try the −v option, preferably on a message that is to travel a long distance.

7. The from command lists the mail headers in your system mailbox without actually starting the mail program. Try it:

§ `from` (Return)

8. The biff utility alerts you when you receive mail. (Believe it or not, this utility was named for a dog that belonged to a graduate student in the Computer Science Department at the University of California at Berkeley.) You can activate biff with the command line

§ `biff y` (Return)

To deactivate biff, enter

§ `biff n` (Return)

When new mail arrives, biff will print a notice, including the login of the sender, the subject line, and the first few lines of the message. Try it.

9. The X client xbiff creates a picture of a mailbox on the screen. When you receive new mail, xbiff emits a sound and raises the flag on the mailbox. You can start xbiff with the command

§ `xbiff &` (Return)

If you are running X, try out xbiff.

10. Study Appendix E to learn how write and talk work. Then find someone with an account on your computer (or on the same network) and practice using write or talk to exchange messages.

19 TUTORIAL: PROCESSING MAIL WITH PINE

In this chapter, you will see how to use the University of Washington's news and mail program pine to send and receive electronic mail. Although pine is not a standard UNIX utility, it is widely available on UNIX systems.

19.1 Starting pine

- **Start pine.** Enter the pine command at the UNIX shell prompt

  § pine (Return)

You should see the pine Main Menu window, as shown in Figure 19–1.

19.2 Composing and Sending a Message

Begin by creating and sending a message to yourself:

1 **Choose the Compose Message option.** Press the *C* key. The COMPOSE MESSAGE screen will appear, as shown in Figure 19–2. Note that the cursor is initially located in the To: field.

You can also use the arrow keys to move the cursor.

2 **Enter the mail address of the recipient.** When you are trying out pine for the first time, type in your own address and press (Return):

  To   : *yourlogin@yourhost* (Return)

The cursor should now be positioned in the Cc: (Carbon copy) field.

3 **Enter addresses of persons who are to receive a copy of the message.** If you do not want to send copies, leave the Cc: field blank. Press (Return):

  Cc   : (Return)

The cursor should now be positioned in the Attchmnt: (Attachment) field.

Version   Screen   Current folder

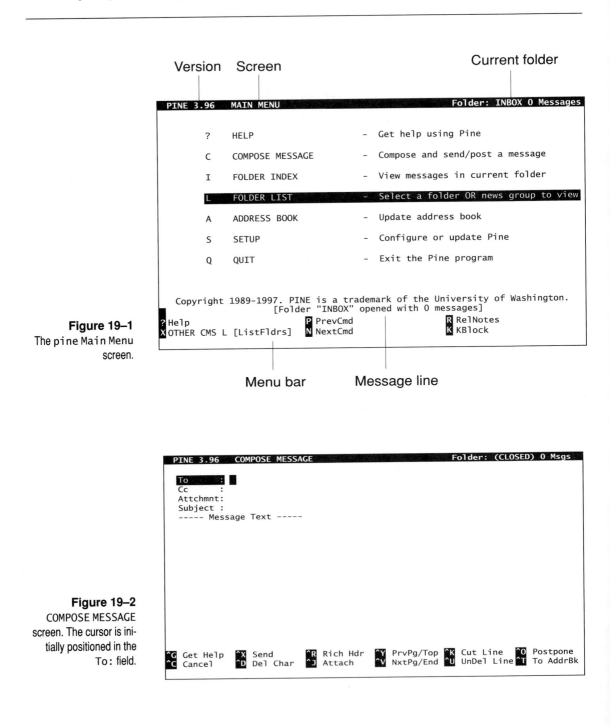

Figure 19–1
The pine Main Menu
screen.

Menu bar   Message line

Figure 19–2
COMPOSE MESSAGE
screen. The cursor is initially positioned in the
To: field.

4   Attach a file. You can attach nearly any UNIX file to your message, even if the format of the file is one that `pine` cannot read. Assuming you still have a file named `poems` in your home directory, enter this file name in the `Attchmnt:` field:

`Attchmnt:poems` (Return)

You should see a message informing you that the file has been attached, and the cursor should now be located in the `Subject:` field.

5   Enter a subject. Choose a short title that summarizes the purpose or content of the message:

`Subject :Test Message #1` (Return)

You might wish to review the chapter on pico.

6   Compose the message. If you have previously used the `pico` text editor, the `pine` editing tools will be familiar. Enter a simple message:

`Do not be alarmed -- this is only a test.`

7   Send the message. The command is ^X:

(Control)–(X)

You will be asked to confirm that you want to send the message:

`Send message?`

8   Confirm. Enter *Y* for "Yes" (or *N* for "No").

You will be returned to the Main Menu. In the Message Line, you will see a message confirming that the mail was sent:

`[Message sent and copied to sent-mail]`

19.3   Listing Your Folders

In `pine`, a *folder* is a file for holding messages. A new user typically has three mail folders:

- `INBOX` holds messages you have received.

- `sent-mail` holds copies of messages you have sent.

- `saved-messages` holds mail you have saved.

The current folder is listed in the upper right corner of the screen. If the INBOX is listed, you can view its contents using the Folder Index command:

Do this if the current folder is the INBOX.

- **Enter the Folder Index command.** From the `Main Menu`, press the *I* key.

  You should see a numbered list of messages received:

+	A 1	Aug 9	Jane Doe	(515K)	Re: Good Book
	D 2	Aug 18	jim@MegaMicro.com	(2,011)	Sale!
+	N 3	Aug 20	Your Name	(1,361)	Test Message #1

These are called mail *headers*

If you see such a list, skip to the next section.

If INBOX is not your current folder, you can use the Folder List command to select it:

1 **Enter the Folder List command.** From the Main Menu screen, press the *L* key:

L

What you see now depends on how your account has been set up. In the simplest scheme, the INBOX, sent-mail, and saved-messages will be listed:

INBOX   sent-mail   saved-messages

A collection *is a group of related folders.*

However, it may be that your system administrator has created separate collections for, say, mail folders and news folders. In that case, you will see a screen that looks something like this:

```
  PINE 3.96    FOLDER LIST                       <mail/[]> sent-mail 0 Msgs

  ------------------------------------------------------------------------
  Folder-collection <mail/[]>  **Default for Saves**                (Local)
  ------------------------------------------------------------------------

                    [ Select Here to See Expanded List ]


  ------------------------------------------------------------------------
  News-collection <News on news.server.edu>                        (Remote)
  ------------------------------------------------------------------------

                    [ Select Here to See Expanded List ]
```

2 **If necessary, view the expanded list in the mail collection.** Under the mail collection, highlight the line

[Select Here to See Expanded List]

and press the *V* key:

V

3 **View the folder.** Use the *P*, *N*, or arrow keys to highlight the INBOX folder, and press *V*:

V

This brings up the FOLDER INDEX screen. You should see a numbered list of mail headers:

<table>
<tr><td>These are called mail headers</td><td>+ A 1 Aug 9 Jane Doe</td><td>(515K)</td><td>Re: Good Book</td></tr>
</table>

These are called *mail headers*

```
+ A 1 Aug  9  Jane Doe            (515K)  Re: Good Book
  S 2 Aug 18  jim@MegaMicro.com   (2,011) Sale!
+ N 3 Aug 20  Your Name           (1,361) Test Message #1
```

19.4   Mail Headers

Let's examine the structure of the mail header:

```
+ N 3 Aug 20  Your Name            (1,361)  Test Message #1
```

The **+** at the beginning of the line indicates that the message was sent directly to you—no one else received a carbon copy. This is followed by a letter indicating the status of the message:

N   New message. You have not yet viewed this particular message.

A   Answered message. You have replied to the sender of the message.

S   Saved message. You have saved a copy of the message.

Next comes the message number (3), followed by the date (Aug 20), the name of the sender (Your Name), the size of the message (1,361), and the Subject (Test Message #1).

19.5   Reading Your Mail

Let's retrieve the message you just sent yourself. Assuming that the current folder is the INBOX, follow these steps:

Use the *P*, *N*, or ↓ ↑ keys to scroll through the list.

1   **Highlight the message of interest**. Scroll up or down the list of mail headers. (This will not be necessary if you have just one message in your INBOX.)

2   **View the message.** Press the *V* key:

V

This will open a MESSAGE TEXT viewer, in which you will see the body of the message (but not the attachment).

19.6   Viewing and Saving an Attachment

1   **View the attachment index.** From the MESSAGE TEXT viewer, press the *V* key again:

V

This brings up the ATTACHMENT INDEX viewer, which shows a list of items. The first item in the list is the body of the message, while the second is the attachment we are looking for.

2   **View the attachment.** Scroll to the second entry and press the *V* key:

V

This brings up the ATTACHED TEXT viewer, in which the text of the attachment appears.

3   **Save the attachment.** You can copy the attachment into a file in your home directory by pressing the *S* key:

S

You will be prompted for a file name:

Copy attachment to file in home directory:

4   **Specify a file.** Enter a valid file name at the prompt:

Copy attachment to file in home directory: poems.mail (Return)

The mail program will confirm that the message was saved in a file.

5   **Return to the message text.** You must exit the ATTACHED TEXT viewer and the ATTACHMENT INDEX viewer. Press the *E* key twice:

E
E

You should now see the MESSAGE TEXT viewer.

19.7   Replying to a Message

Let's reply to the message you just read:

1   **Use the Reply command.** In the MESSAGE TEXT screen, Press the *R* key:

R

You will be asked whether the original message is to be included:

Include original message in Reply?

2   **Answer Yes.** Press the *Y* key:

Y

A COMPOSE MESSAGE screen will appear, with the original message (each line marked by a >) already in place:

On Aug 20 Your Name wrote:

>Do not be alarmed -- this is only a test.
>

3 **Compose your reply.** This is done using the same editing tools you used before:

```
On Aug 20 Your Name wrote:

>Do not be alarmed -- this is only a test.
>
Do not worry -- I am not alarmed by your silly test.
```

4 **Send the message.** Remember, the command is ^X:

> Control – X

As before, you will have to confirm that you really want to send the message.

Note that attachments are not normally sent as part of the reply, even when you include the body of the original message in your reply.

19.8 Saving the Message in a Folder

The Save command allows you to save the current message in a `pine` folder, usually the `saved-messages` folder. You can do this from the MESSAGE TEXT screen:

1 **Use the Save command.** Press the *S* key:

```
S
```

You will be prompted for the folder name:

```
SAVE to folder in <mail/[]> [saved-messages]:
```

The default folder (in this case, `saved-messages`) is listed in square brackets. Unless you specify another folder, the message will go to the default folder.

Skip this step if the default is `saved-messages`.

2 **If necessary, select the correct folder.** Use the To Folders (To Fldrs) command ^T to bring up a list of folders available:

> Control – T

Highlight the `saved-messages` folder and press *S* (for Select):

```
[saved-messages]
S
```

This will return you to the MESSAGE TEXT screen.

The message is copied to `saved-messages` and deleted from INBOX.

3 **Press** Return. You will be told that the message has been copied and deleted:

```
[Message 3 copied to "saved-messages" and deleted]
```

4 **Check the index.** Press the *I* key:

```
I
```

The message will be marked for deletion:

```
+ D 3 Aug 20  Your Name        (1,361)  Test Message #1
```

Expunge means erase.

The message is not actually deleted at this time; in fact, you can decide to "undelete" the message. When you leave pine, you will be asked if you want to *expunge* the deleted messages from the INBOX.

19.9 Getting Help

You probably noticed that the menu bar in every pine screen includes a Help option. The Help screens in pine are *context-sensitive*, meaning that the content of the screen is selected to be appropriate for the screen you are currently viewing.

1. **Select the Help command.** From most screens, simply press the *?* key. (In the COMPOSE MESSAGE screen, the command is ^G.)

2. **Read the Help screen.** You can move to the next page by pressing (Spacebar) (Spc); you can move to the previous page by pressing the – key.

3. **Exit the Help screen.** Press the *E* key:

   E

19.10 Quitting pine

1. **Select the Quit command.** Press the *Q* key:

   Q

   You will be asked to confirm your command:

   Really quit pine?

2. **Answer Yes at the prompt.** Press the *Y* key:

   Y

19.11   Using finger

The `finger` utility tells you the real name of the person who has a particular login name. It can be useful when you are trying to guess a person's e-mail address.

- **Enter the `finger` command, giving the person's login as an argument.** The first time, try it on your own login:

§ `finger yourlogin` `Return`

When entered without an argument, `finger` lists everyone who is currently logged in.

You should see information about the user—in this case, yourself. However, if the `finger` command is not available, the system will say so:

`finger: Command not found`

Some versions of `finger` can tell you the login name, given the user's last name.

- **Enter the `finger` command, giving the person's last name as an argument.** Try it on your own name:

§ `finger yourname` `Return`

This will produce either a list of users having your last name or an error message.

19.12   Command Summary

Starting pine (UNIX shell command)

pine	start pine

Main Menu Screen

?	open Help screen
C	open COMPOSE MESSAGE screen
I	view messages in current folder
L	select a folder to view
Q	exit the pine program

COMPOSE MESSAGE Screen

^G	get Help
^C	cancel message
^X	send message
^D	delete character
^Y	go to previous page
^V	go to next page
^K	cut line
^U	undelete line

MESSAGE TEXT VIEWER

?	get Help
V	view ATTACHMENT or ATTACHMENT INDEX
R	reply to message
E	export message to a UNIX file
S	save message in pine folder

ATTACHMENT INDEX VIEWER

V	view attachment
S	save attachment
E	exit viewer

19.13 Exercises

1. Find someone with an account on your computer (or on the same network) and practice using `pine` to exchange messages.

2. The `pine` mail program allows you to create an address book, containing the names and e-mail addresses of people with whom you correspond frequently. Use the `pine` Help command to see how this is done.

3. One alternative to saving a message in the `saved-messages` folder is to export it to a UNIX file. Use the `pine` Help command to see how this is done.

4. The `from` command lists the mail headers in your system mailbox without actually starting the mail program. Try it:

   § `from` (Return)

5. The `biff` utility alerts you when you receive mail. (Believe it or not, this utility was named for a dog that belonged to a graduate student in the Computer Science Department at the University of California at Berkeley.) You can activate `biff` with the command line

   § `biff y` (Return)

   To deactivate `biff`, enter

   § `biff n` (Return)

   When new mail arrives, `biff` will print a notice, including the login of the sender, the subject line, and the first few lines of the message. Try it.

6. The X client `xbiff` creates a picture of a mailbox on the screen. When you receive new mail, `xbiff` emits a sound and raises the flag on the mailbox. You can start `xbiff` with the command

   § `xbiff &` (Return)

   If you are running X, try out `xbiff`.

7. Study Appendix E to learn how `write` and `talk` work. Then find someone with an account on your computer (or on the same network) and practice using `write` or `talk` to exchange messages.

20 TUTORIAL: PROCESSING MAIL WITH MAILER

Skip this chapter if your system does not run CDE.

The Common Desktop Environment includes Mailer, a powerful program for handling electronic mail. In this chapter, you will see how to use Mailer to compose, send, read, and store messages and attachments.

20.1 Starting Mailer

- **Start Mailer.** Double-click on the Mailer control on the Front Panel. Note that the Mailer icon appears in one of two forms, depending on whether you have received new mail:

(New mail)

The Mailer main window will appear, as shown in Figure 20–1.

Take a moment to identify the parts of the Mailer window:

- ***Window Menu button, Minimize button, and Maximize/Restore button.*** These perform the usual functions on the window.

- ***Title bar.*** The title bar lists the pathname of the *mailbox*, which is a file that holds messages you have received.

- ***Header List.*** Each message has a *mail header* which lists the message's sender, its subject, the date and time it was sent, and its size. The header for the current message is highlighted. You can select the message to view by clicking on its header.

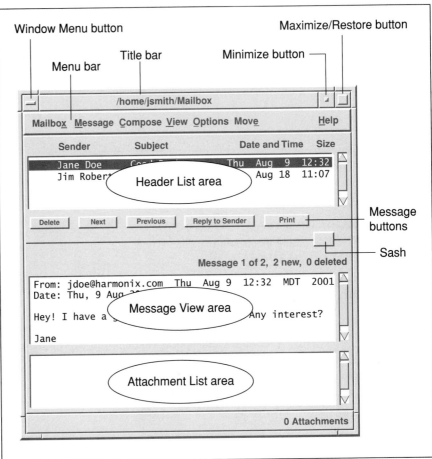

Window Menu button

Maximize/Restore button

Title bar

Minimize button

Menu bar

/home/jsmith/Mailbox

Mailbox Message Compose View Options Move   Help

Sender   Subject   Date and Time   Size

Jane Doe   Cool   Thu   Aug   9 12:32
Jim Rober   Header List area   Aug 18 11:07

Delete   Next   Previous   Reply to Sender   Print

Message buttons

Sash

Message 1 of 2, 2 new, 0 deleted

From: jdoe@harmonix.com Thu Aug 9 12:32 MDT 2001
Date: Thu, 9 Aug
Hey! I have a   Message View area   Any interest?
Jane

Attachment List area

0 Attachments

Figure 20–1
The Mailer main window.

- *Message buttons.* Frequently used commands are available by pressing buttons. These commands are also available from the various menus of the Menu bar.

- *Sash.* By dragging the sash up or down, you can resize the Header List area and the Message View.

- *Message View area.* The header and text of the selected message are shown in this area.

- *Attachment List area.* If there are any attachments to the selected message, their icons will be shown here.

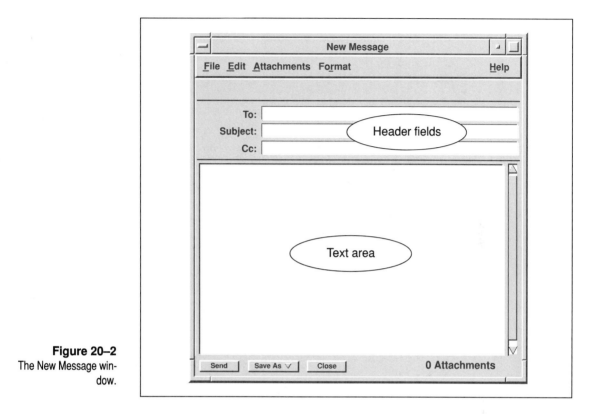

Figure 20–2
The New Message window.

20.2 Composing a Message

If you have a new account, you may not have received any mail yet. However, you can begin by sending a message to yourself:

1 Pull down the Compose menu and choose the New Message option.

The New Message window will appear, as shown in Figure 20–2.

2 Enter the mail address of the recipient in the To: Field. When you are trying out Mailer for the first time, type in your own address and press (Return):

yourlogin@yourhost(Return)

The Subject: field should now be active.

3 Enter a subject in the Subject: field. Choose a short title that summarizes the purpose or content of the message:

Test Message #1 (Return)

The Cc: (Carbon copy) field should now be active.

4 **Enter addresses of persons who are to receive a copy of the message.** If you do not want to send copies, leave the Cc: field blank. Press (Return):

(Return)

The cursor should now be positioned in the Text area.

5 **Compose the message.** Composing in the Mailer is very similar to editing with the Text Editor. Enter a simple message:

`Do not be alarmed -- this is only a test.`

20.3 Adding an Attachment

An *attachment* is a file that is sent along with an e-mail message. Attachments may be used to transmit plain or formatted text, images, sounds, or executable code. Attaching a file is straightforward:

1 **Pull down the Attachments menu and choose Add File.** The Attachment menu is found on the Menu bar of the New Message window.

The Mailer Add dialog box will appear.

2 **Select the file to attach.** Try attaching the file poems from your previous work.

3 **Click Add.**

The dialog box will disappear, an Attachment List area will open up below the Text area, and the attachment's icon will be placed on the list.

If you change your mind, you can remove an attachment by selecting the Delete option on the Attachments menu. And if you change your mind again, you can restore the attachment using the Undelete option.

20.4 Sending the Message

Once you have addressed and composed your message and have added any attachments, you are ready to send it:

• **Send the Message.** Click the Send button on the New Message window.

The New Message window will disappear.

20.5 Reading Your Mail

Let's read the message you just sent yourself:

1 **Pull down the Mailbox menu and select Check for New Mail.**

If the header does not appear, wait and try again.

The new message's header should appear on the Header list.

2 **Highlight the message of interest**. Click on the message's header.

The text of the message will appear in the Message View area.

20.6 Viewing an Attachment

1 **If necessary, open the Attachment list.** Pull down the Attachments menu and select Show List.

The attachment icon should be visible in the Attachment List area.

2 **Open the attachment.** Double-clicking on the attachment icon causes the attachment to open.

20.7 Replying to a Message

Mailer allows you to choose one of four ways to reply to a message:

- *Reply to the sender only.* Your reply goes only to the person who sent the original message.

- *Reply to the sender and include the original message.* Your reply will include a copy of the original message, set off by a symbol such as the right angle bracket (>).

- *Reply to the sender and all recipients.* You reply goes to the sender of the original message and to anyone on the Cc: list of the original message.

- *Reply to the sender and all recipients, and include the original message.* The sender and every recipient of the original message will receive your reply, including a copy of the original message. The original message will be set off by a symbol such as the right angle bracket (>).

Let's reply to the message you just received, including the text of the original message in the reply:

1 **Select the message to which you want to reply.** Simply click on the appropriate header in the Header List.

2 **Pull down the Compose menu and choose Reply to Sender, Include.**

A Compose window will appear, having the To: and Subject: fields already filled in for you.

3 **Compose your reply.** This is done using the same editing tools you used before:

```
On Aug 20 Your Name wrote:
```

```
>Do not be alarmed -- this is only a test.
>
Do not worry -- I am not alarmed by your silly test.
```

4 Add an attachment, if desired.

5 Send the message. Press the Send button.

20.8 Saving a Message in a File

The Save as Text command allows you to save the current message in a file:

1 Select the message to be saved. Click on the message header.

2 Pull down the Message menu and select Save as Text.

A dialog box will appear.

3 Enter the path or folder name, file name, etc.

4 Press Save.

If there are attachments, you will be given a warning that they will not be saved in the file automatically—you must do this yourself.

20.9 Saving an Attachment in a File

You can also use the Save As option on the Attachments menu.

You can also save an attachment in a file:

1 Point to the attachment icon and press the right (#3) button.

A pop-up menu will appear.

2 Select Save As.

A dialog box will open.

3 Enter the path or folder name, file name, etc.

4 Press Save.

20.10 Printing a Message

It is easy to print a hard copy of a message:

1 Select a message. Click on the message header.

The Print One option prints one copy on the default printer.

2 Pull down the Message menu and select the Print... option.

A dialog box will open.

3 Enter the printer name, number of copies, etc.

4   Press Print.

20.11   Deleting a Message

Once you have saved and printed a message, there is no reason to keep it in the in-box:

1   Select the message to be deleted. Click on the message header.

2   Pull down the Message menu and select Delete.

You can also use the Destroy Deleted Messages option on the Mailbox menu.

Deleted messages are not removed from the mailbox immediately—in most cases, they are actually removed (or "destroyed") when you log out. This gives you the chance to retrieve a deleted message using one of the Undelete commands on the Message menu.

20.12   Quitting Mailer

•   **Pull down the Mailbox menu and select Close.**

20.13   Exercises

1.   Find someone with an account on your computer (or on the same network) and practice using Mailer to exchange messages.

2.   The Signature option on the Options menu allows you to enter text that will be included at the end of every message you send. Create your own signature file.

3.   Sometimes you receive a message that you want to pass on to someone else. You can do this by pulling down the Mailbox menu and selecting either Forward or Forward, No Attachments. Try it.

4.   You can set up Mailer so that it will send an automatic reply to anyone who sends you a message. This is usually called *vacation mail* because it is convenient when you have to be away from your office for a time. A typical vacation mail message might look something like this:

```
I am on vacation, and will read your message regarding
'$SUBJECT' when I return.
```

The subject line from the original message is inserted in your reply in place of the string $SUBJECT. You can set up a vacation mail message using Vacation Message on the Options menu.

5.   Using the View menu, you can choose to list messages by Date/Time, Sender, Subject, Size, or Status. Take some time to try out each of these options. What does the Abbreviated Headers option do?

6. Mailer allows you to create additional mailboxes for organizing mail. Refer to the relevant Help volume to find out how to create, open, and close a mailbox.

7. The Search option on the Message menu allows you to search a mailbox for a particular message. Refer to the relevant Help volume to find out how to use Search.

8. A mail *alias* is an alternate name for one or more users. If you regularly send the same message to a group of users, you can save yourself time by creating an alias for the entire group. For example, you might refer to your friends by the alias *friends*. If you then send a message to *friends*, it will be sent to everyone listed under that alias. Refer to the relevant Help volume to find out how to use the Aliases option

21 TUTORIAL: LOGGING IN REMOTELY

Running either the `rlogin` or `telnet` utility on your local host computer, you can log in and work on a remote computer system on which you have an account. The difference is that the `rlogin` utility allows you to connect only to another UNIX system; `telnet` can also connect to non-UNIX hosts. `telnet` can also be used to gain access to certain Internet services that do not require that you have an account on the remote host.

21.1 Running rlogin

In this section you will see how to use `rlogin` to log into your account on a remote UNIX host. (If you do not have an account on another machine, you can practice with your local account.)

1 **Start the `rlogin` program, specifying the remote host and your remote login name.** Thus, if you had an account named `jsmith` on the remote UNIX host `merlin.podunku.edu`, you would type

   § `rlogin merlin.podunku.edu -l jsmith` (Return)

   On some systems, that will be enough to get you into the remote system; no password is needed. Other systems will require that you enter a password:

   `password:`

2 **If necessary, enter the password that you use for the remote host.** This may not be the same as the password used on your local host.

3 **When you finish working on your remote account, log out from that account**. One of the following commands should work (see Chapter 3):

> § logout (Return)
>
> § exit (Return)
>
> § (CONTROL)-(D)

21.2 Running telnet

In this section you will see how to use telnet to log into a remote host—either a UNIX or non-UNIX computer—on which you have an account. (If you do not have an account on another machine, you can practice with your local account.)

1 Start the telnet program.

> § telnet (Return)

You will receive the telnet prompt:

telnet>

2 Enter the Open command, followed by the Internet address of the remote machine. Thus, if you had an account on merlin.podunku.edu, you would type

telnet> open merlin.podunku.edu (Return)

The telnet program will try to connect to the remote host. If the connection is successfully made, the remote host will display a login prompt:

```
Trying . . .
Connected to merlin.podunku.edu.
Escape character is '^]'

SunOS UNIX (merlin.podunku.edu)
login:
```

3 Log into your remote account. Follow the procedure set out in Chapter 3, "Getting Started." Once you have logged in, you can run the usual UNIX commands (but not the X Window System) on the remote host.

21.3 telnet Commands

When you logged in using telnet, you probably noticed a message about an "escape character" that may have looked something like this:

Escape character is '^]'

This means that the telnet program uses the (Control)-(]) key combination as an escape sequence. (This is not to be confused with the (Esc) key that is used with the vi editor.) The telnet escape character allows you to suspend your work on the remote host and give commands to the telnet program itself.

1   **Enter the telnet escape character.** On most systems, this is the ^] combination:

    § (Control)-(])

    The computer will respond with the telnet prompt:

    telnet>

2   **Display the list of telnet commands.** Enter a question mark (?) at the prompt:

    telnet> ? (Return)

    The program will respond with a list of commands:

    ```
    close     close current connection
    display   display operating parameters
    mode      line-by-line or character-at-a-time mode
    open      connect to a site
    quit      exit telnet
    send      transmit special characters
    set       set operating parameters
    toggle    toggle operating parameters
    z         suspend telnet
    ?         print help information
    ```

3   **Display a detailed command description.** To get more information on any of these commands, type the command name followed by a question mark:

    telnet> close ? (Return)

    The telnet program will show you a description of the close command:

    close closes current connection

    That does not tell you anything more than you already knew. However, some of the other commands give you considerably more information; take a moment and try them out.

4   **Exit the telnet command mode.** This is done by pressing the (Return) key at the telnet prompt:

    telnet> (Return)

    This will put you back into your remote UNIX account.

21.4 Ending the telnet Session

Once you have finished working on the remote host, you should log out from that machine and end the `telnet` session.

1 **Log out from your remote account**. This is done the usual way (see Chapter 3). One of the following commands should work:

§ `logout` (Return)

§ `exit` (Return)

§ (CONTROL)-(D)

When you have logged out, you will see a `telnet` prompt:

`telnet>`

At this point you could, if you wish, open another remote session using the open command.

2 **Quit the `telnet` program.** Enter `quit` at the prompt:

`telnet> quit` (Return)

You will see a UNIX shell prompt:

§

21.5 A Shortcut Method

There is a quicker way to run a `telnet` session:

1 **Enter the `telnet` command, followed by the Internet address of the remote machine.** Thus, if you had an account on the host computer `merlin.po-dunku.edu`, you would type

§ `telnet merlin.podunku.edu` (Return)

Eventually, you will see the `login` prompt:

`login:`

2 **Log into your remote account as usual.**

3 **When finished, close the connection.**

`telnet> close` (Return)

This will usually log you out of the remote account and quit `telnet`. You should see a UNIX shell prompt:

§

21.6   Connecting to Guest Accounts

Normally, you must have an account on any remote host to which you want to connect using `telnet`. However, a number of special `telnet` accounts exist on the Internet to provide services to the public. There are two ways to log into such an account.

The first—and perhaps most common—method requires that you connect to the host computer using `telnet`, then log into the account using a special login name and password. (Many systems do not require a password.) For example, you can reach the online catalog of the Washington State University library this way:

§ `telnet griffin.wsu.edu` (Return)

When you reach the server, it will prompt you for a login:

`login:`

The login to be used is `library`; no password is required for this particular service.

The second method is to use `telnet` to log into the server through a special "port," designated by number. It is usually unnecessary to provide either a login or password. For example, Melvyl, the University of California's on-line catalog can be reached using the command line

§ `telnet melvyl.ucop.edu 23` (Return)

Note the number 23; this is the port number.

21.7 Command Summary

Each of these commands is typed in after the UNIX prompt, and each is terminated by a (Return). host represents the address of the remote host.

Remote Login Commands (UNIX shell prompt)

rlogin host	log into a remote UNIX computer named host
telnet host	log into a remote computer named host
telnet	start up the telnet program

Telnet Commands (Telnet Prompt)

open host	open connection to computer host
?	print telnet help
close	close connection to remote host
quit	quit telnet session

21.8 Exercises

1. If you have an account on a remote UNIX machine, log into that account using rlogin.

2. If you have an account on a non-UNIX machine that is connected to the network, log into that account using telnet.

3. Use telnet to connect to the Washington State University library.

4. Use telnet to connect to Melvyl at the University of California.

22 TUTORIAL: TRANSFERRING FILES

Both rcp ("remote copy") and ftp ("file transfer protocol") allow you to transfer files between two computer systems on which you have accounts. The rcp utility is designed to work with two UNIX systems; ftp can also get files from non-UNIX hosts. Moreover, ftp can be used to obtain files from public file servers.

22.1 Running rcp

In this section you will see how to use rcp to obtain a file from a remote UNIX host. For rcp to work, three conditions must be met:

- You must have an account on the remote UNIX host.

- Both hosts must "trust" each other.

- You must have permission to copy the file.

Assuming that these conditions are met, the procedure for copying the file is very simple:

- **Enter the rcp command, specifying the remote host and remote file, then the local host and the new file name.** For example, if you wanted to copy the file myfile from the remote UNIX host farhost.xyz.edu, you would type

  § rcp farhost.xyz.edu:myfile .:mycopy (Return)

  Note that no password is needed. The rcp utility will simply refuse to work if you do not have an account on the remote host or the hosts do not trust each other.

22.2 Running ftp

In this section you will see how to use ftp to copy files from a remote host—either a UNIX or non-UNIX computer—on which you have an account.

1   **Start the** ftp **program.**

§ ftp ⟨Return⟩

You will receive the ftp prompt:

ftp>

2   **Enter the** open **command, followed by the Internet address of the remote machine.** Thus, if you had an account on farhost.xyz.edu, type

ftp> open farhost.xyz.edu ⟨Return⟩

The ftp program will try to connect to the remote host. If the connection is successfully made, the remote host will prompt for your login name:

Connected to farhost.xyz.edu.
220 farhost.xyz.edu FTP server (Version4.179)ready.
Name (farhost.xyz.edu):

3   **Enter your login name.** Be sure to use the login name for the remote account, not that on your local account, if they are different. For example, if you had an account named smithj on the remote host, you would type

Do not enter smithj
(unless that is your login).
Enter *your* login here. ————

Name (farhost.xyz.edu): smithj ⟨Return⟩

The remote host will prompt for your password:

331 Password required for smithj
Password:

4   **Enter your password.** Of course, the password does not show on screen as you type it.

Enter your password here; it
will not appear on the
screen. ————

Password:▓▓▓▓▓▓▓▓

You will be notified when you have successfully logged in:

230 User smithj logged in.
ftp>

22.3   ftp Help

The ftp program takes dozens of commands. Fortunately, one of those commands is help, which lists and describes the set of ftp commands.

1   **Enter the** help **command at the** ftp **prompt.** There are two ways to do this. Either type the word help, or a single question mark (?):

ftp> ? (Return)

The computer will respond with a list of commands:

!	dir	nput	rmdir
$	disconnect	nmap	runique
account	form	ntrans	send
append	get	open	status
ascii	glob	prompt	struct
bell	hash	proxy	sunique
binary	help	sendport	tenex
bye	lcd	put	trace
case	ls	pwd	type
cd	macdef	quit	user
cdup	mdelete	quote	verbose
close	mdir	recv	?
cr	mkdir	remotehelp	
delete	mls	rename	
debug	mode	reset	

Some of these are similar to UNIX commands that are already familiar to you (such as cd, ls, mkdir, and pwd). Others are peculiar to the ftp program.

2   **Obtain a description of a command.** Enter the help or ? command, followed by the command you are interested in. For example, to get a description of the delete command, enter the command line

ftp> ? delete (Return)

The program will respond with a short description of the command that will give you an idea of how it is used:

delete   delete remote file

22.4   Getting a File

One of the reasons to use ftp is to get a copy of a file from a remote host. This is done with the get command.

1   **Move to the remote directory containing the file you want.** Like the UNIX shell, ftp uses the cd command to change the working directory. Thus, if you wanted to get a file from the subdirectory Marsupials, you would type

Enter the pathname of the directory containing the file you want. ─────────/

```
ftp> cd Marsupials (Return)
```

Depending on how ftp has been set up on your system, you may see a message that looks something like this:

```
250 CWD command successful.
```

2   **List the files to find the one you want.** With ftp, as with the UNIX shell, you can do this with the ls command:

```
ftp> ls (Return)
```

This command will list the files in the current directory on the remote host. It usually tells you how many bytes of information were transferred across the network:

```
200 PORT command successful.
150 Opening ASCII mode data connection for file list.
bandicoot
kangaroo
opossum
wombat
226 Transfer complete
38 bytes received in 0.0042 seconds (8.9 Kbytes/sec)
```

3   **Select the file transfer mode.** As far as ftp is concerned, there are two types of files. An *ASCII file* contains text; a *binary file* contains other kinds of information (such as graphics, audio recordings, or compressed text). Depending on the type of information that is in the file, enter either ascii or binary at the ftp prompt:

```
ftp> ascii (Return)
```

The ftp program will confirm your selection:

```
200 Type set to A.
>
```

4   **Get the file.** Enter the get command, followed by the name of the original file, then the name you want to give the local copy. For example, suppose you want to get a copy of the file wombat from the remote host, and that you want to name it wombat.copy on your local host. You would enter this line:

```
ftp> get wombat wombat.copy (Return)
```

In most cases, ftp will inform you that the transfer was successful:

```
200 PORT command successful.
150 Opening ASCII mode data connection for wombat (7014
bytes)
226 Transfer complete
7224 bytes received in 0.8 seconds (8.8 Kbytes/sec)
ftp>
```

22.5   Sending a File

Using ftp, you can also send a file from your local host to the remote host—the reverse of the operation described in the previous section. This is done with the put command.

1   Specify the file type. Remember, ftp distinguishes between ASCII files containing text and binary files containing other kinds of information (graphical, audio, etc.). Select the proper file transfer mode by entering either ascii or binary at the ftp prompt:

```
ftp> ascii (Return)
```

The ftp program will confirm your selection:

```
200 Type set to A.
>
```

2   Send the file. Enter the put command, followed by the name of the original file, then the name you want to give the remote copy. For example, suppose you wanted to send a copy of the file meeting.events from the local host, and that you want to name it meeting.events.copy on your remote host. You would enter this line:

```
ftp> put meeting.events meeting.events.copy (Return)
```

ftp will inform you that the transfer was successful:

```
200 PORT command successful.
150 Opening ASCII mode data connection for meeting.events
226 Transfer complete
local: meeting.events  remote: meeting.events.copy
2878 bytes received in 0.033 seconds (86 Kbytes/sec)
ftp>
```

22.6 Ending the ftp Session

Once you have finished working on the remote host, you should end the `ftp` session.

- **Quit the `ftp` program.** Enter *quit* at the `ftp` prompt:

  ftp> quit (Return)

  You will see a UNIX shell prompt:

  §

22.7 A Shortcut Method

There is a quicker way to run an `ftp` session:

1 **Enter the `ftp` command, followed by the Internet address of the remote machine.** Thus, if you had an account on the host `farhost.xyz.edu`, you would type

   § ftp farhost.xyz.edu (Return)

2 **Log into your remote account as usual.** This will require that you enter your login and password at the appropriate prompts.

3 **When finished, close the connection using the `quit` command.**

   ftp> quit (Return)

   This will log you out and quit `ftp`. You should see a UNIX shell prompt:

   §

22.8 Getting Files with Anonymous ftp

Originally, `ftp` was intended to allow you to transfer files between two computers on which you have accounts. However, *anonymous* `ftp` allows you to get files from hosts on which you do not have an account. These hosts are called *public ftp servers*.

For example, the United States Census Bureau maintains a server that you can reach by anonymous `ftp`.

1 **Start the `ftp` program and specify the server you want.** For example, to connect to the Census Bureau's public `ftp` server, you would enter the command

   § ftp ftp.census.gov (Return)

   When you reach the server, it will identify itself and prompt for your login name:

```
Connected to ftp.census.gov.
220-          U.S. Department of Commerce, Bureau of Census
220-*****************************************************
```

Various warning and
disclaimers appear here.

```
220 blue.census.gov FTP server ready.
Name (ftp.census.gov:yourlogin):
```

2   Enter the guest login name at the prompt. Some servers expect you to enter "guest" as your login; others require "anonymous." For the Census Bureau server, use "anonymous":

Some servers require you
to enter "guest" as your login
name.

```
Name (ftp.census.gov:yourlogin): anonymous (Return)
```

The server will notify you that it has accepted the login name; it may also prompt you for a password:

```
331 Guest login ok, send e-mail address as password.
Password:
```

3   If necessary, enter the guest password. Some systems require no password; others use "guest" or "anonymous." The Census Bureau server asks for your e-mail address. Thus, if your address were jsmith@merlin.podunku.edu, you would enter this at the prompt:

Enter the required guest
password here; it will not
appear on the screen.

```
Password:▮▮▮▮▮▮▮
```

4   Use ftp commands to find and transfer files.

5   When you are finished, quit ftp as before.

22.9 File-Compression Programs

Large files are often compressed to save storage space and decrease the time needed to transfer them over the network. Depending on the file and the compression technique, a compressed text file may occupy as little as 40% of the memory required by the original.

A compressed file is typically distinguished from a normal file by a file name suffix, which indicates the program that was used to compress the file. Some of the more common compression/decompression programs, and their file name suffixes, are listed below:

Compression Program	Decompression Program	File Suffix	Sample File Name
compress	uncompress	.Z	textfile.Z
cpio	cpio	.cpio	textfile.cpio
gzip	gunzip	.gz	textfile.gz
pack	unpack	.z	textfile.z
Stuffit	unsit	.Sit	textfile.Sit
Packit	unpit	.pit	textfile.pit
PKZIP	PKUNZIP	.ZIP	textfile.ZIP
tar	tar	.tar	textfile.tar

Strictly speaking, tar and cpio are not compression programs; they are *file archive programs*. Such programs can combine a number of files and directories into a single file—called an *archive file*—for storage on tape or transferring across the Internet. An archive file is often compressed before it is transferred.

Of the programs listed above, compress and tar are the ones most commonly found on UNIX systems. The procedure for preparing a file or set of files for compression using tar and compress is fairly straightforward, as you will see in the next few sections.

22.10 Creating an Archive File

The tar program is normally used to prepare multiple files and directories for storage or transfer. If you are working with just one file, you will probably not bother with tar; in that case, skip this section.

1 **Create an archive file using tar.** To archive all of the files in a directory, run the tar program with the -cf option, giving a name for the archive file and specifying the directory that is to be processed. Thus, to create an archive file

named `marsupials.tar` containing the files from the `Marsupials` directory, you would enter

§ `tar -cf marsupials.tar Marsupials` (Return)

Here, –c means "create"; the f indicates that a tar file name follows. ───────────/

2   **Check that the `tar` file has been created.** Enter the `ls` command to list the files:

§ `ls` (Return)

You should see the names of both the original directory and the `tar` file:

`Marsupials marsupials.tar`

Note that tar does not alter the original directory.

3   **Verify the contents of the `tar` file.** This is done with the `-t` ("table of contents") option:

§ `tar -tf marsupials.tar` (Return)

The `tar` program will list the files that were bundled together to make the archive file.

22.11   Compressing Files

The most common compression program found on UNIX systems is `compress`, which is very simple to operate:

1   **Compress the file.** This is done by typing the `compress` command, followed by the name of the file to be compressed:

§ `compress marsupials.tar` (Return)

2   **Check that the compressed file has been created.** Once again, enter the `ls` command to list the files:

§ `ls` (Return)

You should see the names of both the original directory and the newly compressed file:

`Marsupials marsupials.tar.Z`

The compress program attaches the .Z suffix automatically.

Once you have compressed the file, it is ready to be transferred by `ftp`. When using `ftp` to send a compressed file, be sure to specify `binary` (not `ascii`) file transfer type.

22.12   Uncompressing Files

Once the compressed file has been transferred to its destination, it must be uncompressed. The uncompress command is used to restore files that have been processed with compress. If you are working with a compressed tar file, you should uncompress it before untarring it.

1   Enter the uncompress command, followed by the name of the file to be restored. The file should have the .Z suffix:

§ uncompress marsupials.tar.Z (Return)

2   List the files. The compressed file will be gone, replaced by its uncompressed version:

§ ls (Return)
marsupials.tar

In this example, the uncompressed file is a tar file; you should restore it next.

22.13   Restoring tar Files

The tar command is used with the -x ("extract") option to restore an archive file:

1   Enter the Extract command. Type tar -xf, followed by the name of the tar file and the name of the directory where you want the untarred file(s) to go:

§ tar -xf marsupials.tar Marsupials (Return)

2   List the files.

§ ls (Return)
Marsupials marsupials.tar

Note that the tar file is not removed.

22.14   Command Summary

Remote Copy Command (UNIX shell prompt)

rcp farhost:file   copy `file` from the remote UNIX host `farhost`; place
    .:mycopy   `mycopy` in current working directory (.)

File Transfer Commands (UNIX shell prompt)

ftp host   log into a remote computer named `host`

ftp   start up the `ftp` program

ftp Commands (ftp Prompt)

open host   open connection to computer `host`

?   print `ftp` help

quit   close connection to remote host

tar Commands (UNIX Shell Prompt)

tar -cf file.tar   create `tar` file named `file.tar` from contents of directo-
    Original   ry `Original`

tar -tf file.tar   print table of contents for the `tar` file named `file.tar`

tar -xf file.tar   extract file(s) from `file.tar` and place the untarred file(s)
    Destination   in the directory `Destination`

compress Commands (UNIX Shell Prompt)

compress file   compress `file` and create new file named `file.Z`

uncompress file.Z   restore `file.Z`

22.15 Exercises

1. Be sure you can define the following terms:

    anonymous `ftp`   archive file   ASCII file

    binary file   `tar` file

2. Use `ftp`'s `help` command to determine what the following commands do:

append	mdelete
bell	mdir
bye	mkdir
cd	mls
cdup	nput
delete	pwd
dir	recv
disconnect	remotehelp
lcd	rmdir
ls	

3. Information on NASA and its programs can be obtained by anonymous `ftp` from the host `explorer.arc.nasa.gov`. Log in as "anonymous" and try to get a list of Frequently Asked Questions (FAQ) related to the requirements for becoming an astronaut.

4. Genealogical information can be obtained by anonymous `ftp` from the host `ftp.cac.psu.edu`. Log in as "anonymous" and see if you can obtain a list of useful tips for beginning genealogists.

5. Larry Landweber, a computer scientist at the University of Wisconsin, collects data on international network connectivity. He maintains a list of the countries that are connected to the Internet, BITNET, FIDONET, or `uucp`. Obtain this list by anonymous `ftp` from `ftp.cs.wisc.edu`. (Hint: Look for a directory named `connectivity_table`.)

23 TUTORIAL: READING THE NEWS

Other news readers are discussed in the exercises.

In this chapter, you will learn how to process Usenet news with rn ("read news"). Although other news readers—such as trn, nn, tin, and xrn—have more features, rn has the advantage of being more widely available on UNIX systems. Once you have mastered rn, you should have no trouble learning to use one of the alternatives.

23.1 Usenet Newsgroups and Hierarchies

Tens of thousands of messages are posted on the Usenet every day. To make it possible for you to keep up with this volume of information, the network news is organized by topic into *newsgroups*. There are several thousand newsgroups, which are further organized into seven top-level groups called *hierarchies*:

comp   The comp ("computer") hierarchy includes several hundred newsgroups devoted to computer issues. For example,

        comp.ai   comp.sys.mac

        comp.compilers   comp.unix.questions

        comp.lang.c

misc   Groups that deal with topics that do not fit neatly into any of the other hierarchies are put in the misc ("miscellaneous") category. Some examples:

        misc.headlines   misc.misc

        misc.jobs.offered   misc.taxes

news   Groups in the news hierarchy deal with the operation of the Usenet itself. This hierarchy includes several newsgroups that are intended for new users of the Usenet:

        news.newusers.questions   news.announce.important

        news.announce.newusers   news.newusers.newgroups

rec   The rec ("recreation") hierarchy comprises newsgroups dedicated to hobbies, sports, arts, and other avocations. A few of the rec newsgroups are

rec.arts.tv	rec.humor
rec.birds	rec.music.classical
rec.games.chess	rec.scuba

sci   The sci ("science") hierarchy includes newsgroups that deal with scientific and research issues. Here are some typical newsgroups in this hierarchy:

sci.astro	sci.lan.japan
sci.bio.technology	sci.skeptic
sci.engr.chem	sci.math.symbolic

soc   Newsgroups dealing with social issues are found in the soc hierarchy. Here is a random sample of the newsgroups in this hierarchy:

soc.couples	soc.misc
soc.culture.jewish	soc.politics
soc.men	soc.women

talk The newsgroups in the talk hierarchy provide a place for people to debate, converse, exchange information, or just sound off:

talk.bizarre	talk.religion.misc
talk.philosophy.misc	talk.politics.misc

23.2   Other Newsgroups and Hierarchies

Your system administrator decides which newsgroups to make available.

The seven major hierarchies described in the previous section form the core of the Usenet, and are widely available. There are a number of other hierarchies that may or may not be available on your system; the decision is usually up to your system administrator. Here are some of the most common popular alternative hierarchies:

alt   This hierarchy includes "alternative" newsgroups. These cover a wide range of interests, as you can see by the following sample:

alt.angst	alt.personals
alt.books.reviews	alt.postmodern
alt.fishing	alt.religion.computers
alt.individualism	alt.stupidity

biz   The biz ("business") hierarchy consists of groups that discuss business issues. Unlike other newsgroups, many of the biz groups allow postings of advertisements, new product announcements, and other commercial materials. Here is a sampling of the `biz` newsgroups:

`biz.sco.announce`   `biz.clarinet.sample`

`biz.jobs.offered`

`ieee` This hierarchy is sponsored by the Institute of Electrical and Electronics Engineers (IEEE), and includes a dozen or so groups dealing with topics of interest to that organization.

`k12` The `k12` hierarchy comprises newsgroups that discuss topics related to teaching (kindergarten through grade 12).

`clari` `ClariNet` is a commercial news service operated by United Press International. This service is not free, and therefore is less likely to be found on your system than some of the other groups.

In addition to these national newsgroups, there are many local and regional groups. Many college campuses, for example, have local newsgroups related to particular departments or courses.

23.3 Creating a .newsrc File

Skip this section if you already have a `.newsrc` file in your home directory.

The first step in preparing to use the `rn` news reader is to create a `.newsrc` ("news run-commands") file. This file will hold a list of the newsgroups you want to follow.

1 Start the `rn` program.

§ `rn` (Return)

If you have not previously run `rn`, it will show you an introductory message that typically looks something like this:

```
                         *** NEWS NEWS ***
Welcome to rn. There are more options to rn than you want to think about,
so we won't list them here. If you want to find out about them, read the
manual page(s). There are some important things to remember, though:
* Rn is not a modified readnews. Don't expect the commands to be identi-
  cal.
* Rn runs in cbreak mode. This means you don't have to type carriage
  return on single-character commands.
* At ANY prompt in rn, you may type 'h' for help. There are many different
  help menus, depending on where you are.
* Typing a space at any prompt means to do the normal thing.
This particular message comes from /usr/local/bin/rn_private/newsnews. You
will not see it again.
[Press space bar to continue.]
```

2 **If necessary, press the space bar to continue.** If rn does not find a .newsrc, it will create one for you:

```
Trying to set up a .newsrc file--running newsetup...
Creating .newsrc to be used by news programs.
Done.
```

Eventually, rn will tell you that there are unread articles in one of the newsgroups, and it will ask whether you want to read them:

```
****** 4 unread articles in alt.stuff--read now? [ynq]
```

3 **Quit the rn program.** Enter q at the prompt:

```
****** 4 unread articles in alt.stuff--read now? [ynq]q
```

Before rn quits, it will create a .newsrc file for you.

23.4 Subscribing to Newsgroups

You should now have a .newsrc file in your home directory. The next step is to edit the .newsrc file to "subscribe" to the newsgroups that interest you.

1 **Use the text editor to open the .newsrc file.**

§ vi .newsrc (Return)

You will see line after line of entries that look like this:

```
news.admin.hierarchies:
news.admin.misc:
news.admin.policy:
```

and so on. A colon (:) following a newsgroup name indicates that you have subscribed to that group; you will notice that you have subscribed to all of them. Since you probably do not want to follow them all, you must "unsubscribe" to them. This is done by replacing the colon with an exclamation point (!).

2 **Use the text editor's global search-and-replace command to cancel subscriptions.** The following vi command line will search for the colons (:) in the file and replace them with exclamation points (!):

:%s/:/!/g (Return)

This will cancel all of the subscriptions, allowing you to choose those groups that interest you.

3 **Search through the file for the group(s) you want.** For example, the group news.newusers.questions is intended to help new users. Use the vi search command to find this group:

/news.newusers.questions! ⟨Return⟩

vi will go to the line containing this newsgroup name.

4   **Subscribe to the group.** Change the exclamation point (!) to a colon (:). Thus, to subscribe to news.newusers.questions, you should have

news.newusers.questions:

5   **Repeat Steps 3 and 4 as necessary.** As a novice user, you should consider subscribing to the following newsgroups:

news.announce.newusers
news.announce.important
news.answers
news.newusers.newgroups
alt.internet.services

6   **When you finish, save the changes and quit the editor.** This is done the usual way:

⟨Esc⟩:wq ⟨Return⟩

23.5   Reading the News

Now that you have set up your .newsrc file and subscribed to newsgroups, you are ready to read the news.

1   **Start the news reader program.**

§ rn ⟨Return⟩

The rn program will examine your .newsrc file to find out which newsgroups you have subscribed to. Then it will check for unread articles in those groups, and ask if you want to read them:

9 unread articles in alt.internet.services--read now? [ynq]

2   **List the titles of the articles in the newsgroups.** Type an equals sign (=) at the prompt:

=

The rn program will print the titles of the unread articles, each identified by a number:

75068 Frequently Asked Questions (FAQ)
75069
75070

```
75071
75072

Press space to continue:
```

3   **Select an article to read.** Enter the number of the article you wish to read:

```
75072  (Return)
```

The news reader will print the article. At the end of the article, you will see a prompt:

```
End of article 75072 (of 75305)--what next? [npq]
```

4   **Repeat Steps 2 and 3 as needed.**

23.6   Saving a News Article

Occasionally, you may want to save a copy of a Usenet article. The Save command puts a copy of the article into a file in a directory named News in your home directory.

1   **Save the article.** At the prompt, type s (for "save"), followed by the name of the file that is to contain the article:

```
--what next? [npq]s newsfile  (Return)
```

The news reader will inform you that the file does not exist, and will ask whether you want to create a file using the "mailbox format."

```
File /home/yourlogin/News/newsfile does not exist--
   use mailbox format? [ynq]
```

2   **Select mailbox format.** At the prompt, type y (for "yes").

```
use mailbox format? [ynq]y  (Return)
```

23.7   Quitting the News Reader

- **When you are finished, quit the news reader.** Type q (for "quit") at the prompt:

```
End of article 75072 (of 75305)--what next? [npq]q  (Return)
```

23.8   Posting News Articles

After you have gotten accustomed to reading Usenet news, you may want to post your own articles. To see how this is done, you should read the following articles, which are posted periodically to the news.answers newsgroup:

"What is Usenet?"

"A Primer on How to Work with the Usenet Community"

"Rules to Posting to Usenet"

"Answers to Frequently Asked Questions about Usenet"

"Hints on Writing Style for Usenet"

23.9   Exercises

1. Be sure you can define the following terms:

    hierarchy   newsgroup   news reader

2. What is your favorite hobby, pastime, or recreation? Scan the newsgroups in the rec hierarchy to find a group dealing with that activity. If you find an appropriate newsgroup, subscribe to it.

3. Obtain and read the following articles, which are posted periodically to the news.answers newsgroup:

    "What is Usenet?"

    "A Primer on How to Work with the Usenet Community"

    "Rules to Posting to Usenet"

    "Answers to Frequently Asked Questions about Usenet"

    "Hints on Writing Style for Usenet"

4. After reading the articles listed in the previous exercise, post an article to one of the newsgroups that you have followed.

5. The menu-driven news reader nn ("*No n*ews [is good news]") is preferred by many users over rn. Refer to the man pages for information on how nn works, then use it to process the articles in one of your favorite newsgroups. In your opinion, how does nn compare with rn?

6. In Usenet terminology, the word *thread* refers to both a news topic and a series of articles dealing with that topic. *Threaded* news readers such as trn ("*t*hreaded *r*ead *n*ews") and tin sort articles by topic and by date, which makes it easier

to follow a thread. Read the appropriate man pages to learn how trn or tin works, then use one of these to read the articles in one of your favorite newsgroups.

7. The X client xrn is a basic window-based news reader. If xrn is available on your system, use it to read the articles in one of your favorite newsgroups.

8. The mail reader pine also doubles as a news reader. If you have been using pine to read your mail, try it for news as well.

24 TUTORIAL: BROWSING THE WWW

You cannot use Netscape without a GUI, but you may be able to use a text-based browser such as lynx— see Exercise 11.

In this chapter, you will learn how to use Netscape, a powerful World Wide Web (WWW) browser. Netscape is not the only WWW browser available, but it is the most widely used. Versions of Netscape are available for the Apple Macintosh, for IBM-compatible personal computers running Microsoft Windows, and for UNIX machines running the X Window System.

A word of warning: It seems that nothing on the World Wide Web stays the same for long. Do not be surprised, therefore, if some of the Web documents are no longer where we say they are, or if their appearance is not exactly as shown.

24.1 Starting Netscape

How you start the Netscape browser depends on whether you are working with the Common Desktop Environment (CDE) or X/Motif. If you are a CDE user, try the following:

- **Click on the Browser control on the Front Panel.** In some cases, the Front Panel clock may double as the Browser control.

Or

- **Open the Links subpanel and click on the Browser control.**

If you are working with Motif, try the following procedure:

1 **If necessary, start X and the window manager.** You will not be able to use Netscape on a text-only display.

2 **Select the Netscape option on one of the pop-up menus.** This assumes, of course, that such an option has been provided on your system.

3 **If Netscape is not available as a menu option, start the program from the command line.** At the shell prompt, type netscape, an ampersand (&), and (Return).

§ `netscape &` Return

It may take a moment or two for Netscape to start up. Eventually, you will see your *default home page*. Generally, this will be either the Netscape company home page or a local home page (Figure 24–1). Note that the Universal Resource Locator (URL) for this page is shown in the Location field.

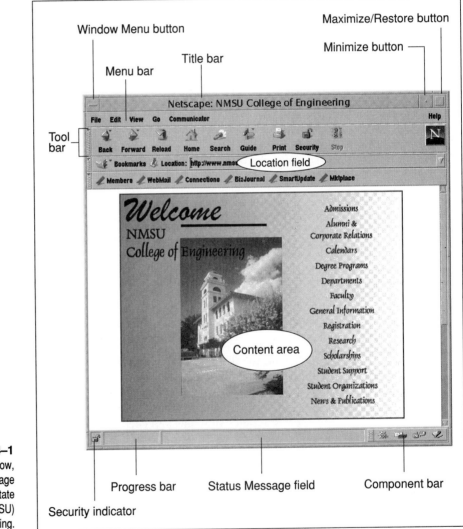

Figure 24–1
Netscape window, showing the home page of the New Mexico State University (NMSU) College of Engineering.

24.2   The Netscape Window

Take a moment to acquaint yourself with the various parts of the Netscape window. Be sure you can locate and identify the following:

* *Menu Bar.* Six pull-down menus are available from the menu bar near the top of the window. Reading from left to right, these are the File, Edit, View, Go, Communicator, and Help menus.

* *Toolbar buttons.* Nine buttons are located in a row beneath the menu bar. These are labeled Back, Forward, Reload, Home, Search, Guide, Print, Security, and Stop.

* *Netscape logo.* This is located to the right of the toolbar buttons. (Clicking on this logo will take you to the Netscape home page.)

* *Location field.* The URL of the currently displayed page appears in this area. You can also move to another page by inserting its URL here.

* *Bookmarks button.* This button opens the Bookmarks QuickFile.

* *Content area.* The Web pages are displayed in this part of the window.

* *Security indicator.* This is an icon representing a padlock. When the browser displays a web page that is encrypted, the padlock is shown closed; when the page is unencrypted, the padlock appears open. If you click on the padlock, the page's security information is displayed.

* *Status Message field.* Whenever the browser sends or receives information over the Web, it prints an appropriate message in the Status Message field to let you know what is happening.

* *Component bar.* The icons on this bar allow you to switch between the various components of Netscape Communicator: Navigator (Web browser), Messenger (e-mail program), Collabra (discussion groups), and Page Composer.

24.3   Specifying a Document by Its URL

It is easy to obtain a WWW document if you know its URL. The Library of Congress home page is a good place to start when you are getting used to running Netscape.

1   **Enter the URL in the Location field.** For the Library of Congress, the URL is

    `http://lcweb.loc.gov/homepage/lchp.html`

    Note that the label on the field becomes **Go To:**.

2   **Press** (Return).

    It may take a minute or so for the Library of Congress home page to appear. During this time, "shooting stars" move across the Netscape logo and the

Progress bar indicates that the program is working. At the same time, a message appears in the Message Status field. Eventually, you should see the home page of the Library of Congress.

24.4 Selecting Hypertext Links

Hypertext links appear on a Web page as underlined text, buttons, or icons (Figure 24–2). Clicking on one of these will lead you to another hypertext document.

Figure 24–2
Hypertext links. Underlined text, buttons, and icons are used to indicate links to other documents.

Note that the cursor assumes the shape of a pointing finger when it is placed over an active link:

Take time now to explore the hypertext documents available from the Library of Congress server.

24.5 Examining Cached Documents

When the Netscape client obtains a document from the Web, it places a copy of that document in a temporary storage area called a *cache*. You can return to documents in the cache by pressing the Forward and Back buttons in the Netscape toolbar:

These buttons move you through the pages you have recently visited.

Try the Back and Forward buttons to reexamine the hypertext documents you obtained from the Library of Congress.

24.6   Setting a Bookmark

After you have been using the WWW awhile, there may be a Web page you wish to visit frequently. Rather than having to enter the URL each time, you can create a menu link—called a *bookmark*—which leads directly to that page. It is easy to set a bookmark:

1   Go to the page you wish to mark.

You can also pull down the Communicator menu, open the Bookmarks submenu, and select Add Bookmark.

2   Open the Bookmarks QuickFile. The Bookmarks button can be found to the left of the Location Field.

The QuickFile will open.

3   Click on Add Bookmark.

The new bookmark will be added to the list.

Once you have marked a page, you can return to that page simply by selecting it from the list of bookmarks.

24.7   Getting Help

Netscape offers more features than can be covered in a single chapter. Fortunately, you can get on-line Help:

•   **Pull down the Help menu and select Help Contents.**

The NetHelp window will appear (Figure 24–3). It initially opens on the Overview section, which provides useful information on how the various parts of Netscape Communicator work.

You can read the Help pages section by section, if you wish. Or you can look for Help on a specific topic:

1   Click on the Index button.

An alphabetical list of topics will appear.

You can also scroll down the list of topics and select the topic you want.

2   Look for a topic. Suppose, for example, that you wanted to know how to print a Web page. Enter the word *print* in the "Look for" box.

A shorter list of topics dealing with printing will appear.

3   Click on the desired topic.

The requested help page will open in the Current page area.

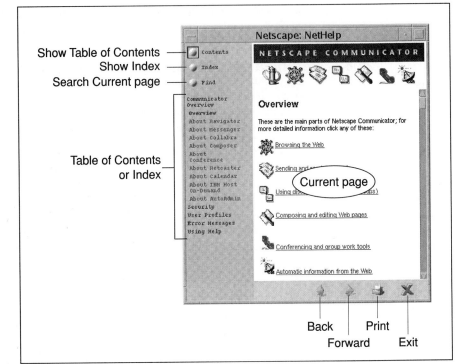

Show Table of Contents
Show Index
Search Current page

Table of Contents
or Index

Current page

Back
Forward
Print
Exit

Figure 24–3
NetHelp window.

24.8 Searching the Web

A number of services have been created to help you find information on the World Wide Web. The Netscape browser has a built-in button that allows you to call up the most widely used search engines.

Suppose, for example, that someone told you that there are Web sites that show live shots from outdoor video cameras. Let's see how you might find such a site.

1 Click on the Search button.

The Netcenter Search page will appear.

2 Choose a search engine. Click on Infoseek.

The Infoseek window will appear.

3 Enter appropriate keyword(s) in the box. If you are interested in outdoor cameras, it would make sense to enter *outdoor cameras*. (The word *camera* by itself is probably too general.) Try it.

4 Click on Go. Alternatively, you can press (**Return**).

Either way, Infoseek will show you a list of outdoor- and camera-related topics, as well as a list of links to specific Web sites. Note that Infoseek "scores" the Web sites by how well they fit the search keywords, and lists the sites accordingly.

5 **Select a hypertext link.** Look down the list of links to find one that seems to offer what you are looking for. Click on the link.

24.9 Quitting Netscape

1 **Pull down the File menu.**

2 **Select the Exit option.**

24.10 Exercises

1. Refer to the Help pages to find out how to print a Web document on a printer or into a file.

2. Netscape may be used to process electronic mail. Refer to the Help pages to see how this is done.

3. Netscape may be used to read network news. Refer to the Help pages to see how this is done.

4. Refer to the Netscape Help pages to determine the functions of the Reload, Home, Guide, Security, and Stop buttons.

5. *PC Magazine* maintains a list of Top 100 Web Sites, as chosen by their editors. Examine the list at `http://www.pcmag.com`.

6. Find the home pages for the following organizations:

   Apple Computer

   Boeing Aircraft

   Brigham Young University

   New Mexico State University

   Purdue University Schools of Engineering

   Smithsonian Institution

   Sun Microsystems

   White House

7. Find a map and photographs of the Apache Point Observatory in southern New Mexico.

8. What is in Room 350 of the Clyde Building at Brigham Young University?

9. You may have noticed that Infoseek offers a link labeled <u>Search tips</u>. Select this and learn about search methods. Then search the Web for the following information:

Gross domestic product (GDP) of Guatemala

Biographical data on Sam Houston

Soft drinks currently available in the vending machine in the Computer Science Department at the University of California, Berkeley

Retail price of the *Oxford English Dictionary*

Map of Howland Island

Retailers of equipment and supplies for amateur telescope makers

Violent crime rate in the United States

Job openings in the industry of your choice

Material safety data sheet for cupric sulfate ($CuSO_4$)

The current weather report

10. Try out one of the other search tools available on the Web:

Alta Vista (`http://altavista.digital.com`)

Excite (`http://www.excite.com`)

Galaxy (`http://galaxy.tradewave.com`)

GoTo (`http://GoTo.com`)

HotBot (`http://HotBot.com`)

Looksmart (`http://www.looksmart.com`)

Lycos (`http://www.lycos.com`)

Snap! (`http://www.home.snap.com`)

Yahoo (`http://www.yahoo.com`)

11. If your system does not have a graphical user interface, you cannot run Netscape. There are, however, a number of text-based WWW browsers that do not require a GUI, the most popular being a program called `lynx`. Refer to your system's manual pages to see how `lynx` works, then use it to gain access to the home page of the Library of Congress.

PART VI:
STARTUP FILES

25 STARTUP FILES

A *startup file* contains commands for the shell to execute when it begins running. Startup files greatly increase the convenience and flexibility of the shell by performing routine tasks such as setting up your terminal, customizing the shell prompt, and reminding you of upcoming events.

25.1 Login and Shell Initialization Files

There are two types of startup files. A *login initialization file* contains commands that are executed when you first log in. If your login shell is the Bourne Shell (sh) or Korn Shell (ksh), this file will be called .profile; if your login shell is the C Shell (csh), it will be called .login.

The second type of startup file is the *shell initialization file*, which contains commands that are executed when a new ksh or csh process is started. This happens when you log in if you are using ksh or csh as your login shell. It also happens whenever you start ksh or csh as a subshell. You can run ksh as a subshell simply by entering the command line

§ /bin/ksh (Return)

The rc ending stands for "run command."

When you do this, the new ksh shell process looks for commands in a file named .kshrc.

Likewise, you can run csh as a subshell with the command line

§ /bin/csh (Return)

The new csh process looks for commands in a file named .cshrc.

Control Files

Note that the various startup files are hidden files—their names begin with a period (.)—meaning that they will not be listed by the simple `ls` command. Most hidden files are used to control the way the system works. For this reason, they are sometimes called *control files*. Some of the more common control files are listed below, along with a description of their contents:

.cshrc	Commands to be run when a new shell starts up (`csh` only)
.exrc	Settings for `vi` editor
.forward	Addresses to which e-mail is forwarded
.kshrc	Commands to be run when a new shell starts up (`ksh` only)
.login	Commands to be run when you log in (`csh` only)
.logout	Commands to be run when you log out (`csh` only)
.mailrc	Mail aliases
.mwmrc	Commands to configure the Motif Window Manager (`mwm`)
.newsrc	List of newsgroups and messages read
.plan	Information displayed by `finger` command
.profile	Commands to be run when you log in (`sh` & `ksh`)
.xinitrc	Commands to configure the X Window System
.dtprofile	Commands to configure the CDE Desktop

A subshell is sometimes started for you by the login shell. For instance, when you run your own program or shell script, the login shell actually calls up a subshell to run the program. The same thing happens when you group several commands together using parentheses. In either case, the new subshell executes the commands it finds in the `.kshrc` or `.cshrc` file.

25.2 Startup Files Thus Far

Let's summarize what we have learned about startup files:

- `sh` uses one startup file, named `.profile`. The shell executes the commands in this file only once, when you first log in.

- `ksh` uses two startup files. It executes the instructions in `.profile` and `.kshrc` when you first log in. After that, every `ksh` subshell executes the commands in `.kshrc`.

- csh also uses two startup files. It executes the instructions in .cshrc and .login when you first log in. After that, every csh subshell executes the commands it finds in .cshrc.

25.3 Variables

One of the most important uses for a startup file is to set the values of variables used by the shell. A *variable* is a named storage location that can hold a value. Three types of variables are commonly used by the shell:

- *Environment Variables.* Also called *special shell variables*, *keyword variables*, *predefined shell variables*, or *standard shell variables*, they hold information about the computer system that the shell needs to operate correctly.

- *User-created Variables.* You can name your own variables and assign them values. These are also called *personal variables*.

- *Positional Parameters.* These are used in shell programs.

In this chapter we will discuss the environment and user-created variables. We will discuss positional parameters when we take up shell scripts in Chapter 28.

25.4 Environment Variables

The environment shell variables provide information to the shell about the way your account is set up. Here are some of the more common environment variables:

Variable	Contents
HOME	Pathname of your home directory
PATH	Directories where shell is to look for commands
TERM	The termcap code for your terminal
USER	Your user name
PWD	Your current working directory
MAIL	Pathname of your system mailbox
SHELL	Pathname of shell

25.5 Setting the Environment Variables

Some of the standard shell variables (such as HOME and SHELL) are set automatically for you when you log in. Others (such as TERM) you may have to set yourself. This is usually done in your login initialization file.

If you are using either sh or ksh as your login shell, you can put instructions in your .profile for setting up the values of the shell variables. For example, you could set the terminal type to be a vt100 by including the following command line in your .profile:

There are no spaces around the equals sign.

TERM=vt100

This line would suffice to tell the login shell that you are working on a vt100, but you also need to get this information to any subshells that might be created. To do this, you must include the export command in your .profile:

export TERM

This will ensure that the subshells are given the value of TERM. If for some reason you did not want the subshells to know what kind of terminal you are using, you could simply omit the export command.

The csh works a bit differently. You can set the terminal type and "export" it all at once by putting the setenv ("set environment") command in your .login file:

setenv does not take an equals sign (=).

setenv TERM vt100

25.6   Listing the Environment Variables

There are several ways to examine the value of a standard shell variable once it is set. If you are using sh or ksh, the set command without arguments will list the values of all the environment variables:

(sh or ksh)

§ set (Return)

If you are using csh, the setenv command will accomplish the same thing:

(csh)

§ setenv (Return)

You can also view the values of the individual variables one at a time with the echo command. For example, the following command line will display the current value of TERM:

§ echo $TERM (Return)
vt100

Note the dollar sign ($) preceding TERM; this is a special character that tells echo you want to see the *contents* of the variable TERM, not just its name. If you omitted the dollar sign, this is what you would see:

§ echo TERM (Return)
TERM

25.7   The Search Path

In Chapter 10, we summarized how the shell processes commands:

1. **The shell displays a prompt symbol on the screen.** The prompt tells you the shell is ready to receive your commands.

2. **You type in a command.** As you type, the system stores the characters and also echoes them back to the terminal screen.

3. **You type** (Return). This is the signal for the shell to interpret the command and start working on it.

4. **The shell looks for the appropriate software to run your command.** In most cases, it looks for a file having the same name as the command. If the shell can't find the right software, it gives you an error message; otherwise, the shell asks the kernel to run it.

5. **The kernel runs the requested software**. While the command is running, the shell "goes to sleep." When the kernel finishes, it "wakes up" the shell.

6. **The shell again displays a prompt symbol**. This indicates that the shell is once again ready to receive your commands.

How does the shell know where to find software to run (Step 4)? The answer is that the shell examines the value of the environment variable PATH. This variable holds the *search path,* which is a list of pathnames telling the shell where to look.

If you are using either sh or ksh, the pathnames of the search path are separated by colons (:). The PATH variable can be set like this:

sh and ksh use colons to separate pathnames.

```
PATH=/bin:/usr/bin:/usr/yourlogin/bin:
export PATH
```

This tells the shell to look first in the /bin directory. If it cannot find the right software in that directory, it is to search /usr/bin, then /usr/yourlogin/bin, and finally, the current directory. (Placing a colon by itself at the beginning or end of the path, or two colons in a row within the path, tells the shell to search the current directory.)

A csh search path uses spaces instead of colons to separate the directory pathnames, and it uses the setenv command to set the value of PATH:

csh uses spaces to separate pathnames.

```
setenv PATH ( /bin /usr/bin /usr/yourlogin/bin . )
```

This tells csh to search /bin, then /usr/bin, then /usr/yourlogin/bin, and finally, the current directory (.).

25.8   User-Defined Variables

In addition to the standard shell variables, you can define your own variables. This is done by giving the variable a name and a value. Suppose, for example, that you were frequently using a long directory name such as `/usera/george/bin/stuff` and would prefer not to have to type it out each time. If you are using the `sh` or `ksh`, you could place the following line in your `.profile` to define a variable to hold the pathname:

Neither `sh` or `ksh` allows spaces around the equals sign.

```
stuff=/usera/george/bin/stuff
```

This creates a variable named `stuff`, and gives it the pathname as a value. This variable will be known only to the login shell; if you also want it to be available to any subshells, you will have to "export" it:

```
export stuff
```

(If you are a `ksh` user, you could also make `stuff` available to the subshells by defining it in the `.kshrc` file.)

`csh` handles user-defined variables somewhat differently. To create the variable `stuff` you could use the `set` command in your `.login` file:

`csh` allows spaces around the equals sign.

```
set stuff = /usera/george/bin/stuff
```

This would define `stuff` for the login shell, but the definition would not carry over to any subshells. If you want your subshells to be able to use this variable, you have two choices. First, you could use the `setenv` command in your `.login` file:

Do not use an equals sign with `setenv`.

```
setenv stuff /usera/george/bin/stuff
```

Or you could use the `set` command in your `.cshrc` file:

```
set stuff = /usera/george/bin/stuff
```

Remember, any command in your `.cshrc` is run each time a new shell process is started, including subshells.

Having defined the variable `stuff` and given it a value, you can use it to save keystrokes. For example, you could list the files in the directory `/usera/george/bin/stuff` with the following command line:

Note the dollar sign preceding the variable name.

§ `ls $stuff` (Return)

Traditionally, user-defined variable names are spelled in lowercase letters, to distinguish them from the standard shell variables.

25.9   The calendar Utility

Do not confuse this with the cal utility, which displays a calendar on the screen.

Most UNIX systems offer the calendar utility, a kind of electronic datebook that can remind you of important assignments, appointments, project deadlines, and so on. If you want to use calendar, you must include the following line in your startup file:

    calendar

This command tells UNIX to search through a file named calendar for any lines that contain today's date or tomorrow's date; it then displays those lines on the screen. (On weekends, it also displays Monday's messages.) Suppose you wanted to remember to call Adam Smith on April 12. You might put the following line in cal-endar, which will be displayed when you log in on April 11:

    Call Adam Smith April 12

The same line will be displayed when you log in on April 12. Any of the following messages would have the same effect:

    Call Adam Smith on 4/12

    April 12: call Adam Smith

    Call Adam Smith on Apr 12

The date may appear anywhere on the line, and it may be spelled out (April 12), abbreviated (Apr 12), or written in numerals (4/12). However, you must put the month before the date. (Do not write 12 April, 12 Apr, or 12/4). If you include the year, it will be ignored; calendar always assumes the current year.

25.10   The history Mechanism (csh and ksh)

The Bourne Shell does not have a history mechanism.

Another useful feature of the C Shell and the Korn Shell is the history mechanism, which keeps track of the most recent commands you have issued and gives you a quick way to repeat those commands.

You can specify how many commands you want history to remember for you. If you are a csh user, you can set history to remember the last ten commands by putting the following line in your .cshrc file:

csh allows spaces around the equals sign.

    set history = 10

To set ksh to remember the last ten commands, you would put the following line in your .kshrc file to set the value of the variable HISTSIZE:

ksh does not allow spaces around the equals sign.

    HISTSIZE=10

If you do not give a value to the HISTSIZE variable, ksh will remember 128 commands by default.

Once the history mechanism is set up, typing

§ history ⟨Return⟩

will produce a numbered list of the ten commands you have used most recently, including history itself:

```
1   who | sort
2   ls
3   cal
4   cd
5   ls -l
6   mkdir Stuff
7   cd Stuff
8   vi newstuff
9   spell newstuff
10  history
```

You can repeat any of these commands by number. In csh, you simply type an exclamation mark (!) followed by the number. Thus, to repeat command number 5 on the history list, you would type

Repeat command #5 (csh).

§ !5 ⟨Return⟩

The command will appear on the screen just as if you typed it again:

```
ls -l
```

You can repeat the most recent command by entering two exclamation marks:

Repeat last command (csh).

§ !! ⟨Return⟩

The ksh history command uses r (for "repeat") instead of an exclamation mark. Thus, to repeat the fifth command on the history list, you would type:

Repeat command #5 (ksh).

§ r 5 ⟨Return⟩

The command is echoed on the screen:

```
ls -l
```

You can repeat the most recent command by entering the r command without a number:

Repeat last command (ksh).

§ r ⟨Return⟩

25.11 Command Aliases (csh and ksh)

The C and Korn Shells allow you to rename UNIX commands. A renamed command —called an *alias*—may be used to shorten long commands or to protect you from accidentally deleting an important file. Most users set up a list of aliases in their shell initialization file (.kshrc or .cshrc), so that the aliases are defined automatically each time a new shell is started.

The alias command is used to define aliases in csh. Placing the following line in the .cshrc file tells the shell to treat m as an alias for the mailx command:

(csh)   `alias m mailx`

The alias command works a bit differently with ksh. The following line may be placed in the .kshrc file to create a ksh alias for the mailx command:

(ksh)   `alias m='mailx'`

Once the alias is set, you could send mail to the user bfranklin with the command line

§ m bfranklin (Return)

You can remove an alias with the unalias command:

§ unalias m (Return)

25.12 Protecting Existing Files (csh and ksh)

One of the common uses of command aliases is to protect files from being deleted accidentally. When you specify the -i ("interactive") option with the cp, mv, or rm command, you will be asked to confirm your intentions if you try to do something that would destroy an existing file. For example, suppose you tried to remove a file named oldfile using the rm -i command:

§ rm -i oldfile (Return)

The command will prompt you to confirm that this is what you want:

rm: remove oldfile?

If you enter a *y* (for "yes"), the file will be removed. Otherwise, no action will be taken. The -i option works similarly with the cp or mv commands, should you try to overwrite an existing file.

If you are a csh user, you can create a "safe" alias for rm by placing the following line in the .cshrc file:

(csh)   `alias rm 'rm -i'`

If you use ksh, you would put this line in your .kshrc file:

(ksh)   `alias rm='rm -i'`

Alternatively, you could put the following line in your `.profile`, using the `-x` option to export the command to all subshells:

The `-x` *option exports the alias* (`ksh`).

`alias -x rm='rm -i'`

25.13   Comment Lines

A *comment* is text in a startup file (or a program) that is ignored by the shell when the file is executed. Comments are useful for reminding you of the file's purpose. In shell startup files, a comment begins with a pound sign (#). For example,

`# This is a comment line`

25.14   Exercises

1. Be sure you can define the following terms:

startup file	login initialization file	shell initialization file
subshell	variable	special shell variable
environment variable	alias	

2. Be sure you can explain the function or contents of each of the following files:

`.cshrc`	`.exrc`	`.forward`	`.kshrc`
`.login`	`.logout`	`.mailrc`	`.mwmrc`
`.newsrc`	`.plan`	`.profile`	`.xinitrc`

3. Be sure you can explain the purpose of each of the following variables:

HOME	MAIL	PATH
PWD	SHELL	TERM

4. Suppose a `sh` user wanted to create a variable named `myhome` to hold the pathname of his or her home directory.

    a. What command(s) should be put in the login initialization file so that `myhome` will be usable by the login shell only?

    b. What command(s) will ensure that `myhome` will be available to all subshells? (The variable HOME contains the pathname of the home directory.)

5. Repeat the previous problem, assuming that `ksh` is the login shell.

6. Repeat the previous problem, assuming that `csh` is the login shell.

26 TUTORIAL: USING SH OR KSH STARTUP FILES

Skip this chapter if you are a C Shell user.

If you use either the Bourne Shell (sh) or the Korn Shell (ksh), your login initialization file will be named .profile. If you are a Korn Shell user, you may also have a shell initialization file named .kshrc. In this chapter, you will learn how to make and modify such files.

26.1 Listing the Variables with set

- **List the current settings of the environment variables.** This is done with the set command, used without arguments:

The $ is the default prompt for sh and ksh, and will be used in this chapter.

```
$ set (Return)
```

The shell will display a list of variables and their current settings. Some variables you might see include the following:

Variable	Contents
HOME	Pathname of your home directory
MAIL	Pathname of your system mailbox
PATH	Directories where shell is to look for commands
PS1	"Prompt string 1"—primary prompt (default: $)
PS2	"Prompt string 2"—secondary prompt (default: >)
PWD	Your current working directory
SHELL	Pathname of shell (/bin/sh or /bin/ksh)
TERM	The termcap code for your terminal
USER	Your user name

26.2 Showing the Value of a Variable with echo

You can examine the values of these variables one at a time using the echo command.

- **Enter the echo command, specifying the variable you wish to examine.**
  You must enter a dollar sign ($) as a prefix to the variable name. Thus, to view
  the contents of the PS2 variable, type

```
$ echo $PS2 Return
```

The secondary prompt is discussed in the next section.

PS2 contains the secondary prompt. Its default value is

```
>
```

If you omit the dollar sign prefix, the *name* of the variable, not its contents, will
be displayed:

```
$ echo PS2 Return
PS2
```

26.3 The Secondary Prompt

The secondary prompt is a symbol that indicates that the shell is waiting for you to
finish an incomplete command line. In this section, you will see how this works.

1 **Enter an incomplete command line.** Try the following line, making sure not
to type any closing quotes:

```
$ echo "This is an Return
```

Because you did not provide the closing quotes, the shell assumes that there is
more to come, and it displays the secondary prompt stored in PS2:

```
>
```

2 **Enter the rest of the command line.** Be sure to finish it off with double quotes,
before pressing Return:

```
>incomplete command line." Return
```

The shell will echo back the entire message:

```
This is an
incomplete command line.
```

26.4 Making Backups of the Startup Files

The first step in creating a .profile is to see whether you already have such a file. If so, you should prepare a backup copy.

1 **If necessary, go to your home directory.** Remember, the cd command without arguments will take you to your home directory:

```
$ cd (Return)
```

2 **List all files in your home directory.** Enter the ls -a ("list -all") command:

```
$ ls -a (Return)
```

If you see a file named .profile it means that one was placed in your home directory when your account was created. You may want to consult with your instructor or system administrator before editing this file. If you are a ksh user, also note whether you already have a .kshrc file.

3 **Make a backup copy of the existing startup file(s).**

```
$ cp .profile .profile.BAK (Return)
$ cp .kshrc .kshrc.BAK (Return)
```

26.5 A Login Message

In this section you will create a .profile file (or edit an existing file) to display a message on the screen every time you log in. You will use the echo command to do this.

1 **Try out the login message.** Type

```
$ echo "Your wish is my command, Oh Great One." (Return)
```

The shell should respond with the appropriate message:

```
Your wish is my command, Oh Great One.
```

2 **Use your text editor to open the** .profile **file.**

```
$ vi .profile (Return)
```

3 **Insert a comment showing the modification date.** Put the following line at the top of .profile:

```
# This file was last modified on [today's date].
```

The # at the beginning of the line makes this a comment. This shows a typical use of comments, which is to tell you when the file was last edited.

4 **Add the message command to the file.**

```
echo "Your wish is my command, Oh Great One."
```

5   Write the file and quit the editor.

26.6   Running the Startup File

At this point, you *could* log out and log back in again to see if your .profile works. However, there is an easier way: Use the "dot" command.

- **Run the "dot" command.** Type a period, a space, and the name of the file:

```
$ . .profile (Return)
```

This will cause the shell to execute the commands in .profile, as if you had just logged in. You should see the login message:

```
Your wish is my command, Oh Great One.
```

The shell will display this message each time you log in, unless you change it or delete it from your .profile.

26.7   Changing the Prompt Symbol

The default primary prompt symbol for sh or ksh is the dollar sign ($). You can change the prompt symbol by changing the value of the variable PS1. In this section, you will try out various prompts, then edit .profile to display one of the new prompts.

1   Change the value of the PS1 variable. Type the following line, making sure not to put spaces around the equals sign:

```
$ PS1=# (Return)
```

This will change your shell prompt to the pound sign:

```
#
```

2   Try out another prompt. You can include spaces and special characters in the prompt string if you quote it:

```
# PS1="Your Majesty? " (Return)
```

The prompt will change to the new string:

```
Your Majesty?
```

3   Include shell variables in your prompt. Some users like to display the pathname of their home directory as part of their prompt. Remember, your home directory's pathname is stored by the shell in a variable named HOME. Try the following command (don't type Your Majesty?—it is the prompt):

```
Your Majesty? PS1="$HOME > " (Return)
```

Without the dollar sign, the
word HOME would appear
instead of the pathname.

The dollar sign placed in front of HOME tells the shell to put the contents of HOME in the prompt. Now your prompt should show the absolute pathname of your home directory, followed by an arrow (>). For example, if the absolute pathname of your home directory were /home/you, the prompt would now be

```
/home/you >
```

Let's put this prompt into your .profile.

4   Use the text editor to edit the startup file. Add the following to .profile:

```
PS1="$HOME > "
export PS1
```

5   Write to the file and quit the editor.

6   Use the "dot" command to run the commands in .profile.

```
/home/you > . .profile (Return)
```

Your prompt should now consist of your home directory's pathname, followed by an arrow. Thus, if your home directory were /home/you, you would see your login message, then the prompt

```
/home/you >
```

26.8   Setting the Terminal Type

Having to set your terminal type each time you log in is a nuisance—especially if you use the same kind of terminal all of the time. You can set the terminal in your .profile file.

1   Edit your .profile to set the terminal type. Insert the following lines, substituting your terminal's termcap code for vt100:

```
TERM=vt100
export TERM
echo "Terminal set to $TERM"
```

2   Write and quit the editor.

3   Apply the "dot" command to .profile:

```
/home/you > . .profile (Return)
```

Your login message should appear, then the message about the terminal type:

```
Terminal set to vt100
```

26.9 Making a calendar File

The `calendar` utility will remind you of upcoming events. This requires that you have a `calendar` file in your home directory, and that you modify `.profile` to read the `calendar` file.

1 **Edit your `.profile` with the text editor.** Add the following line:

`calendar`

2 **Write the change into the file and quit the editor.**

3 **Use the text editor to create a `calendar` file.** Be sure to use this exact spelling of `calendar`, in lowercase letters. Otherwise, the shell won't recognize the file.

4 **Add a message to the `calendar` file.** Include today's date in the message. For example, if today is April 12, type

Write the date in the form April 12, Apr 12, or 4/12.

`This is a test for April 12`

5 **Write the changes into the `calendar` file and quit the editor.**

6 **Use the "dot" command to run the `.profile` file.**

`/home/you > . .profile` (Return)

You should see your login message, the message about your terminal type, and the `calendar` message:

```
Your wish is my command, Oh Great One.
Terminal set to vt100
This is a test for April 12
```

26.10 Creating a .kshrc File (ksh only)

If you are a `ksh` user, you may create a shell initialization file named `.kshrc`. This file is typically used for setting up command aliases and the `history` mechanism. Before doing this, however, you need to edit `.profile`:

1 **Use the text editor to edit `.profile`.** Add the following lines to the file:

```
ENV=$HOME/.kshrc
export ENV
```

This tells `ksh` that it should look for `.kshrc` in your home directory. If the ENV variable is not set, `ksh` will not execute `.kshrc`.

2 **Write and quit the editor.**

3 **Use the text editor to edit the `.kshrc` file.** Start by inserting a comment line, giving today's date:

```
# This file was last modified on [today's date]
```

26.11   Creating an Alias (ksh)

One of the uses for `.kshrc` is to create aliases. In this section, you will create a one-letter alias for the `history` command.

1   Use the text editor to edit the `.kshrc` file. Add the following line to the file to create an alias for the `history` command:

```
alias -x h=history
```

The `-x` option tells `alias` to export the alias to all subshells.

2   Write the changes to the file and quit the editor.

3   Use the "dot" command to run the `.kshrc` file.

```
/home/you > . .kshrc (Return)
```

At this point, the alias should be set. In the next section, you will see how to use the alias to run the `history` command.

26.12   Using the history Mechanism (ksh)

The `history` mechanism keeps a list of the commands you have used most recently, and it allows you to view and repeat commands on the list.

1   Run the `history` command using its alias. Type h followed by (Return) to run the `history` command:

```
/home/you > h (Return)
```

If you correctly set up the alias for `history`, you should see a numbered list of the most recently executed commands. Note that the history command itself will appear as the last item on the list:

```
1   set
2   echo $PS2
3   echo PS2
4   echo "This is an incomplete command line."
5   ls -a
6   echo "Your wish is my command, Oh Great One."
7   vi .profile
8   . .profile
9   PS1=#
10  PS1="Your Majesty? "
11  PS1="$HOME >"
12  vi .profile
```

```
13  . .profile
14  vi .profile
15  . .profile
16  vi .profile
17  vi calendar
18  vi .kshrc
19  . .kshrc
20  h
```

2 Repeat the most recent command on the list. This is done by typing an r at the prompt. Try it:

```
/home/you > r (Return)
```

You should see another listing of commands, as before:

```
1   set
2   echo $PS2
3   echo PS2
4   echo "This is an incomplete command line."
5   ls -a
6   echo "Your wish is my command, Oh Great One."
7   vi .profile
8   . .profile
9   PS1=#
10  PS1="Your Majesty? "
11  PS1="$HOME >"
12  vi .profile
13  . .profile
14  vi .profile
15  . .profile
16  vi .profile
17  vi calendar
18  vi .kshrc
19  . .kshrc
20  h
21  h
```

3 Repeat a command by number. Thus, to repeat the sixth command on the list, type

```
/home/you > r 6 (Return)
```

The command line will appear on the screen, and the command will be run.

```
echo "Your wish is my command, Oh Great One."
Your wish is my command, Oh Great One.
```

4 Repeat a command by entering the first letter(s) of the command line. Thus, to repeat a command line that starts with the letter *s*, type

```
/home/you > r s Return
```

The most recent command beginning with *s* is the set command; it should list the values of the environment variables.

```
set
```

26.13   Command Summary

Checking the Values of Variables

set	list the valuables of all variables
echo $var	print value of variable var

Setting Values of Variables

var=value	set variable var to value
var="A string"	store string A string in variable var
export var	export contents of var to all subshells

Executing a Startup File

. .profile	execute .profile

Changing Prompts

PS1="Prompt string" export PS1	set primary prompt to Prompt string

Creating Command Aliases (ksh)

alias c=command	define c as an alias for command
alias -x c=command	define c as an alias for command and export
unalias c	remove c as an alias for command

Using the history Mechanism (ksh)

history	print history list
r	repeat the most recent event on history list
r *n*	repeat the *n*th event on history list
r *abc*	repeat the most recent event starting with letters *abc*

26.14   Exercises

1. The `date` command prints the date and current time. Add the following line to your `.profile`, making sure to use backquotes around `date`:

    ```
    echo "The date and time are `date`."
    ```

    Exit the editor and run the `.profile` using the "dot" command. What happens?

2. The backquotes were needed in the previous exercise to tell the shell that `date` was to be interpreted as a command, not as a word. What happens if the backquotes are omitted? Try it. Open `.profile` and remove the backquotes from `date`:

    ```
    echo "The date and time are date"
    ```

    Exit the editor and run the `.profile` using the "dot" command. What happens? (Now open up the file and replace the backquotes.)

3. What is your search path (PATH)?

4. What is the complete pathname for your shell?

5. The `rm`, `cp`, and `mv` commands are dangerous because they can overwrite or remove existing files. The `-i` ("interactive") option will ask you to confirm that this is what you want. If this option is available to you, add the following lines to your `.kshrc` file:

    ```
    alias -x rm="rm -i"

    alias -x cp="cp -i"

    alias -x mv="mv -i"
    ```

6. Explain what the following lines would do if they were placed in your `.kshrc` file:

    ```
    alias -x m=more

    alias -x f=finger

    alias -x ls="ls -R"
    ```

7. Most users set up their `history` mechanism to remember about 100 commands. To do this yourself, open your `.kshrc` file and insert this line:

    ```
    HISTSIZE=100
    ```

    If you neglect to set the `HISTSIZE` variable, `ksh` will remember the most recent 128 commands by default.

27 TUTORIAL: USING CSH STARTUP FILES

If you use the C Shell (`csh`) as your login shell, your login initialization file will be named `.login,` and your shell initialization file will be named `.cshrc`. In this chapter, you will learn how to make and modify these files.

27.1 Listing the Environment Variables

- **List the current settings of the environment variables.** This is done with the `setenv` command, used without arguments:

The percent sign is the default prompt for `csh`, and will be used in this chapter.

```
% setenv (Return)
```

The shell will display a list of variables and their current settings. Some variables you might see include the following:

Variable	Contents
HOME	Pathname of your home directory
MAIL	Pathname of your system mailbox
PATH	Directories where shell is to look for commands
PWD	Your current working directory
SHELL	Pathname of shell (`/bin/csh`)
TERM	The `termcap` code for your terminal
USER	Your user name

You can examine the values of these variables one at a time using the `echo` command.

- **Enter the** echo **command, specifying the variable you wish to examine.**
  You must enter a dollar sign ($) as a prefix to the variable name. Thus, to view the contents of the SHELL variable, type

% echo $SHELL ⟨Return⟩

This will display the absolute pathname of csh:

/bin/csh

If you omit the dollar sign prefix, the *name* of the variable, not its contents, will be displayed:

% echo SHELL ⟨Return⟩
SHELL

27.2 Checking the Special csh Variables

The C Shell uses the same environment variables as the Bourne Shell and Korn Shell, but it also has some special shell variables of its own. You can check the settings of these variables using the set command.

- **Enter the** set **command without arguments.**

% set ⟨Return⟩

This will list the special shell variables and their current settings. For example:

Variable	Contents
cwd	Pathname of current working directory
history	Size of history list
home	Pathname of your home directory
path	Directories where shell is to look for commands
prompt	Current prompt symbol (default: %)
shell	Pathname of shell (/bin/csh)
term	The termcap code for your terminal
user	Your user name

These special shell variables are used only by csh, not by sh or ksh.

Note that the csh special variables are written in lowercase letters to distinguish them from the environment variables.

27.3   Setting the Special csh Variables

The set command is used to assign a value to a variable.

1   Enter the set command. For example, to set the value of the history variable, type the following:

```
% set history = 100 (Return)
```

2   Check the setting with echo.

Do not omit the $ sign.

```
% echo $history (Return)
```

This should show the value stored in history:

```
100
```

The special csh variables home, path, shell, term, and user have a special relationship with their uppercase counterparts. When you change the value of the lowercase variable, the uppercase variable is changed as well. If you change the value of term, for example, the value of TERM is changed automatically to match.

27.4   Making Backups of the Startup Files

The first step in creating or editing .login or .cshrc is to see whether you already have such files. If so, you should prepare backup copies.

1   If necessary, go to your home directory. Remember, the cd command without arguments will take you to your home directory:

```
% cd (Return)
```

2   List all files in your home directory. Enter the ls -a ("list -all") command:

```
% ls -a (Return)
```

If you see files named .login and .cshrc, these were probably placed in your home directory when your account was created. You may want to consult with your instructor or system administrator before editing them.

3   Make a backup copy of the existing startup file(s).

```
% cp .login .login.BAK (Return)
% cp .cshrc .cshrc.BAK (Return)
```

27.5   A Login Message

In this section you will create a .login file (or edit an existing file) to display a message on the screen every time you log in. You will use the echo command to do this.

1   **Try out the login message.** Type

```
% echo "Your wish is my command, Oh Great One." (Return)
```

The shell should respond with the appropriate message:

```
Your wish is my command, Oh Great One.
```

2   **Use your text editor to open the** `.login` **file.**

```
% vi .login (Return)
```

3   **Insert a comment showing the modification date.** Put the following line at the top of `.login`:

```
# This file was last modified on [today's date].
```

The # at the beginning of the line makes this a comment. This shows a typical use of comments, which is to tell you when the file was last edited.

4   **Add the message command to the file.**

```
echo "Your wish is my command, Oh Great One."
```

5   **Write the file and quit the editor.**

27.6   Running the Startup File

At this point, you *could* log out and log back in again to see if your `.login` works. However, there is an easier way: Use the `source` command.

•   **Run the** `source` **command on the file.** Thus, to run the commands in `.login`, type:

```
% source .login (Return)
```

This will cause the shell to execute the commands in `.login`, as if you had just logged in. You should see the login message:

```
Your wish is my command, Oh Great One.
```

The shell will display this message each time you log in, unless you change it or delete it from your `.login`.

27.7   Changing the Prompt Symbol

The default primary prompt symbol for `csh` is the percent sign (%). You can change the prompt symbol by changing the value of the variable `prompt`. In this section, you will try out various prompts, then edit `.login` to display one of the new prompts.

1 **Change the value of the** `prompt` **variable.** Type the following line:

`% set prompt = #`(Return)

This will change your shell prompt to the pound sign:

`#`

2 **Try out another prompt.** You can include spaces and special characters in the prompt string if you quote it:

`# set prompt = 'Your Majesty? '`(Return)

The prompt will change to the new string:

`Your Majesty?`

3 **Include shell variables in your prompt.** Some users like to display the pathname of their home directory as part of their prompt. Remember, your home directory's pathname is stored by the shell in a variable named `home`. Try the following command (don't type `Your Majesty?`—it is the prompt):

`Your Majesty? set prompt = "$home > "`(Return)

The dollar sign placed in front of `home` tells the shell to put the contents of `home` in the prompt. Now your prompt should show the absolute pathname of your home directory, followed by an arrow (>). For example, if the absolute pathname of your home directory were `/home/you`, the prompt would now be

`/home/you >`

Let's put this prompt into your `.login`.

4 **Use the text editor to edit the startup file.** Add the following to `.login`:

`set prompt = "$home > "`

5 **Write to the file and quit the editor.**

6 **Use the** `source` **command to run the commands in** `.login`.

`/home/you > source .login`(Return)

Your prompt should now consist of your home directory's pathname, followed by an arrow. Thus, if your home directory were `/home/you`, you would see your login message, then the prompt

`/home/you >`

27.8 Setting the Terminal Type

Having to set your terminal each time you log in is a nuisance—especially if you use the same kind of terminal all of the time. You can set the terminal in your `.login` file.

1 **Edit your `.login` to set the terminal type.** Insert the following lines, substituting your terminal's termcap code for **vt100**:

```
set term = vt100
echo "Terminal set to $term"
```

2 **Write and quit the editor.**

3 **Apply the source command to `.login`:**

```
/home/you > source .login (Return)
```

Your login message should appear, then the message:

```
Terminal set to vt100
```

27.9 Making a calendar File

The `calendar` utility will remind you of upcoming events. This requires that you have a `calendar` file in your home directory and that you modify `.login` to read the `calendar` file.

1 **Edit your `.login` with the text editor.** Add the following line:

```
calendar
```

2 **Write the change into the file and quit the editor.**

3 **Use the text editor to create a `calendar` file.** Be sure to use this exact spelling of `calendar`, in lowercase letters. Otherwise, the shell won't recognize the file.

4 **Add a message to the `calendar` file.** Include today's date in the message. For example, if today is April 12, write:

```
This is a test for April 12
```

Write the date in the form April 12, Apr 12, or 4/12.

5 **Write the changes into the `calendar` file and quit the editor.**

6 **Use the source command to run the `.login` file.**

```
/home/you > source .login (Return)
```

You should see your login message, the message about the terminal type, and the `calendar` message:

```
Your wish is my command, Oh Great One.
Terminal set to vt100
This is a test for April 12
```

27.10   Creating a .cshrc File

If you are a csh user, you may create a shell initialization file named .cshrc. This file is typically used for setting up command aliases and the history mechanism. In this section, you will create a one-letter alias for the history command.

1   **Use the text editor to edit the** .cshrc **file.** Start by inserting a comment line, giving today's date:

```
# This file was last modified on [today's date]
```

2   **Use the text editor to define an alias.** Add the following line to the .cshrc file to create an alias for the history command:

```
alias h history
```

3   **Write the changes to the file and quit the editor.**

4   **Use the** source **command to run the** .cshrc **file.**

```
/home/you > source .cshrc (Return)
```

At this point, the alias should be set. In the next section, you will see how to use the alias to run the history command.

27.11   Using the history Mechanism

The history mechanism keeps a list of the commands you have used most recently, and it allows you to view and repeat commands on the list.

1   **Run the** history **command using its alias.** Type h followed by (Return) to run the history command:

```
/home/you > h (Return)
```

If you correctly set up the alias for history, you should see a numbered list of the most recently executed commands. Note that the history command itself will appear as the last item on the list:

```
1   set history = 100
2   echo $history
3   cd
4   ls -a
5   cp .login .login.BAK
6   cp .cshrc .cshrc.BAK
```

```
 7  echo "Your wish is my command, Oh Great One."
 8  vi .login
 9  source .login
10 set prompt = #
11 set prompt = 'Your Majesty? '
12 vi .login
13 source .login
14 vi .login
15 source .login
16 vi calendar
17 source .login
18 vi .cshrc
19 . .cshrc
20 h
```

2 **Repeat the most recent command on the list.** This is done by typing two exclamation marks at the prompt. Try it:

```
/home/you > !! (Return)
```

You should see another listing of commands, as before.

3 **Repeat a command by number.** Thus, to repeat the seventh command on the list, type

```
/home/you > !7 (Return)
```

The command line will appear on the screen, and the command will be run.

```
echo "Your wish is my command, Oh Great One."
Your wish is my command, Oh Great One.
```

4 **Repeat a command by entering the first letter(s) of the command line.** Thus, to repeat a command line that starts with the letter *s*, type

```
/home/you > !s (Return)
```

The most recent command beginning with *s* is the **source** command:

```
source .login
```

27.12 Command Summary

Checking the Values of Variables

`setenv`	list the values of environment variables
`set`	list the values of special `csh` variables
`echo $var`	print value of variable `var`

Setting Values of Variables

`set var = value`	set variable `var` to `value`
`set var = "A word"`	store string `A word` in variable `var`
`setenv VAR value`	set environment variable VAR to `value`

Executing a Startup File

`source .login`	execute `.login`

Changing Prompts

`set prompt = "Prompt string"`	set prompt to `Prompt string`

Creating Command Aliases (`csh`)

`alias c command`	make `c` an alias for `command`
`unalias c`	remove `c` as an alias for `command`

Using the history Mechanism (`csh`)

`history`	print `history` list
`!!`	repeat most recent event on `history` list
`!n`	repeat the *n*th event on `history` list
`!abc`	repeat the most recent event starting with letters *abc*

27.13 Exercises

1. The `date` command prints the date and current time. Add the following line to your `.login`, making sure to use backquotes around `date`:

    ```
    echo "The date and time are `date`."
    ```

    Exit the editor and run the `.login` using the `source` command. What happens?

2. The backquotes were needed in the previous exercise to tell the shell that date was to be interpreted as a command, not as a word. What happens if the backquotes are omitted? Try it. Open up your .login and remove the backquotes from date:

```
echo "The date and time are date"
```

Exit the editor and run the .login using the source command. What happens? (Now open up the file and replace the backquotes.)

3. What are your search paths (path and PATH)?

4. What is the complete pathname for your shell?

5. Change your prompt so that it always displays the current working directory.

6. The rm, cp, and mv commands are dangerous because they can overwrite or remove existing files. The −i ("interactive") option will ask you to confirm that this is what you want. If the −i option is available to you, put the following lines in your .cshrc file:

```
alias rm "rm -i"
```

```
alias cp "cp -i"
```

```
alias mv "mv -i"
```

7. Explain what the following lines would do if they were placed in your .cshrc file:

```
alias m more
```

```
alias f finger
```

```
alias ls "ls -R"
```

8. To prevent files from being overwritten by the redirection operation, place the following line in your .cshrc:

```
set noclobber
```

Does this work as expected?

PART VII:
SHELL SCRIPTS

28 SHELL SCRIPTS

Until now, you have been giving commands to the UNIX shell by typing them on the keyboard. When used this way, the shell is said to be a command interpreter. The shell can also be used as a high-level programming language. Instead of entering commands one at a time in response to the shell prompt, you can put a number of commands in a file, to be executed all at once by the shell. A program consisting of shell commands is called a *shell script*. This chapter will introduce you to shell scripts for the Bourne Shell.

28.1 Simple Shell Script

Suppose you were to make up a file named `commands` containing the following lines:

```
# A simple shell script
cal
date
who
```

The first line in this file begins with a # symbol, which indicates a *comment line*. Anything following the # is ignored by the shell. The remaining three lines are shell commands: the first produces a calendar for the current month, the second gives the current date and time, and the third lists the users currently logged onto your system.

One way to get the Bourne Shell (`sh`) to run these commands is to type

§ sh < commands (Return)

The redirection operator (<) tells the shell to read from the file `commands` instead of from the standard input. It turns out, however, that the redirection symbol is not really needed in this case. Thus, you can also run the `commands` file by typing

§ sh commands (Return)

Is there any way to set up `commands` so that you can run it without explicitly invoking the shell? In other words, can you run `commands` without first typing `sh`, `csh`, or `ksh`? The answer is yes, but you first have to make the file *executable*. The `chmod` utility does this:

chmod is described in
Appendix D.

§ `chmod u+x commands` (Return)

The argument `u+x` tells `chmod` that you want to add (+) permission for the user (u) to execute (x) the shell script in the file. Now all you need do is type the file name

§ `commands` (Return)

and the shell will run the commands in the file.

28.2 Subshells

The new shell process is a
subshell or *child* of the
original shell.

When you tell the shell to run a script such as the `commands` file, your login shell actually calls up another shell process to run the script. (Remember, the shell is just another program, and UNIX can run more than one program at a time.) The parent shell waits for its child to finish, then takes over and gives you a prompt:

§

Incidentally, a subshell can be different from its parent shell. For example, you can have `csh` or `ksh` as your login shell, but use `sh` to run your shell scripts. Many users in fact do this. When it comes time to run a script, the `csh` or `ksh` simply calls up `sh` as a subshell to do the job.

We will always use `sh` for running shell scripts. To make sure that `sh` is used, we will include the following line at the top of each shell script file:

In this case, the # does *not*
mark a comment.

`#!/bin/sh`

Thus, our `commands` file would look something like this:

```
#!/bin/sh
# A simple shell script
cal
date
who
```

28.3　The Shell as a Programming Language

The sample script commands is almost trivial—it does nothing more than execute three simple commands that you could just as easily type into the standard input. The shell can actually do much more. It is, in fact, a sophisticated programming language, with many of the same features found in other programming languages, including

- Variables

- Input/output functions

- Arithmetic operations

- Conditional expressions

- Selection structures

- Repetition structures

We will discuss each of these in order.

28.4　Variables

There are three types of variables commonly used in Bourne Shell scripts:

- ***Environment Variables.*** Sometimes called special shell variables, keyword variables, predefined shell variables, or standard shell variables, they are used to tailor the operating environment to suit your needs. Examples include TERM, HOME, and MAIL.

- ***User-created Variables.*** These are variables that you create yourself.

- ***Positional Parameters.*** These are used by the shell to store the values of command-line arguments.

Of these, the environment variables and user-created variables have been introduced already. The positional parameters, however, are new, and since they are very useful in shell programming, we will examine them in some detail now.

The positional parameters are also called *read-only variables*, or *automatic variables*, because the shell sets them for you automatically. They "capture" the values of the command-line arguments that are to be used by a shell script. The positional parameters are numbered 0, 1, 2, 3, ... , 9. To illustrate their use, consider the following shell script, and assume that it is contained in an executable file named echo.args:

```
#!/bin/sh
# Illustrate the use of positional parameters
echo $0 $1 $2 $3 $4 $5 $6 $7 $8 $9
```

Suppose you run the script by typing the command line

```
§ echo.args We like UNIX. (Return)
```

The shell stores the name of the command ("echo.args") in the parameter $0; it puts the argument "We" in the parameter $1; it puts "like" in the parameter $2, and "UNIX." in parameter $3. Since that takes care of all the arguments, the rest of the parameters are left empty. Then the script prints the contents of the variables:

```
echo.args We like UNIX.
```

What if the user types in more than nine arguments? The positional parameter $* contains all of the arguments $1, $2, $3, ... $9, and any arguments beyond these nine. Thus, we can rewrite echo.args to handle any number of arguments:

```
#!/bin/sh
# Illustrate the use of positional parameters
echo $*
```

The parameter $# contains the number of arguments that the user typed. We can modify the script echo.args once again to use this parameter:

```
#!/bin/sh
# Illustrate the use of positional parameters
echo You typed $# arguments: $*
```

Suppose we were then to type the command line

```
§ echo.args To be or not to be  (Return)
```

The computer would respond with

$ does not contain $0, so echo.args is neither counted nor printed.*

```
You typed 6 arguments: To be or not to be
```

28.5   Input Using the read Statement

The positional parameters are useful for capturing command-line arguments but they have a limitation: once the script begins running, the positional parameters cannot be used for obtaining more input from the standard input. For this you have to use the read statement. Let's modify the previous program to make use of read:

```
#!/bin/sh
# Illustrate the use of positional parameters, user-defined
# variables and the read command.
echo 'What is your name?'
read name
echo "Well, $name, you typed $# arguments:"
echo "$*"
```

In this script, name is a user-defined variable. The read command obtains the user's response and stores it in name. With this modification, the script echo.args works something like this:

§ echo.args To be or not to be (Return)

The shell script would respond by prompting you for your name:

What is your name?

Suppose you were to type

Rumpelstiltskin (Return)

The computer would respond with

Well, Rumpelstiltskin, you typed 6 arguments:
To be or not to be

28.6 The set Command

The positional parameters are sometimes called *read-only variables*, because the shell sets their values for you when you type arguments to the script. However, you can also set their values using the set command. To illustrate this, consider the following shell script, which we will assume is in the file setdate:

```
#!/bin/sh
# Demonstrate the set command
set `date`
echo "Time: $4 $5"
echo "Day: $1"
echo "Date: $3 $2 $6"
```

Assuming that setdate has been made executable with the chmod command, we can run the script by typing the command

§ setdate (Return)

The output will look something like this:

```
Time: 10:56:08 EST
Day: Fri
Date: 10 Aug 2001
```

What happened? Consider the command line

set `date`

The backquotes run the date command, which produces output something like this:

Fri Aug 10 10:56:08 EST 2001

This does not appear on the screen. Instead, the `set` command catches the output and stores it in the positional parameters $1 through $6:

$1 *contains* `Fri`
$2 *contains* `Aug`
$3 *contains* `10`
$4 *contains* `10:56:08`
$5 *contains* `EST`
$6 *contains* `2001`

28.7 Arithmetic Operations Using the expr Utility

The shell is not intended for numerical work—if you have to do a lot of calculations, you should consider C, FORTRAN, or Pascal. Nevertheless, the `expr` utility may be used to perform simple arithmetic operations on integers. (`expr` is not a shell command, but rather a separate UNIX utility; however, it is most often used in shell scripts.) To use it in a shell script, you simply surround the expression with backquotes. For example, let's write a simple script called `add` that adds two numbers typed as arguments:

```
#!/bin/sh
# Add two numbers
sum=`expr $1 + $2`
echo $sum
```

Here we defined a variable `sum` to hold the result of the operation. (Note the spaces around the plus sign, but not around the equals sign.) To run this script, we might type the following line:

§ add 4 3 ⏎(Return)

The first argument (4) is stored in $1, and the second (3) is stored in $2. The `expr` utility then adds these quantities and stores the result in `sum`. Finally, the contents of `sum` are echoed on the screen:

```
7
§
```

The `expr` command only works on integers (i.e., whole numbers). It can perform addition (+), subtraction (−), multiplication (*), integer division (/), and integer remainder (%).

28.8   Control Structures

Normally, the shell processes the commands in a script sequentially, one after another in the order they are written in the file. Often, however, you will want to change the way that commands are processed. You may want to choose to run one command or another, depending on the circumstances; or you may want to run a command more than once.

To alter the normal sequential execution of commands, the shell offers a variety of control structures. There are two types of *selection structures*, which allow a choice between alternative commands:

- `if/then/elif/else/fi`

- `case`

There are three types of *repetition* or *iteration structures* for carrying out commands more than once:

- `for`

- `while`

- `until`

28.9   The if Statement and test Command

The `if` statement lets you choose whether to run a particular command (or group of commands), depending on some condition. The simplest version of this structure has the general form

```
if conditional expression
then
    command(s)
fi
```

When the shell encounters a structure such as this, it first checks to see whether the conditional expression is true. If so, the shell runs any commands that it finds between the `then` and the `fi` (which is just *if* spelled backwards). If the conditional expression is not true, the shell skips the commands between `then` and `fi`. Here is an example of a shell script that uses a simple `if` statement:

```
#!/bin/sh
set `date`
if test $1 = Fri
then
    echo "Thank goodness it's Friday!"
fi
```

Here we have used the `test` command in our conditional expression. The expression

```
test $1 = Fri
```

checks to see if the parameter `$1` contains `Fri`; if it does, the `test` command reports that the condition is true, and the message is printed.

The `test` command can carry out a variety of tests; some of the arguments it takes are listed below:

Argument	Test is true if . . .
`-d file`	`file` is a directory
`-f file`	`file` is an ordinary file
`-r file`	`file` is readable
`-s file`	`file` size is greater than zero
`-w file`	`file` is writable
`-x file`	`file` is executable
`n1 -eq n2`	integer n1 equals integer n2
`n1 -ge n2`	integer n1 greater than or equal to integer n2
`n1 -gt n2`	integer n1 greater than integer n2
`n1 -le n2`	integer n1 less than or equal to integer n2
`n1 -ne n2`	integer n1 not equal to integer n2
`n1 -lt n2`	integer n1 less than integer n2
`s1 = s2`	string s1 equals string s2
`s1 != s2`	string s1 not equal to string s2

28.10   The elif and else Statements

We can make the selection structures much more elaborate by combining the if with the elif ("else if") and else statements. Here is a simple example:

```
#!/bin/sh
set `date`
if test $1 = Fri
then
    echo "Thank goodness it's Friday!"
elif test $1 = Sat  || test $1 = Sun
then
    echo "You should not be here working."
    echo "Log off and go home."
else
    echo "It is not yet the weekend."
    echo "Get to work!"
fi
```

Here, the first conditional expression is tested to see if the day is a Friday. If it is, the message "Thank goodness it's Friday!" is printed, and the shell script is finished. If not, the second conditional expression is tested. Note that we have used the OR operator (||) in this expression to test whether the day is a Saturday or Sunday, in which case the second set of messages will be printed, and the script is finished. Otherwise, the third set of messages is printed.

We could make even more elaborate selection structures by including more elif clauses. The important thing to note about such structures is that only one of the alternatives may be chosen; as soon as one is, the remaining choices are skipped.

28.11   The case Statement

The shell provides another selection structure that may run faster than the if statement on some UNIX systems. This is the case statement, and it has the following general form:

```
case  word in
pattern1)  command(s) ;;
pattern2)  command(s) ;;
...
patternN)  command(s) ;;
esac
```

The case statement compares word with pattern1; if they match, the shell runs the command(s) on the first line. Otherwise, the shell checks the remaining patterns, one by one, until it finds one that matches the word; it then runs the command(s) on that line.

Here is a simple shell script that uses the `case` statement:

```
#!/bin/sh
set `date`
case $1 in
Fri) echo "Thank goodness it's Friday!";;
Sat | Sun) echo "You should not be here working";
           echo "Log off and go home!";;
*)   echo "It is not yet the weekend.";
     echo "Get to work!";;
esac
```

There are a few points to note about this structure. First, commands are separated by semicolons (`;`), and the end of a group of commands is indicated by two semicolons (`;;`). The OR symbol used in `case` statements is a single vertical line (`|`), not the double vertical lines (`||`) used in the `if` statement. The last pattern (`*`) marks the *default case*, which is selected if no other pattern is matched.

28.12   for Loops

Sometimes we want to run a command (or group of commands) over and over. This is called *iteration*, *repetition*, or *looping*. The most commonly used shell repetition structure is the `for` loop, which has the general form

```
for variable in list
do
    command(s)
done
```

Here is a simple application of the `for` loop:

```
#!/bin/sh
#
for name in $*
do
    finger $name
done
```

Each time through the `for` loop, the user-defined variable `name` takes on the value of the next argument in the list `$*`. This is then used as the argument to the `finger` command. Assuming this script is contained in the executable file `fingerall`, it would be run by typing the name of the file, followed by the login names you wish to finger:

§ `fingerall johnp maryl frederick` (Return)

28.13   while Loops

The general form of the `while` loop is

```
while condition
do
    command(s)
done
```

As long as the condition is true, the commands between the do and the done are executed. Here is an example of a shell script that uses the `expr` utility with the `while` loop to print a message ten times:

```
#!/bin/sh
# Print a message ten times
count=10
while test $count -gt 0
do
    echo $*
    count=`expr $count - 1`
done
```

28.14   until Loop

Another kind of iteration structure is the `until` loop. It has the general form

```
until condition
do
    command(s)
done
```

This loop continues to execute the command(s) between the do and done until the condition is true. We can rewrite the previous script using an `until` loop instead of the `while` loop:

```
#!/bin/sh
# Print a message ten times
count=10
until test $count -eq 0
do
    echo $*
    count=`expr $count - 1`
done
```

28.15   Exercises

1.   Be sure you can define each of the following terms:

shell script	comment	subshell
child process	positional parameter	selection structure
default case	repetition structure	iteration
loop		

2.   If you have not already done so, read about the chmod utility in Appendix D. Suppose you have a file named myfile. Write the commands you would use to accomplish the following:

   a.   Make myfile executable (but not readable or writable) by everyone.

   b.   Allow the owner to read, write, or execute myfile; allow the group to read or execute the file; allow everyone else to execute the file only.

   c.   Add write permissions for members of the group.

   d.   Remove all permissions from everyone. (Why might you want to do this?)

29 TUTORIAL: CREATING SHELL SCRIPTS

In this chapter we present a number of shell scripts that make use of the programming features discussed in the previous chapter.

Before listing the actual code for each script, we will follow the general outline of the man pages and present the name of the script, a brief synopsis of how the script is used, and an outline of the script.

29.1 Making a File Executable: chex

If you are planning to write a lot of shell scripts, you will find it convenient to have a script that makes files executable. If we were to write our own man page for such a script, it might look like this:

```
NAME
      chex—change a file to be executable

SYNOPSIS
      chex filename

DESCRIPTION
     This is the outline for chex:

            Select sh
            Apply chmod u+x to file named as argument ($1)
            Inform user that file is executable
            Use ls -l to show the file modes
```

Listing 29–1A
Summary of the chex script.

The shell script itself is shown in Listing 29–1B. Take a moment to study the outline, then create the script:

Listing 29–1B
The chex script.

```
#!/bin/sh
# Make a file executable
chmod u+x $1
echo $1 is now executable:
ls -l $1
```

1   **Use the text editor to create the script file.** Open a file named chex and enter the script shown in the listing. Write and quit the file when finished.

2   **Make the chex file executable.** This requires you to change the access privileges on the file. One way to do this is to tell the shell to run chex on itself. Try this command line:

§ sh chex chex ⏎(Return)

This tells the shell to run chex, taking chex itself as the argument. The result is that chex makes itself executable. The output from this command will look something like this:

```
chex is now executable:
-rwxr-xr-x     1     yourlogin 59   Date time   chex
```

Now you can use chex to change the protections on other files.

29.2   Labeling the Output from wc: mywc

The wc ("word count") filter counts the words, lines, and characters in a file. For example, try running wc on the chex file you have just created:

```
§ wc chex (Return)
5    17    84     chex
§
```

The output tells us that there are 5 lines, 17 words, and 84 characters in the file chex. This can be very useful information, but it would be a bit more convenient to use if the output were labeled.

```
NAME
     mywc-labeled word count

SYNOPSIS
     mywc filename

DESCRIPTION
     This is the outline for mywc:

          Select sh
          Run wc on $1 and capture output with set
          Print the filename ($4)
          Print the number of lines ($1)
          Print the number of words ($2)
          Print the number of characters ($3)
```

Listing 29–2A
Summary of the mywc script.

The shell script that implements the outline is shown in Listing 29–2B.

```
#!/bin/sh
# Label the output from wc
set `wc $1`
echo "File: $4"
echo "Lines: $1"
echo "Words: $2"
echo "Characters: $3"
```

Listing 29–2B
The mywc script.

1   **Use the text editor to create the script file.** Open a file named mywc and enter the script shown in Listing 29–2B. Write and quit the file when finished.

2   **Make the script executable.** Use chex for this:

§ chex mywc ⟨**Return**⟩

mywc is now executable:
```
-rwxr-xr-x   1  yourlogin   59   Date   time   mywc
```

3   **Test the new script.** You might run mywc on the file chex:

§ mywc chex ⟨**Return**⟩

```
File: chex
Lines: 5
Words: 17
Characters: 84
```

29.3 Removing Files Safely: del

The rm command can be very dangerous because it allows you to remove a file, but does not give you a way of getting back a file you may have removed accidentally. If you are a csh or ksh user, you can create an alias for the rm with the −i ("interactive") option; it will ask you if you are sure you want to remove the file in question. But sh does not allow aliases. Let's create a script that will duplicate the effect of the rm −i command. The script will also tell what action has been taken.

```
NAME
     del-delete a file interactively

SYNOPSIS
     del filename

DESCRIPTION
     This is the outline for del:

          Select sh
          Get the filename from the command line ($1)

          If there is no file with that name
             print an error message
          Otherwise
             Ask if the user wants to delete the file
             Read the user's choice (y/n)

          If the choice is yes (y)
             remove the file & print a message
          otherwise
             print a message
```

Listing 29–3A
Summary of the del
script.

After studying the outline, create the script:

1 **Use the text editor to create the script file.** Open a file named del and enter the script shown in Listing 29–3B. Write and quit the file when finished.

2 **Make the script executable.** Use chex for this:

§ chex del (Return)

del is now executable:
-rwxr-xr-x   1   yourlogin   347   Date time   del

3 **Test the new script.** Use del on a file you no longer need.

```
#!/bin/sh
# Delete a file interactively
filename=$1
if test ! -f $filename
then
    echo "There is no file \"$filename\"."
else
        echo "Do you want to delete \"$filename\"?"
        read choice
    if  test  $choice = y
    then
        rm $filename
        echo "\"$filename\" deleted."
    else
        echo "\"$filename\" not deleted."
    fi
fi
```

Listing 29–3B

The del script

29.4   A Daily Reminder System: tickle

We have already seen how you can use the calendar utility to remind yourself of important events. One limitation of calendar is that you have to enter each event individually, along with its date. This can be a problem for routine events that happen every day or every week. For reminding yourself of such events, the following tickle script can be very useful. It uses the date command to check the day of the week, then prints out an appropriate message.

```
NAME
    tickle-a daily reminder service

SYNOPSIS
    tickle

DESCRIPTION
    Here is the outline for tickle:

        Select sh
        Use set to capture the output from date
        Print a message
        Check day ($1) and print an appropriate message
```

Listing 29–4A

Summary of the
tickle script.

```
#!/bin/sh
# A daily reminder service
set `date`
echo "Remember for today:"
case $1 in
    Mon) echo "Plan the week.";;
    Tue) echo "Take clothes to the cleaners.";;
    Wed) echo "Attend group meeting.";;
    Thu) echo "Make plans for the weekend.";
         echo "Pick up clothes at the cleaners.";;
    Fri) echo "Answer e-mail.";;
    Sat) echo "You should not be here working.";
         echo "Finish your work and log off.";;
    Sun) echo "Call Grandma and Grandpa.";;
esac
```

Listing 29–4B
The `tickle` script.

After studying the outline, create the script:

1 **Use the text editor to create the script file.** Open a file named `tickle` and enter the script shown in Listing 29–4B. Write and quit the file when finished.

2 **Make the script executable.** Use `chex` for this:

§ chex tickle (Return)

tickle is now executable:
-rwxr-xr-x 1   yourlogin 457   Date time   tickle

3 **Test the new script.** Enter the `tickle` command:

§ tickle (Return)

This should print out the appropriate message for the day. However, we are not finished yet. A reminder service is not much good if you have to remember to type "tickle" to use it. It would be better to have the shell run the script automatically each time you log in.

4 **If necessary, move the file `tickle` to your home directory.** Recall that the variable HOME contains the pathname of your home directory:

§ mv tickle $HOME (Return)

5 **Modify your login initialization file to execute `tickle`.** Using the text editor, add the following line to your `.login` or `.profile`:

tickle

6 **Execute your login initialization file.** Use the `source` or "dot" command, as appropriate:

```
§ source .login Return
```

```
§ . .profile Return
```

Your tickle message should appear.

29.5 An Improved spell Program: myspell

The spell program is very useful, but it has a serious limitation: it lists the (possibly) misspelled words in a file, but does not tell you where in the file the misspelled words reside. Listing 29–5A outlines a script that will correct this problem.

```
NAME
      myspell–an improved spelling-checker

SYNOPSIS
      myspell file

DESCRIPTION
      Here is the outline for myspell:

            Select sh
            Run spell on the file; for each misspelling
            do
                  Run grep to find lines with misspellings
                  Print the misspelled word
                  Print the line(s) containing the misspellings
            done
```

Listing 29–5A
Summary of the myspell script.

```
#!/bin/sh
# An improved spelling-checker
file=$1
for word in `spell $file`
    do
        line=`grep -n $word $file`
        echo "     "
        echo "Misspelled word: $word"
        echo "$line"
    done
```

Figure 29–5B
The myspell script.

After studying the outline, create the script:

1   **Use the text editor to create the script file.** Open a file named myspell and enter the script shown in Listing 29–5B. Write and quit the file when finished.

2 **Make the script executable.** Use chex for this:

§ chex myspell (Return)

myspell is now executable:
-rwxr-xr-x 1   yourlogin 140   Date time   myspell

3 **Test the new script.** Try myspell on a file that contains a spelling error:

§ myspell *file* (Return)

29.6 Echo the Arguments Multiple Times: echo.by

The standard echo command echoes its arguments just once. The script presented here echoes its arguments as many times as the user chooses.

```
NAME
      echo.by–echo the arguments n times

SYNOPSIS
      echo.by n arguments(s)

DESCRIPTION
      Here is the outline for echo.by:

            Select sh
            Get $count from the command line ($1)
            Use shift to get rid of the first argument
            Get the message from the command line ($*)

            While $count is greater than 0
            do
               print the message
               subtract 1 from $count
            done
```

Listing 29–6A
Summary of the
echo.by script.

Be sure you understand the outline in Listing 29–6A, then create the script:

1 **Use the text editor to create the script file.** Open a file named echo.by and enter the script shown in Listing 29–6B. Write and quit the file when finished.

2 **Make the script executable.** Use chex for this:

§ chex echo.by (Return)

```
#!/bin/sh
# Echo a line n times
count=$1
shift
message=$*

while test $count -gt 0
do
        echo $message
        count=`expr $count - 1`
done
```

Figure 29–6B
The myspell script.

echo.by is now executable:
-rwxr-xr-x 1   yourlogin 111   Date time   echo.by

3   Test the new script. Try this:

§ echo.by 5 Play it again, Sam. (Return)

The first argument (5) will be read in, then the rest of the command line will be repeated five times:

Play it again, Sam.
Play it again, Sam.
Play it again, Sam.
Play it again, Sam.
Play it again, Sam.

29.7   Exercises

1.   Write a shell script chnoex that reverses the effects of chex by removing the execution permissions on a file.

2.   Write a shell script private that uses chmod to change the access permissions on a file so that only the owner may read, write, or execute it. Be sure to label the output to show what was done to the file.

3.   Write a shell script public that reverses the effect of the private script you wrote in the previous exercise.

4.   Modify the del script so that it detects whether the user has specified a directory to be deleted. (Hint: use test with the –d option to test for a directory.)

5. Rewrite `tickle` to use an `if/then/elif.../fi` structure.

6. Rewrite `echo.by` to use an `until` loop.

7. If you haven't already done so, write and run the sample shell scripts in the previous chapter.

PART VIII:
PROGRAMMING UNDER UNIX

30 PROGRAMMING UNDER UNIX

UNIX was originally written by professional programmers for the use of other professional programmers. It is not surprising, therefore, that UNIX provides a number of excellent programming tools. Traditionally, UNIX systems have come equipped with the C programming language. (UNIX itself is written in C.) Many UNIX systems also offer the Fortran and Pascal languages, and other languages as well.

In this chapter, we will see how Fortran, Pascal, and C programs can be written and run under UNIX.

30.1 Programming Languages

A *computer program* is a set of coded instructions that tell the computer how to perform some task. Computers do not (yet) understand English or any other human language. Instead, computers respond to what is called *machine language*, in which everything is represented by binary numbers—combinations of 0s and 1s. Consider, for example, how a segment of a program might appear in binary form:

```
00000000011000110000000000011000
00000000000000000001110000010010
00000000111000100001000000100000
00100000110001100000000000000001
```

Obviously, it would be tedious to program in a binary code such as this. A better alternative would be to program in *assembly language*, which represents each of the machine's binary instructions symbolically. For example, the previous four lines of binary code might be represented by the following four lines of assembly language:

```
mult $6, $6
mflo $7
add $2, $7, $2
addi $6, $6, 1
```

Assembly language is clearly a step up from binary, but it is still fairly difficult to master. Moreover, programs written in assembly language are not portable because every type of computer has its own assembly language.

Fortunately, high-level programming languages are available that make programming much easier. For example, the previous assembly-language code could be written in the C programming language like this:

```
sum = sum + i * i;
i = i + 1;
```

Not only is this much easier to write and understand than the assembly-language code; it is also much more portable because C programs can be run on nearly any kind of computer.

30.2 Program Design

The first step in creating a program is to design it. That is, you plan what the program is to do, and how. This is perhaps the most important and the most difficult part of programming. Entire volumes have been devoted to this topic; obviously, we can only scratch the surface in this short book.

Program design often begins with the definition of the problem to be solved. To illustrate, let's see how we would design a program to calculate the reciprocal of a number. The problem is simple to define:

Problem: Create a program to calculate the reciprocals of numbers entered by the user at the keyboard; display the results on the terminal screen.

A common tool used in program design is *pseudocode*, which is an outline of the code written in abbreviated English. Pseudocode is laid out to resemble the structure of the actual program. Thus, the pseudocode for our reciprocal program might be:

prompt the user for a number x
read x
calculate 1/x
display the answer

30.3 Source Code

Once you are satisfied with your program design, you can begin to write the solution to the problem using a programming language. Listing 30–1 shows how the reciprocal program might appear when written in C.

```
/* Compute reciprocals */

#include <stdio.h>

main()
{
    double x, recip;
    printf("This program computes reciprocals.\n");
    printf("Enter a number: ");
    scanf("%lf", &x);
    recip = 1.0/x;
    printf("The reciprocal of %f is %f.\n", x, recip);
}
```

Listing 30–1
C code for computing reciprocals.

A program written in a high-level language is often called *source code*. Typically, you will use a text editor such as vi to prepare a file containing the source code. You will follow the usual naming rules for this file, but with one additional rule: files containing source code always have a suffix that indicates the language in which they are written. The suffix *.c* indicates C-language source code, the suffix *.p* indicates Pascal source code, and the suffix *.f* indicates Fortran code. Thus, for our program to compute reciprocals, we might have

recip.c (C version)

recip.p (Pascal version)

recip.f (Fortran version)

30.4   Compiling and Linking

Once you have finished the source code, you must translate it into machine language. This is called *compiling* the code, and the program that performs this task is called a *compiler*. If you are programming in C, compilation is actually a three-step process:

Neither Fortran nor Pascal has a preprocessor.

1. **Preprocessing.** The *preprocessor* goes through your source code and makes certain changes to the code.

2. **Compilation.** The compiler translates your modified source code into machine language. The output from the compiler is called *object code*.

3. **Linking.** Although object code consists of machine language, it is not yet a complete program. The *linker* combines your object code with code from the system software libraries to produce *executable code*.

30.5 Program Execution

The file containing the executable code is given the name `a.out` by the linker (unless you specify another name). To execute the program, all you have to do is type

§ `a.out` (Return)

If you want to save the executable code, you can use the `mv` command to give this file an appropriate name.

30.6 Errors

The easiest thing about programming is making errors. Programming errors come in several varieties:

The computer cannot think, so you have to do the thinking for it.

- *Logic errors.* The computer does what you tell it to do, not what you want it to do. If you specify the wrong way to solve the problem—if you multiply when you should have divided, for instance—your program may run and produce output, but the output will not be correct.

- *Syntax errors.* A syntax error results when you violate one of the rules of the programming language. Such errors are often called *compilation errors* because they will be detected by the compiler when you try to compile the program.

Runtime errors are more commonly called *bugs*.

- *Runtime errors.* More insidious than syntax errors are those errors that escape detection by the compiler. These are called *runtime errors* because they usually are not discovered until you run the program a few times. (And perhaps not even then—many runtime errors are never tracked down.)

30.7 Debugging

A serious runtime error, such as dividing by zero or taking the square root of a negative number, may cause the program to crash. When this happens, the program quits running and the UNIX shell sends you an error message of some sort. Usually, these messages are not very informative: they tell you that the program crashed, but they don't always tell you the reason.

When a program aborts because of a runtime error, the system produces a *core dump*, which is a file containing a "snapshot" of the main memory at the time the program failed. This is put into a file named `core`.

The `core` file contains machine code, so it is not something you would try to read directly yourself. However, most UNIX systems include special programs called *debuggers* that are designed to help you exterminate bugs in your programs. A debugger can use the information in the `core` file to determine what the bug was and where it occurred. One debugger found on many UNIX systems is called dbx; it is described in Appendix F.

30.8 The make Utility

You can learn about make by reading Appendix G.

When writing large programs, it is the usual practice to divide the source code up among several different files. This allows different programmers to work on different parts of the program. It is also more efficient to change and recompile one part of the program at a time, rather than having to compile the entire program whenever a small change is made. The make program is used to keep track of the files making up a large program and to recompile parts of the program as needed. Although make is most often used with programs, it can also be useful in updating any project consisting of multiple files.

30.9 Other Programming Tools

Most UNIX systems come equipped with a battery of programming utilities, most of which are designed for use in creating C programs:

Utility	Description	Function
cb	C beautifier	Formats C source code
cflow	Flow analyzer	Shows flow of control in C programs
ctrace	Execution tracer	Traces execution of a C program
cxref	C tracer	Lists references to variables in C programs
lint	C verifier	Warns of potential bugs, portability problems
prof	Profiler	Tests efficiency
time	Program timer	Times program execution
timex	Program timer	Times program execution

30.10 Exercises

1. Be sure you can define the following terms:

computer program	machine language	assembly language
pseudocode	compiler	source code
preprocessor	object code	executable code
linker	logic error	syntax error
runtime error	core file	debugger

2. Write pseudocode for a program to compute square roots.

31 TUTORIAL: PROGRAMMING IN C

It is a good idea to keep a C
book handy as you read
through this chapter.

C is the "native language" of UNIX—most of the UNIX operating system is written in C. It is not surprising, therefore, that for many applications C is the preferred language of UNIX programmers. In this chapter, you will see how to take advantage of some of the features that make programming in C possible. This is not intended to teach you C; for that, you should consult a standard text on C.

31.1 The hello.c Program

We will begin with the program shown in Listing 31–1, which prints a message on the standard output.

```
/* Traditional first C program. */

#include <stdio.h>

main()
{
    printf("Hello, world!\n");
}
```

Listing 31–1
The hello.c program.

Let's examine this program in more detail:

- `/* Traditional first C program. */`

Any text appearing between /* and */ is treated as a comment and is ignored by the compiler. Comments are included for the benefit of the programmer and anyone else who may read the program later.

- `#include <stdio.h>`

Lines that begin with a pound sign (#) in the first column are taken to be instructions to the preprocessor. These are usually called *preprocessor directives* or *control lines*. In this case, the directive tells the preprocessor to include the contents of the file `stdio.h` ("standard input/output header" file) in the program before it is compiled. The angle brackets `< >` tell the preprocessor to search for `stdio.h` in the "usual place," which for most UNIX systems is the directory `/usr/include`. You can also tell the preprocessor to include files that you have written yourself, in which case you would surround the file's pathname by double quotes. Thus the line

```
#include "/home/mylogin/myfile.h"
```

would direct the preprocessor to include `/home/mylogin/myfile.h` in the program before it is compiled.

- `main()`

C programs consist of one or more units called *functions*. Every C program must include a function named `main()` where execution begins. We know that `main()` is the name of a function because of the parentheses.

- `{`

Each function body begins with a left brace. Braces are also used within the function body to group lines of code together.

- `printf("Hello, world!\n");`

`printf()` is a standard C library function used to "print" output on the standard output. The argument to the function is a group of characters enclosed by double quotes, which is called a *string constant* or *string literal*. At the end of the string (but inside the double quotes) are the two characters `\n`, which together stand for a NEWLINE or (Return). The entire line is terminated by a semicolon.

- `}`

The function body ends with a right brace, which matches the left brace at the beginning of the function body. The compiler will consider it an error if you omit either brace.

31.2 Creating and Running hello.c

Remember that the file name must end in *.c*.

1 **Create a source file.** Use the `vi` editor to create a file named `hello.c`:

§ `vi hello.c` (Return)

Enter the program exactly as shown in Listing 31–1, then write to the file and quit the editor.

2   **Compile the source code.** The standard C compiler is called `cc`. To compile the file, simply type `cc` followed by the name of the file:

§ `cc hello.c`(Return)

3   **If necessary, correct any compiler errors and repeat Step 2**. If the compiler cannot compile your code because of syntax errors, it will try to tell you where the errors are located. Reopen the file and correct the errors.

4   **Run the program.** By default, the linker gives the name `a.out` to the executable file. To run the program, type

§ `a.out` (Return)

You should see the message

`Hello, world!`
§

The shell prompt appears when the program finishes, indicating that the shell is ready for your next command.

31.3   Review of the Compilation Process

Recall the command you used to compile the `hello.c` program:

§ `cc hello.c` (Return)

The `cc` command appears simple, but it starts a fairly complicated chain of events involving three separate programs:

The preprocessor works on a copy of the code; it does not actually alter `hello.c`.

1.   The C preprocessor goes through the file `hello.c` and looks for preprocessor directives, which are marked by a leading pound sign (#). The preprocessor makes the requested changes and passes the altered code to the compiler.

2.   The compiler translates the C code into object code, which it places in a file named `hello.o`. (If there are syntax errors, the compiler will not produce object code; instead, it will try to tell you where the errors are to be found.)

3.   The linker combines your object code with any code your program may need from the standard libraries to produce executable code. In this case, the program calls the library function `printf()`. The executable code is placed in a file named `a.out`. (In some cases, the object file `hello.o` is deleted automatically.)

31.4   Renaming the Executable File

Note that the file containing the executable code is given the name a.out by the
linker. If you want to save the executable code, you must use the mv command to
give this file another name—otherwise, it will be overwritten the next time you use
the cc compiler.

1   Use the mv command to rename the executable file. It is common practice to
give the executable code the same name as the source code, but without the .c
suffix:

§ mv a.out hello (Return)

2   Run the program. Enter the new name of the executable file:

§ hello (Return)
Hello, world!
§

As we shall see, you can compile the source code and rename the executable file all
at once using cc with the -o option:

§ cc hello.c -o hello (Return)

Note that the arguments can be written in a different order:

§ cc -o hello hello.c (Return)

31.5   The recip.c Program

Our next program calculates reciprocals of numbers entered by the user at the keyboard. A pseudocode outline for this program is shown in Listing 31–2A; the corresponding C code is shown in Listing 31–2B.

Listing 31–2A
Pseudocode for the re-
cip.c program.

Print a brief message about what the program does
Prompt the user for an integer n
Read n
Calculate 1/n
Display the answer

```
/* Compute reciprocals */

#include <stdio.h>

main()
{
    int n, recip;
    printf("This program computes reciprocals.\n");
    printf("Enter a number: ");
    scanf("%d", &n);
    recip = 1/n;
    printf("The reciprocal of %d is %d.\n", n, recip);
}
```

Listing 31–2B
C code for the
`recip.c` program.

This program introduces a few new features that were not in the previous program:

•   `int n, recip;`

This is a *declaration*. It tells the compiler to create two variables to hold integers (`int`) and to give them the names n and `recip`. C requires that you declare all variables before you use them.

•   `scanf("%d", &n);`

A common mistake is to omit the address operator &.

`scanf()` is a standard C library function, used to get input from the standard input. In this example, the function takes two arguments, `"%d"` and &n. The first argument (`"%d"`) is called a *control string*; it tells the compiler about the format of the input. In this case, the format specification %d stands for a single decimal integer. The second argument (&n) tells `scanf()` to store the integer that it reads in the variable n. The ampersand (&) is the address operator; it is required in this context.

•   `recip = 1/n;`

This is how we compute the reciprocal. The computer first divides the integer 1 by the contents of the variable n, and then assigns the result to the variable `recip`. In C, = is called the *assignment operator*; it tells the computer to take the value of the expression on the right and assign it to the variable on the left.

•   `printf("The reciprocal of %d is %d.\n", n, recip);`

This is another `printf()` function call, with a difference. There are three arguments this time instead of one. The first argument is a string containing two formats (%d and %d). The other two arguments are variables (n and `recip`). The `printf()` function prints out the string, substituting the contents of n and `recip` for the two formats.

31.6   Creating and Running recip.c

1   **Create a source file.** Use the vi editor to create a file named `recip.c`:

§ vi recip.c (Return)

Enter the program exactly as shown in Listing 31–2B, then write to the file and quit the editor.

2   **Compile the source code.** The default name for an executable file is `a.out`. You can specify another name using cc with the −o option. For the executable file, let's use the name `recip` (without the `.c` suffix):

§ cc -o recip recip.c (Return)

This tells cc to compile `recip.c` and put the executable in the file `recip`.

3   **If necessary, correct any syntax errors and repeat Step 2.**

4   **Run the program.** To run the program, enter the name of the executable file:

§ recip (Return)

You should see a message and a prompt:

This program computes reciprocals.
Enter a number:

5   **Enter a number at the prompt.** Try the number 2:

Enter a number: 2 (Return)

The program will respond:

The reciprocal of 2 is 0.
§

This is obviously wrong: the reciprocal of 2 is 1/2, not 0. In fact, `recip.c` gives the correct answer only when you enter −1 or 1 as an input. The reason has to do with the way that the computer stores and uses integers. To repair this defect, you should revise the program to use variables of type `float` or `double` rather than type `int`. (We leave this as an exercise.)

31.7   Arithmetic Exceptions and Core Dumps

How does the `recip.c` program handle division by zero?

1   **Run the program.**

§ recip (Return)

The program will print a message and a prompt:

This program computes reciprocals.
Enter a number:

2   **Enter zero at the prompt.**

Enter a number: 0 (Return)

You should receive an error message, something like this:

Arithmetic exception (core dumped)

What happened? It is not hard to figure out. Division by zero is an undefined operation that caused the program to crash.

3   **Check for a** core **file.** If you list the files in your directory, you should see a file named core:

§ ls (Return)

Since you cannot read the core file, and because it takes up so much room, you should delete it.

4   **Remove the** core **file.**

§ rm core (Return)

31.8   Setting up recip.c for Debugging

Although you cannot read a core file as you would a normal UNIX text file, you can use a debugger such as dbx to examine the file and determine what caused the program to crash.

•   **Compile the program using the debug option.** With most compilers, the –g option indicates "debug":

§ cc -g recip.c (Return)

This causes the compiler to include additional information in the compiled code that can be used by dbx. If you would like to see how dbx is used, refer to Appendix F.

31.9   The sqroot.c Program

Our next program calculates the square roots of numbers entered by the user at the keyboard. A pseudocode outline for this program is shown in Listing 31–3A, and the C code itself is shown in Listing 31–3B.

Listing 31–3A

Pseudocode for the
sqroot.c program.

> *Print a brief message about what the program does*
> *Prompt the user for a number x*
> *Read x*
> *Compute the square root of x*
> *Display the answer*

Listing 31–3B

C code for the
sqroot.c program.

```
/* Compute square roots */

#include <stdio.h>
#include <math.h>

main()
{
    double n, root;
    printf("This program computes square roots.\n");
    printf("Enter a number: ");
    scanf("%lf", &n);
    root = sqrt(n);
    printf("The square root of %f is %f.\n", n, root);
}
```

This program introduces some interesting new elements:

- `#include <math.h>`

This control line tells the preprocessor to include the contents of the file `math.h` (standard math header file) in the program before it is compiled. As before, the angle brackets `< >` tell the preprocessor to search for the file in the "usual place," most likely the directory `/usr/include`.

- `double n, root;`

This declaration tells the compiler to create two variables to hold `double` values and to give them the names `n` and `root`.

- `scanf("%lf", &n);`

The control string in this `scanf()` function call contains the format specification `%lf`, which stands for "long float," a synonym for `double`.

- `root = sqrt(n);`

This statement calls the library function `sqrt()` to compute the square root of `n`, then assigns the result to the variable `root`.

31.10 Creating and Running sqroot.c

1 **Create a source file.** Use the vi editor to create a file named sqroot.c:

§ vi sqroot.c (Return)

Enter the program exactly as shown in Listing 31–3B, then write to the file and quit the editor.

2 **Compile the source code.** The program sqroot.c uses the math library function sqrt(). The −1m option tells the linker to combine compiled code from the math library with your object code:

§ cc -o sqroot sqroot.c -1m(Return)

Note that the −1m option comes at the end of the command line because it is an instruction to the linker rather than the compiler.

3 **If necessary, correct any syntax errors and repeat Step 2.**

4 **Run the program.** To run the program, enter the name of the executable file:

§ sqroot (Return)

The program will print a message and the prompt:

This program computes square roots.
Enter a number:

5 **Test the program.** Enter a 4 at the prompt:

Enter a number: 4 (Return)

You should see something like this:

The square root of 4 is 2.
§

31.11 The Trip Program

Our next sample program illustrates the use of separate source files for putting together a large program. Large programs are often the work of more than one programmer; it is common for each programmer to work on his or her own files, which then are assembled to make a complete program.

It is convenient to group the source files for a program in the same directory.

1 **Create a directory to hold the program.** Use mkdir to create a directory named Trip:

§ mkdir Trip (Return)

2   **Move to the new directory.**

§ cd Trip (Return)

All of the files making up the Trip program will be put in the Trip directory.

31.12   The main.c Function

Every C program must have one main() function, where execution begins. As shown in Listing 31–4, main() is a simple function. All main() does is call two other functions, indiana() and chicago().

Listing 31–4
C code for the
main.c file.

```
/* Illustrate multiple source files */

void chicago(void);
void indiana(void);

main()
{
    chicago();
    indiana();
    chicago();
}
```

There is a new feature to note here:

•   void chicago(void);

This is a *function prototype* (also called a *function declaration*). It tells the compiler that the function chicago() takes no arguments and returns no value.

31.13   Creating and Compiling main.c

As we just saw, main() is a simple function. All it does is call two other functions, indiana() and chicago(). We have not yet written either of these two functions, so the program is not complete. Nevertheless, we can still run main.c through the compiler to check for syntax errors and produce an object file.

1   **Use the text editor to create a new source file.** Open a file named main.c and enter the code shown in Listing 31–4.

2   **Compile the function without linking.** Invoke cc with the -c ("compile only") option:

§ cc -c main.c (Return)

If the compilation is successful, this creates an object file named `main.o`. On the other hand, if the compiler detects an error in the file, it will give you an error message, and it will not create an object file.

3   If necessary, correct any errors in the file and repeat Step 2.

31.14   Creating and Compiling chicago.c

Listing 31–5 shows the source code for the `chicago()` function.

Listing 31–5
C code for the chi-
cago.c file.

```
/* The chicago() function */

void chicago(void)
{
    printf("\nI'm waiting at O'Hare International,\n");
    printf("the busiest airport in the world.\n");
}
```

1   Create a source file. Use your text editor to create a file named `chicago.c`:

§ `vi chicago.c` (Return)

2   Enter the C code as shown in Listing 31–5.

3   Compile without linking. Invoke `cc` with the `-c` ("compile only") option:

§ `cc -c chicago.c`(Return)

4   If necessary, correct syntax errors and compile again.

5   Verify that the object file has been created. Listing the files should show the source and object files:

§ `ls`(Return)
`chicago.c  chicago.o  main.c  main.o`

31.15   Creating indiana.c and indy.c

We are not yet finished with the program. Listings 31–6 and 31–7 show the C code for `indiana()` and `indianapolis()`.

```
/* The indiana() function */

void indianapolis(void);

void indiana(void)
{
    printf("\nBack home again, Indiana.\n");
    indianapolis();
    printf("\nWander Indiana--come back soon.\n");
}
```

Listing 31–6

C code for the indiana.c file.

```
/* The indianapolis() function */

#define  POP90  1.2      /* Population in millions */

void indianapolis(void)
{
    printf("\nWelcome to Indianapolis, Indiana.\n");
    printf("Population: %f million.\n", POP90);
}
```

Listing 31–7

C code for the indy.c file.

Perhaps the most interesting feature introduced in Listing 31–7 is the #define preprocessor directive:

•   #define POP90 1.2   /* Population in millions */

This directive tells the preprocessor to search through the file and replace every occurrence of the string POP90 with 1.2, the population (in millions) of Indianapolis in 1990.

1   **Create the source files** indiana.c **and** indy.c. Use your text editor as you have done before to enter the C code shown in Listings 31–6 and 31–7.

2   **Compile (but do not link) the files** indiana.c **and** indy.c. If necessary, review the previous section to remind yourself of how this is done.

31.16   Linking and Running the Trip Program

If you have done everything correctly, you should now have four files of C source code and four files of object code in the directory Trip. In this section, you will see how to link the object files to create an executable file.

1   **Verify that the object files exist.** Enter the `ls` command:

§ `ls` (Return)

You should see something like this:

```
chicago.c  indiana.c  indy.c  main.c
chicago.o  indiana.o  indy.o  main.o
```

2   **Link the object files to make an executable file.** The `cc` command will do the trick:

§ `cc *.o`(Return)

This will create an executable file named `a.out`.

3   **Run the program.** Simply enter the name of the executable file:

§ `a.out` (Return)

The output will be something like this:

```
I'm waiting at O'Hare International,
the busiest airport in the world.

Back home again, Indiana.

Welcome to Indianapolis, Indiana.
Population: 1.20000 million.

Wander Indiana--come back soon.

I'm waiting at O'Hare International,
the busiest airport in the world.
```

31.17   Compiling and Linking in One Step

In the previous section you linked four files of object code that you had previously compiled. However, it is not necessary to separate the compilation and linking steps. In this section, you will see how to compile and link multiple source files all at once.

1   **Compile and link the source code.** The `cc` command will do this:

§ `cc *.c` (Return)

This will create an executable file named `a.out`.

2   **Run the program as before.**

§ `a.out` (Return)

31.18 Maintaining a Program with make

One advantage to breaking up a large program into multiple source files is that it allows you to modify and recompile one source file without having to recompile the entire program. The UNIX make program is useful in keeping track of the changes you make in the program files. You can learn about make by reading Appendix G.

31.19 Command Summary

Each of these commands is entered at the shell prompt and is terminated by a (Return).

cc file.c	compile and link the source code in file.c
cc -c file.c	compile but do not link; put output in file.o
cc -g file.c	compile file.c; set up for the debugger
cc -o file file.c	compile file.c; put executable code in file
cc file.c -o file	same as previous
cc file.c -lm	compile file.c and link with code from standard math library

31.20 Exercises

1. The cc compiler available on most systems takes a number of options. Refer to the UNIX manual to determine what each of the following commands will do:

   cc -c source.c

   cc -O source.c

   cc -S source.c

   cc source -l*name*

2. The system() function allows a C program to execute UNIX commands. For example, the statement

   system("date");

   runs the UNIX date command. Revise the hello.c program so that it displays the date, lists the files in your home directory and the users logged into the system, then prints the message "Hello, world!"

3. Rewrite recip.c to employ double or float variables. (Listing 30–1 shows how this might be done.)

4. Refer to your C book to see how to format the output from `printf()`. Revise `sqroot.c` using the %f, %e, and/or %g formats to control the spacing of the output line.

5. Even if you have rewritten `recip.c` to use `double` or `float` data, it may still not handle an input of zero correctly. Read your C book about the `if-else` statement, then rewrite the `recip.c` program so that it prints the message "The reciprocal of 0 is not defined" if the user enters a zero.

6. C is a very powerful language, but C compilers traditionally have tended to be lax at checking for some kinds of errors. UNIX offers a tool called `lint` that can find errors that the compiler might miss. `lint` does not produce executable code. Instead, it examines your source code and prints warnings about bad programming practices and potential portability problems. To run `lint` on the source file `file.c`, type the command line

§ `lint file.c` (Return)

Run `lint` on each of the C source files you created in this chapter, and note the kinds of messages it gives you. Note that `lint` tends to be very picky and will often warn you about things that really aren't errors.

7. Refer to your C book to see how to correct the problems `lint` warned you about in the previous exercise.

8. The `cb` ("C beautifier") utility will format C source code to conform to one of the standard layout styles. You can format `file.c` and put the result into `file2.c` with the command line

§ `cb file.c > file2.c` (Return)

Use the `man` command to learn about the various options that `cb` takes. Then try out this utility on one of your source files.

9. The `ctrace` utility takes C source code and inserts additional `printf()` statements to aid in debugging. You can run `ctrace` like this:

§ `ctrace sqroot.c > sqroot.trace.c` (Return)

You can then compile and run `sqroot.trace.c` the usual way:

§ `cc sqroot.trace.c` (Return)
§ `a.out` (Return)

The additional `printf()` statements will display the program's executable statements and the values of the variables as they are changed. Try `ctrace` on one of your source files to see how it works.

10. The `time` utility measures the time required to execute a program or shell script. You can time the execution of `a.out` with the command line

§ `time a.out` (Return)

Use the `man` command to learn how `time` works. Then try out this utility on one of your source files.

32 TUTORIAL: PROGRAMMING IN FORTRAN

It is a good idea to keep a Fortran book handy as you read through this chapter.

Fortran ("FORmula TRANslation") was one of the first and most successful programming languages. Although it was developed in the 1950s, it has been repeatedly updated over the years, and it is still popular with scientists and engineers. The latest version of Fortran is called Fortran 90; however, the most widely used version is still Fortran 77. Neither Fortran 77 nor Fortran 90 is a standard part of UNIX, but one or both are often found on UNIX systems.

In this chapter, you will see how to write, compile, and run Fortran 77 programs on a UNIX system. This is not intended to teach you Fortran; for that, you should consult a standard text on Fortran.

32.1 The hello.f Program

We will begin with the program shown in Listing 32–1, which prints a message on the standard output.

```
* First Fortran program.
*234567

      PROGRAM HELLO
      WRITE(*,*) 'Hello, world!'
      END
```

Listing 32–1
The hello.f program.

Let's examine this program in more detail:

- `* First Fortran program.`

Any line of text that begins with an asterisk (*) in the first column is treated as a comment and is ignored by the compiler. Comments are for the benefit of the programmer and anyone else who may read the program later.

- `*234567`

This is another comment line, included to help you identify the first seven columns. Fortran 77 requires statements to begin in the seventh column.

- `PROGRAM HELLO`

The `PROGRAM` statement marks the beginning of the program and gives the program a name (`HELLO`). Traditionally, Fortran statements have been written entirely in uppercase letters, and this practice continues, although many Fortran compilers also will accept lowercase letters. Thus, on many compilers the `PROGRAM` statement could also be written as `program hello`.

- `WRITE(*,*) 'Hello, world!'`

The `WRITE` statement is used to print output on the screen.

- `END`

The `END` statement marks the end of the program.

32.2 Creating and Running hello.f

1 **Create a source file.** Use the `vi` editor to create a file named `hello.f`:

§ `vi hello.f` (Return)

Enter the program exactly as shown in Listing 32–1, then write to the file and quit the editor.

2 **Compile the source code.** The standard Fortran compiler is called `f77`. To compile the file, simply type `f77` followed by the name of the file. Remember that the file name must end in `.f`:

§ `f77 hello.f` (Return)

3 **If necessary, correct any compiler errors and repeat Step 2**. If the compiler cannot compile your code because of syntax errors, it will try to tell you where the errors are located. Reopen the file and correct the errors.

4 **Run the program.** By default, the linker gives the name `a.out` to the executable file. To run the program, type

§ `a.out` (Return)

You should see the message

`Hello, world!`

The shell prompt appears when the program finishes, indicating that the shell is ready for your next command:

§

32.3 Review of the Compilation Process

Recall the command you used to compile the hello.f program:

§ f77 hello.f (Return)

The f77 command appears simple, but it starts a fairly complicated chain of events involving three separate programs:

The compiler works on a copy of the code; it does not actually alter hello.f.

1. The Fortran 77 compiler goes through the source code in the file hello.f and makes certain substitutions specified by the PARAMETER statements, if there are any.

2. The Fortran 77 compiler translates the Fortran source code into object code, which it places in a file named hello.o. (If there are syntax errors, the compiler will not produce object code; instead, it will try to tell you where the errors are to be found.)

3. The linker combines your object code with any code your program may need from the UNIX standard libraries to produce executable code. The executable code is placed in a file named a.out. (In some cases, the object file hello.o is deleted automatically.)

32.4 Renaming the Executable File

Note that the file containing the executable code is given the name a.out by the linker. If you want to save the executable code, you must use the mv command to give this file another name—otherwise, it will be overwritten the next time you use the f77 compiler.

1   Use the mv command to rename the executable file. It is common practice to give the executable code the same name as the source code, but without the .f suffix:

§ mv a.out hello (Return)

2   Run the program. Enter the new name of the executable file:

§ hello (Return)
Hello, world!
§

As we shall see, you can compile the source code and rename the executable file all at once using f77 with the -o option:

§ f77 hello.f -o hello ⟨Return⟩

32.5 The recip.f Program

Our next program calculates reciprocals of numbers entered by the user at the keyboard. A pseudocode outline for this program is shown in Listing 32–2A; the corresponding Fortran code is shown in Listing 32–2B.

Listing 32–2A
Pseudocode for the
recip.f program.

Print a brief message about what the program does
Prompt the user for an integer n
Read n
Calculate 1/n
Display the answer

Listing 32–2B
Fortran code for the
recip.f program.

```
C Compute reciprocals
C234567

      PROGRAM RECIPROCAL

      INTEGER N, RECIP

      WRITE(*,*) 'This program computes reciprocals.'
      WRITE(*,*) 'Enter a number: '

      READ(*,*) N

      RECIP = 1/N
      WRITE(*,*) 'The reciprocal of ', N, ' is ', RECIP
      END
```

32.6 Creating and Running recip.f

1   **Create a source file.** Use the vi editor to create a file named recip.f:

§ vi recip.f ⟨Return⟩

Enter the program exactly as shown in Listing 32–2B, then write to the file and quit the editor.

2 **Compile the source code.** The default name for an executable file is `a.out`. You can specify another name using `f77` with the `-o` option. For the executable file, let's use the name `recip` (without the `.f` suffix):

§ `f77 -o recip recip.f` (Return)

This tells `f77` to compile `recip.f` and put the executable in the file `recip`.

3 **If necessary, correct any syntax errors and repeat Step 2.**

4 **Run the program.** To run the program, enter the name of the executable file:

§ `recip` (Return)

You should see a message and a prompt:

```
This program computes reciprocals.
Enter a number:
```

5 **Enter a number at the prompt.** Try the number 2:

```
Enter a number:
2  (Return)
```

The program will respond:

```
The reciprocal of 2 is 0
§
```

This is obviously wrong: the reciprocal of 2 is 1/2, not 0. In fact, `recip.f` gives the correct answer only when you enter −1 or 1 as an input. The reason has to do with the way that the computer stores and uses integers. To repair this defect, you should revise the program to use variables of type REAL rather than type INTEGER. (We leave this as an exercise.)

32.7 Arithmetic Exceptions and Core Dumps

How does the `recip.f` program handle division by zero?

1 **Run the program.**

§ `recip` (Return)

The program will print a message and a prompt:

```
This program computes reciprocals.
Enter a number:
```

2 **Enter zero at the prompt.**

```
Enter a number:
0 (Return)
```

You should receive an error message, something like this:

```
Arithmetic exception (core dumped)
```

What happened? It is not hard to figure out. Division by zero is an undefined operation that caused the program to crash.

3 **Check for a core file.** If you list the files in your directory, you should see a file named core:

§ ls Return

Since you cannot read the core file, and because it takes up so much room, you should delete it.

4 **Remove the core file.**

§ rm core Return

32.8 Setting up recip.f for Debugging

Although you cannot read a core file as you would a normal UNIX text file, you can use a debugger such as dbx to examine the file and determine what caused the program to crash.

• **Compile the program using the debug option.** With most compilers, the −g option indicates "debug":

§ f77 −g recip.f Return

This causes the compiler to include additional information in the compiled code that can be used by dbx. If you would like to see how dbx is used, refer to Appendix F.

32.9 The Trip Program

Our next sample program illustrates the use of separate source files for putting together a large program. Large programs are often the work of more than one programmer; it is common for each programmer to work on his or her own files, which then are assembled to make a complete program.

It is convenient to group the source files for a program in the same directory.

1 **Create a directory to hold the program.** Use mkdir to create a directory named Trip:

§ mkdir Trip Return

2 **Move to the new directory.**

§ cd Trip (Return)

All of the files making up the Trip program will be put in the Trip directory.

32.10   The main.f Program

The Trip program will consist of a MAIN program and several subroutines. The Fortran code for the MAIN program is shown in Listing 32–3.

```
* Trip
*234567

      PROGRAM MAIN
      CALL CHICAGO()
      CALL INDIANA()
      CALL CHICAGO()
      END
```

32.11   Creating and Compiling main.f

MAIN calls two subroutines, INDIANA and CHICAGO. We have not yet written either of these subroutines, so the program is not complete. Nevertheless, we can still run main.f through the compiler to check for syntax errors and produce an object file.

1   **Use the text editor to create a new source file.** Open a file named main.f and enter the code shown in Listing 32–3.

2   **Compile the function without linking.** Invoke f77 with the –c ("compile only") option:

§ f77 -c main.f (Return)

If the compilation is successful, this creates an object file named main.o. On the other hand, if the compiler detects an error in the file, it will give you an error message, and it will not create an object file.

3   **If necessary, correct any errors in the file and repeat Step 2.**

32.12   The chicago.f Subprogram

Listing 32–4 shows the source code for the subroutine CHICAGO.

There are two interesting features to note about the WRITE statement in this program:

•   WRITE(*,*) 'I''m waiting at O''Hare International,

Listing 32–4
Fortran code for the
`chicago.f` file.

```
*234567
      SUBROUTINE CHICAGO
      WRITE(*,*)'I''m waiting at O''Hare International,
     +the busiest airport in the world.'
      END
```

Single quotes or apostrophes ('. . .') are placed around a string. If you want to include a single quote or apostrophe as part of the string, you must place two single quotes together. (Note that these are two single quotes, not a double quote symbol.)

- `+the busiest airport in the world.'`

Any character other than a space or a zero placed in the sixth column of a Fortran line indicates that it is a *continuation* of the previous line. This is useful because Fortran statements are not allowed to extend beyond column 72.

32.13 Creating and Compiling chicago.f

1. **Create a source file.** Use your text editor to create a file named `chicago.f`:

   § `vi chicago.f` (Return)

2. **Enter the Fortran code as shown in Listing 32–4.**

3. **Compile without linking.** Invoke `f77` with the `-c` ("compile only") option:

   § `f77 -c chicago.f`(Return)

4. **If necessary, correct syntax errors and compile again.**

5. **Verify that the object file has been created.** Listing the files should show the source and object files:

   § `ls` (Return)
   `chicago.f  chicago.o  main.f  main.o`

32.14 Creating and Compiling indiana.f and indy.f

We are not yet finished with the program. Listings 32–5 and 32–6 show the Fortran code for INDIANA and INDY.

Listing 32–5
Fortran code for the
indiana.f file.

```
*234567
      SUBROUTINE INDIANA
      WRITE(*,*) 'Back home again, Indiana.'
      CALL INDY
      WRITE(*,*) 'Wander Indiana--come back soon.'
      END
```

Listing 32–6
Fortran code for the
indy.f file.

```
*234567
      SUBROUTINE INDY
      PARAMETER  (POP90 = 1.2)
      WRITE(*,*) 'Welcome to Indianapolis, Indiana.'
      WRITE(*,*) 'Population: ', POP90, ' million.'
      END
```

Perhaps the most interesting feature shown in Listing 32–6 is the PARAMETER statement:

- PARAMETER (POP90 = 1.2)

This statement causes the Fortran compiler to search through the subroutine and replace every occurrence of the string POP90 with 1.2, the population (in millions) of Indianapolis in 1990.

1 **Create the source files** indiana.f **and** indy.f. Use your text editor as you have done before to enter the Fortran code shown in Listings 32–5 and 32–6.

2 **Compile (but do not link) the files** indiana.f **and** indy.f. If necessary, review the previous section to remind yourself of how this is done.

32.15   Linking and Running the Trip Program

If you have done everything correctly, you should now have four files of Fortran source code and four files of object code in the directory Trip. In this section, you will see how to link the object files to create an executable file.

1 **Verify that the object files exist.** Enter the ls command:

§ ls ⏎(Return)

You should see something like this:

```
chicago.f  indiana.f  indy.f  main.f
chicago.o  indiana.o  indy.o  main.o
```

2 **Link the object files to make an executable file.** The f77 command will do the trick:

§ f77 *.o (Return)

This will create an executable file named a.out.

3 **Run the program.** Simply enter the name of the executable file:

§ a.out (Return)

The output will be something like this:

```
I'm waiting at O'Hare International,
the busiest airport in the world.

Back home again, Indiana.

Welcome to Indianapolis, Indiana.
Population: 1.20000 million.

Wander Indiana--come back soon.

I'm waiting at O'Hare International,
the busiest airport in the world.
```

32.16 Compiling and Linking in One Step

In the previous section you linked four files of object code that you had previously compiled. However, it is not necessary to separate the compilation and linking steps. In this section, you will see how to compile and link multiple source files all at once.

1 **Compile and link the source code.** The f77 command will do this:

§ f77 *.f (Return)

This will create an executable file named a.out.

2 **Run the program as before.**

§ a.out (Return)

32.17 Maintaining a Program with make

One advantage to breaking up a large program into multiple source files is that it allows you to modify and recompile one source file without having to recompile the entire program. The UNIX make program is useful in keeping track of the changes you make in the program files. You can learn about make by reading Appendix G.

32.18   Command Summary

Each of these commands is entered at the shell prompt and is terminated by a
(Return).

`f77 file.f`	compile and link the source code in `file.f`
`f77 -c file.f`	compile but do not link; put output in `file.o`
`f77 -g file.f`	compile `file.f`; set up for the debugger
`f77 -o file file.f`	compile `file.f`; put executable code in `file`
`f77 file.f -o file`	same as previous

32.19   Exercises

1. The `f77` compiler available on most systems takes a number of options. Refer
    to the UNIX manual to determine the options that your Fortran compiler will
    take.

2. Rewrite `recip.f` to employ REAL variables.

3. Refer to your Fortran book to see how to format the output. Revise `recip.f`
    using formatted output to control the spacing of the output line.

4. Even if you have rewritten `recip.f` to use REAL data, it may still not handle an
    input of zero correctly. Read your Fortran book about the IF–THEN statement,
    then rewrite the `recip.f` program so that it prints the message "The reciprocal
    of 0 is not defined" if the user enters a zero.

5. Write a program named `sqroot.f` to compute the square roots of values en-
    tered by the user at the standard input. (Refer to your Fortran book to see how
    to compute square roots.)

6. The `time` utility measures the time required to execute a program or shell script.
    You can time the execution of `a.out` with the command line

    § `time a.out` (Return)

    Use the `man` command to learn how `time` works. Then try out this utility on
    one of your source files.

33 TUTORIAL: PROGRAMMING IN PASCAL

It is a good idea to keep a Pascal book handy as you read through this chapter.

Pascal was developed by Niklaus Wirth during the late 1960s and early 1970s for teaching good programming style. It has since become one of the most popular computer languages. Although Pascal is not a standard part of UNIX, it is found on many UNIX systems.

In this chapter, you will see how to write, compile, and run Pascal programs. This is not intended to teach you Pascal; for that, you should consult a standard text on Pascal. Indeed, it is a good idea to keep a Pascal book handy as you read through this chapter.

33.1 The hello.p Program

We will begin with the program shown in Listing 33–1, which prints a message on the standard output.

Listing 33–1
The hello.p program.

```
(* Traditional first Pascal program. *)

program HelloWorld(output);
begin
    writeln('Hello, world!')
end.
```

Let's examine this program in more detail:

- `(* Traditional first Pascal program. *)`

Any text appearing between (* and *) is a *comment* and is ignored by the compiler. Comments are included for the benefit of the programmer and anyone else who may read the program later.

- `program HelloWorld(output);`

Every Pascal program must begin with the word `program`, which is a *reserved word* in Pascal. This means that `program` has a predefined meaning in Pascal and cannot be used any other way by the programmer. Every program must also have a name or *identifier*—in this case, `HelloWorld`. The predefined textfile `output` represents the standard output. The semicolon (`;`) at the end of the line is used to separate statements.

- `begin`

The beginning of the program body is indicated by the reserved word `begin`.

- `writeln('Hello, world!')`

`writeln` is a standard Pascal procedure used to "write" a line on the standard output. The argument to the procedure is a group of characters enclosed by single quotes, which is called a *string*.

- `end.`

The program body ends with the reserved word `end` and a period (`.`).

33.2 Creating and Running hello.p

1 **Create a source file.** Use the `vi` editor to create a file named `hello.p`:

§ `vi hello.p` (Return)

Enter the program exactly as shown in Listing 33–1, then write to the file and quit the editor.

2 **Compile the source code.** On most systems, the Pascal compiler is called `pc`. To compile the file, simply type `pc` followed by the name of the file. Remember that the file name must end in `.p`:

§ `pc hello.p`(Return)

3 **If necessary, correct any compiler errors and repeat Step 2**. If the compiler cannot compile your code because of syntax errors, it will try to tell you where the errors are located. Reopen the file and correct the errors.

4 **Run the program.** By default, the executable file is given the name `a.out`. To run the program, type

§ `a.out` (Return)

You should see the message

`Hello, world!`
§

The shell prompt appears when the program finishes, indicating that the shell is ready for your next command.

33.3   Renaming the Executable File

Note that the file containing the executable code is given the name a.out. If you want to save the executable code, you must use the mv command to give this file another name—otherwise, it will be overwritten the next time you use the pc compiler.

1   Use the mv command to rename the executable file. It is common practice to give the executable code the same name as the source code, but without the .p suffix:

§ mv a.out hello (Return)

2   Run the program. Enter the new name of the executable file:

§ hello (Return)
Hello, world!
§

As we shall see, you can compile the source code and rename the executable file all at once using pc with the -o option:

§ pc hello.p -o hello (Return)

Note that the arguments can be written in a different order:

§ pc -o hello hello.p (Return)

33.4   The recip.p Program

Our next program calculates reciprocals of numbers entered by the user at the keyboard. A pseudocode outline for this program is shown in Listing 33–2A; the corresponding Pascal code is shown in Listing 33–2B.

Listing 33–2A
Pseudocode for the
recip.p program.

Print a brief message about what the program does
Prompt the user for an integer n
Read n
Calculate 1/n
Display the answer

```
{ Compute reciprocals }

program reciprocal(input, output);
var n, recip: integer;
begin
    writeln('This program computes reciprocals.');
    write('Enter a number: ');
    readln(n);
    recip := 1 div n;
    writeln('The reciprocal of ', n, ' is ', recip)
end.
```

Listing 33–2B
Pascal code for the
recip.p program.

This program introduces a few features that were not in the previous program:

- `{ Compute reciprocals }`

An alternative way to write comments is to surround the comment with braces {...}.

- `var n, recip: integer;`

This is a *declaration*. It tells the compiler to create two variables (`var`) to hold integers and to give them the names n and `recip`. Pascal requires that you declare all variables before you use them. A semicolon is placed at the end of this line to separate it from those that follow.

- `write('Enter a number: ');`

`write` is a standard Pascal procedure, used to write output on the standard output. Unlike `writeln`, `write` does not start a new line after it finishes printing.

- `readln(n);`

This `readln` statement obtains the user's input from the standard input and stores it in the variable n.

- `recip := 1 div n;`

This line computes the reciprocal. The computer first divides the integer 1 by the contents of the variable n, then assigns the result to the variable `recip`. In Pascal, `div` is used for dividing two integers. The pair of symbols `:=` is treated as one operator, called the *assignment operator*. It assigns the value of the expression `1 div n` to the variable `recip`.

- `writeln('The reciprocal of ', n, ' is ', recip)`

This is a `writeln` with four arguments. It will print out the string `'The reciprocal of '`, followed by the value of the variable n, the string `' is '`, and finally the value of the variable `recip`.

33.5 Creating and Running recip.p

1   **Create a source file.** Use the vi editor to create a file named recip.p:

    § vi recip.p (Return)

Enter the program exactly as shown in Listing 33–2B, then write to the file and quit the editor.

2   **Compile the source code.** The default name for an executable file is a.out. You can specify another name using pc with the –o option. For the executable file, let's use the name recip (without the .p suffix):

    § pc -o recip recip.p (Return)

This tells pc to compile recip.p and put the executable in the file recip.

3   **If necessary, correct any syntax errors and repeat Step 2**.

4   **Run the program.** To run the program, enter the name of the executable file:

    § recip (Return)

You should see a message and a prompt:

```
This program computes reciprocals.
Enter a number:
```

5   **Enter a number at the prompt.** Try the number 2:

```
Enter a number: 2  (Return)
```

The program will respond:

```
The reciprocal of          2 is          0
§
```

This is obviously wrong: the reciprocal of 2 is 1/2, not 0. In fact, recip.p gives the correct answer only when you enter –1 or 1 as an input. The reason has to do with the way that the computer stores and uses integers. To repair this defect, you should revise the program to use variables of type real rather than type integer. (We leave this as an exercise.)

33.6 Arithmetic Exceptions and Core Dumps

How does the recip.p program handle division by zero?

1   **Run the program.**

    § recip (Return)

The program will print a message and a prompt:

```
This program computes reciprocals.
Enter a number:
```

2 **Enter zero at the prompt.**

```
Enter a number: 0 (Return)
```
You should receive an error message, something like this:

```
Arithmetic exception (core dumped)
```

What happened? It is not hard to figure out. Division by zero is an undefined operation that caused the program to crash.

3 **Check for a core file.** If you list the files in your directory, you should see a file named core:

§ `ls` (Return)

Since you cannot read the core file, and because it takes up so much room, you should delete it.

4 **Remove the core file.**

§ `rm core` (Return)

33.7 Setting up recip.p for Debugging

Although you cannot read a core file as you would a normal UNIX text file, you can use a debugger such as dbx to examine the file and determine what caused the program to crash.

- **Compile the program using the debug option.** With most compilers, the -g option indicates "debug":

  § `pc -g recip.p` (Return)

  This causes the compiler to include additional information in the compiled code that can be used by dbx. If you would like to see how dbx is used, refer to Appendix F.

33.8   Command Summary

Each of these commands is entered at the shell prompt and is terminated by a
(Return).

pc file.p	compile and link the source code in file.p
pc -g file.p	compile file.p; set up for the debugger
pc -o file file.p	compile file.p; put executable code in file
pc file.p -o file	same as previous

33.9   Exercises

1. The pc compiler available on most systems takes a number of options. Refer to
    the UNIX manual to determine the options that your Pascal compiler will take.

2. Rewrite recip.p to employ real variables. Be sure to use the real division op-
    erator (/) instead of the integer division operator (div).

3. Even if you have rewritten recip.p to use real variables, it may still not han-
    dle an input of zero correctly. Read your Pascal book about the if-then state-
    ment, then rewrite the recip.p program so that it prints the message "The
    reciprocal of 0 is not defined" if the user enters a zero.

4. The output from recip.p is not as attractive as it might be because of the large
    spaces preceding the numbers. Refer to your Pascal book to see how to format
    the output, then revise recip.p to control the spacing of the output line.

5. The time utility measures the time required to execute a program or shell script.
    You can time the execution of a.out with the command line

    § time a.out (Return)

    Use the man command to learn how time works. Then try out this utility on one
    of your source files.

6. Write a Pascal program sqroot.p to compute the square roots of numbers en-
    tered by the user at the keyboard. (Refer to your Pascal book to see how to com-
    pute square roots.)

APPENDICES

A APPENDIX: TAMING YOUR TERMINAL

The `stty` ("set terminal") command allows you to set parameters that affect the operation of your terminal. In this appendix you will see how to use `stty` to perform the following tasks:

- Set your terminal to handle lowercase input.

- Define the erase key.

- Ensure that the terminal echoes your input properly.

A.1 Correcting Uppercase-Only Output

Sometimes the system may behave as if your terminal can handle only uppercase letters. (This can occur if you accidentally press the "Caps Lock" key before logging in.) The following command will correct the problem:

§ STTY -LCASE (Return)

A.2 Defining the Erase Key

Most users expect the (Backspace) key to erase characters on the command line. (Others prefer to use (Delete) or (Control)-(H) for this.) The following command will make (Backspace) the character-erase key:

§ stty erase (Backspace) (Return)

The following command will set (Delete) as the character-erase key:

§ stty erase (Delete) (Return)

To set the (Control)-(H) key combination as the character-erase key, use the command line

§ `stty erase ^h` (**Return**)

Note that the caret (∧) is used to represent the (**Control**) key.

A.3   Setting the Terminal Echo

As you type characters on the keyboard, the system is supposed to echo them back to you on the terminal screen (except when you are entering your password). If what you type does not appear on the screen, you can turn on the echo using the following command:

§ `stty echo` (**Return**)

On the other hand, if every character is being echoed *twice*, you should turn off the echo:

§ `stty -echo` (**Return**)

B APPENDIX: THE UNIX MANUAL

The UNIX system is described in detail in a massive document called the UNIX Programmer's Manual or User's Reference Manual, or simply the User's Manual. Your UNIX installation may have a printed (paper) copy of this manual, an on-line (electronic) version, or both.

The UNIX manual has the reputation of being difficult to read. It has been said that if you can read the manual, you do not need the manual. That is a bit of an exaggeration, but the manual is terse and takes some getting used to. Even so, it is a good idea to get familiar with the manual—it can be very useful.

B.1 Organization of the Manual

Most UNIX manuals have eight sections:

Section 1	User Commands
Section 2	UNIX and C System Calls
Section 3	Library Calls
Section 4	Device Drivers and Special Files
Section 5	File Formats and Conventions
Section 6	Games
Section 7	Miscellany
Section 8	System Administration Commands and Procedures

Your system's manuals may be arranged a bit differently. (For example, it is not uncommon to find that some spoilsport has deleted the games from the system.)

In addition to the usual eight manual sections, you may find supplementary articles and technical papers describing the UNIX system. These are usually grouped together and called something like "Documents for Use with the UNIX System," or "UNIX User's Supplement," or perhaps "UNIX Programmer's Manual, Volume 2." We won't say much about this second part of the manual—if you happen to find a copy, you might want to browse through it to see if it contains anything of interest to you.

B.2 Using the man Command

If your system has an on-line manual, you can read it using the man command, which has the general form

§ man *command* (Return)

For example, to read the manual entry for the cal command, you would type

§ man cal (Return)

If your system has an on-line manual, this command will list a man page for cal, as shown in Listing B–1.

B.3 Organization of a Manual Entry

All manual entries follow much the same format. Let's examine the various parts of the entry for the cal command:

- CAL(1)   USER COMMANDS   CAL(1)

The first line begins and ends with the name of the command, written entirely in caps (CAL). The number in parentheses (1) gives the section of the manual in which this entry is found.

- NAME
       cal - display a calendar

The name and a one-line description of the command are listed next.

- SYNOPSIS
       cal [[**month**] **year**]

This is probably the most useful part of the man page. It shows how the command is actually used. Anything shown in square brackets [] is optional. In this case, the brackets show that you can use the cal command either by itself, with the year only, or with the month and year. Thus, each of the following commands would be legal:

```
CAL(1)                    USER COMMANDS                    CAL(1)

NAME
        cal - display a calendar

SYNOPSIS
        cal [ [ month ] year ]

DESCRIPTION
        cal displays a calendar for the specified year. If
        a month is also specified, a calendar for that
        month only is displayed. If neither is specified, a
        calendar for the present month is displayed.

        year can be between 1 and 9999. Be aware that 'cal
        78' refers to the early Christian era, not the 20th
        century. Also, the year is always considered to
        start in January, even though this is historically
        naive.

        month is a number between 1 and 12.

        The calendar produced is that for England and her
        colonies.


        Try September 1752.
```

Listing B–1
The manual page for
the cal command.

§ cal (Return)
§ cal 2001 (Return)
§ cal 5 2001 (Return)

Some commands take various options, which are typically preceded by a hyphen. The options will be shown here, along with the other arguments.

• DESCRIPTION

Next comes a written description of the command. This description may be as short as a paragraph, or it may go on for several pages, depending on the command.

B.4 Other Categories

The manual entry for the `cal` command is rather simple because the `cal` command itself is rather simple. Entries for other commands may contain still more headings. Depending on the command, you may see one or more of the following:

- FILES—Files used or created by the command are listed here under this heading.

- SEE ALSO—This entry will direct you to other entries in the manual that are related to the current topic.

- DIAGNOSTICS—Some UNIX commands generate error messages. The more important or cryptic error messages will be described under this heading.

- BUGS—Believe it or not, some UNIX commands contain minor errors—usually called "bugs"—that have been identified but yet not eliminated. If you are lucky, such bugs will be listed here.

B.5 Reading Longer Manual Pages

The manual entry for `cal` will probably fit entirely on your screen. Other manual entries are too long to be shown on the typical terminal screen all at once. For example, try reading the manual entry describing `man` itself:

§ man man ⟨**Return**⟩

If the entire manual entry is too long to fit on the screen, you can pipe the output from the `man` command through the `more` or `pg` utility:

§ man man | more ⟨**Return**⟩

or

§ man man | pg ⟨**Return**⟩

The vertical line is called the *pipe symbol*.

C Appendix: Starting X and Motif

If your system does not have a display manager that starts the X server and window manager automatically, you will have to start them yourself. To do this, you should first log in according to the procedure presented in Sections 3.1 through 3.5.

C.1 Starting X

1 **Look for evidence of windows on your screen.** If you see one or more windows, the X server is already running, and you can skip to Section C.2.

2 **Start X.** One of the following commands should work:

§ xinit (Return)

If none of these commands works, ask your system administrator for help.

§ startx (Return)

§ openwin (Return)

3 **Wait for an xterm window to appear.** It should look something like the window shown in Figure C–1.

C.2 Starting the Motif Window Manager

1 **If necessary, select the xterm window.** Use the mouse to move the pointer to the xterm window.

2 **Start the window manager.** Enter the following command line:

§ mwm & (Return)

The ampersand (&) at the end of the command line causes mwm to be run "in the background." (Remember, UNIX is a multitasking OS.) This way, mwm will not interfere with any other programs you run.

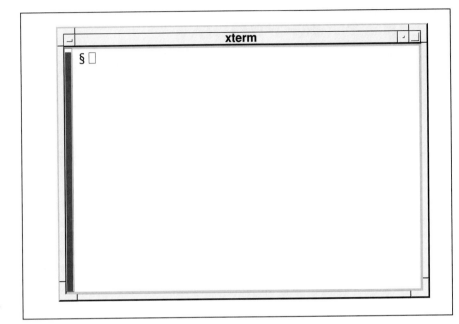

Figure C–1
An xterm window.

C.3 Logging Out

Some systems are configured to allow you to log out with a menu option. If your system does not offer such an option, logging out may be somewhat more complicated.

It is a good idea to ask your system administrator about the logout procedure.

1   **Quit the window manager.** There should be an option marked "Exit" or "Quit" on one of the pop-up menus. In some cases, this option will also stop X and log you out.

2   **If necessary, stop X.** Closing the original xterm window will do the trick.

3   **If necessary, log out.** One of the following commands should work:

§ logout (Return)

§ exit (Return)

§ (Control)-(D)

D APPENDIX: ACCESS PRIVILEGES

Anything you can do to one of your own files you could potentially do to files belonging to another user. Obviously, it would not be good if everyone were able to change someone else's files without permission. To prevent chaos, and to preserve privacy, UNIX allows users to restrict access to their files.

D.1 The Long Listing

To see the access permissions on a file or directory, use the `ls -l` ("list –long") command:

§ `ls -l` (**Return**)

You should see listings that look something like this:

```
drwxrwx---   2 you engr     12 Apr  1 15:53 Cal
-rw-rw----   1 you engr    997 Mar 31 10:53 fun
-rw-rw----   1 you engr    401 Mar 31 10:30 summer.2001
```

Let's decipher the first listing:

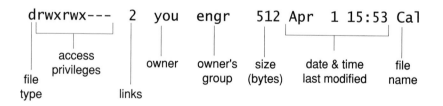

- **File type.** A *d* in the leftmost position indicates a directory. An ordinary file will have a hyphen (–) in this position.

401

- *Access privileges.* These nine positions show who has permission to do what with the file or directory. More about this later.

- *Links.* A *link* is a pseudonym for a file or directory. Directory files always have at least two links, because each directory contains the hidden entry "dot" as a pseudonym for itself. Most ordinary files have just one link. You can create more links yourself, although this is beyond the scope of this book; if you are interested, see the manual entry for the ln command.

- *Owner.* This is the login of the person who owns the file.

- *Owner's group.* A *group* is a collection of users to which the owner of the file belongs. (On Berkeley systems, ls -l does not list the group name; to see it, you have to use the ls -lg command.)

- *Size.* The size of the file is given in bytes.

- *Date and time.* The date and time the file was last modified is shown here.

- *File name.* The name of the file or directory is listed last.

D.2   Access Permissions

The nine entries showing the access permissions deserve a closer look:

rwxrwx---

Basically, there are three things that can be done to an ordinary file:

r   *Read.* Examine (but not change) the contents of the file.

w   *Write.* Change the contents of a file.

x   *Execute.* If the file contains a program, run that program.

Likewise, there are three things that can be done to a directory:

r   *Read.* List the contents of the directory using the ls command.

w   *Write.* Change the contents of the directory by creating new files or removing existing files. (To edit an existing file requires write permission on that file.)

x   *Execute.* "Search" the directory using ls -l. Also, move to the directory from another directory, and copy files from the directory.

When deciding who can have access to a file, UNIX recognizes three categories of users:

- *Owner.* The owner of the file or directory.

- *Group.* Other users belonging to the user's group.

- *Public.* All other users on the system.

The first three permissions show what the owner may do; the next three show what the group may do; the last three show what the public may do. For example,

rwxrwx---   owner has read, write, and execute privileges

                    group has read, write, and execute privileges

                    public has no privileges

rw-rw----   owner has read and write privileges

                    group has read and write privileges

                    public has no privileges

r--r--r--   owner has read privileges only

                    group has read privileges only

                    public has read privileges only

D.3 Changing File Modes

The access privileges are sometimes called the *mode* of the file or directory. To change the mode, you use the chmod ("change mode") command. chmod uses the following notation:

u   user (owner) of the file

g   group

o   others (public)

a   all (owner, group, and public)

=   assign a permission

+   add a permission

–   remove a permission

A few examples will help you see how chmod is used. To give the owner execute permission without changing any other permissions, you would use

§ chmod u+x *filename* (Return)

Note that there are no spaces between u and +, or between + and x.

To remove read and write permissions from group members, you would use

§ chmod g-rw *filename* (Return)

The following command will give everyone read permissions while removing any other permissions:

§ chmod a=r *filename* (Return)

To give everyone read and write permissions, you could use

§ chmod a=rw *filename* (Return)

E APPENDIX: WRITE AND TALK

The write and talk utilities are similar to each other in that both allow you to communicate directly with a user who is logged into the system. Whatever either of you types on your keyboard appears simultaneously on both screens. Of the two utilities, write is less convenient because the messages can become garbled if both of you try to type at the same time. talk separates the messages, even if both of you type simultaneously.

E.1 Sending and Receiving Messages

Using either write or talk is a five-step process:

1 **The first user requests a session with the second user.** Suppose, for example, that the user george wishes to communicate with martha. To do this, he would type

    § talk martha (Return)

    or

    § write martha (Return)

2 **The second user is notified.** Thus, if martha is logged in and receiving messages, she will be alerted:

    Message from george...

3 **The second user agrees to answer.** martha would have to type

    § talk george (Return)

    or

    § write george (Return)

4   **The two users exchange messages.** Anything that either user types will be displayed on both terminals. Most people using `write` work out a convention whereby only one types at a time, signaling the end of a thought with an o (for "over").

5   **When finished, they break off communication.** To quit `talk`, one of the parties has to type (Control)-(C). To quit `write`, however, both users must type (Control)-(D).

E.2   Refusing and Accepting Messages

You can refuse to accept `write` or `talk` messages with the command

§ mesg n

which is short for "messages—no." Anyone trying to establish contact with you using `write` or `talk` will get the message:

Your party is refusing messages.

(Electronic mail will still get through, however.) To accept messages again, you would use the command

§ mesg y

F APPENDIX: USING DBX

The standard UNIX debugger dbx can debug programs written in C, Fortran, or Pascal. To use dbx, you must compile your program using the −g option. For example, to debug the C program recip.c (Sections 31.5, 32.5, and 33.4) you would use the command

§ cc -g recip.c (Return)

to compile the program. Once this is done, you can run dbx on the executable file:

§ dbx a.out (Return)

The computer will respond with a cryptic message (which you can ignore), something like

Reading symbolic information...

Then it will give you a prompt that shows you are inside dbx:

(dbx)

F.1 Getting Help with dbx

The first thing to try is the help command. At the dbx prompt type:

(dbx) help (Return)

The computer should respond with a listing of the various dbx commands:

Command Summary

Execution and Tracing

catch	clear	cont	delete	ignore
next	rerun	run	status	step
stop	trace	when		

and so on. Take a moment to look over the entire list. You may notice a few UNIX shell commands (cd, pwd, setenv, sh), and some other commands whose purpose you can probably guess. (edit, for example, calls up the text editor so you can edit the source file from within dbx.) We will not try to go over all of the available commands; you can do quite a lot with just the following dozen commands:

cont	display	help	print	quit	rerun
run	sh	step	stop	trace	where

You can use the help command to find out more information on any of these commands. Try using help on itself:

(dbx) help help Ⓡⓔⓣⓤⓡⓝ

You should see a brief synopsis of the help command. (Note that <cmd> stands for any dbx command, <topic> stands for any topic, and so forth.) Although the help command does not provide much information on any of the commands, it is better than nothing.

F.2 Running the Program

The command to run the program is, appropriately enough, run. Try this:

(dbx) run ⓇⒺⓉⓊⓇⓃ

Except for some additional information printed by dbx itself, your program should run as usual:

```
Running: a.out
(Access id 3431)
This program computes reciprocals.
Enter a number:
```

Enter the number 1 and press Ⓡⓔⓣⓤⓡⓝ:

```
Enter a number: 1 Ⓡⓔⓣⓤⓡⓝ
```

The output should resemble the following:

The output on your system may not be exactly like this.

```
The reciprocal of 1 is 1.
execution completed, exit code is 1
(dbx)
```

The message "exit code is 1" simply tells you that the program completed successfully.

Running a program from inside dbx doesn't seem too useful—after all, it is easier to run the program directly, without first calling up the debugger to do the job. What dbx allows you to do is step through the program, one line at a time, and examine the values of the variables and expressions as they change.

F.3   Listing the Source Code

The list command will show you the source code. Try it:

(dbx) list 1, 15 (Return)

This tells dbx that you wish to see the source code from line 1 to line 15. dbx will display the file, numbering the lines as it does so. (The line numbers are not actually added to the source file.)

F.4   Setting Breakpoints

A *breakpoint* is a place in the program where you want the execution to halt. Breakpoints may be set using the stop command. Let's set a breakpoint at line 8:

(dbx) stop at 8 (Return)

dbx will tell you that it has set the breakpoint:

stop at "recip.c":8

Now use the run command to begin execution:

(dbx) run (Return)

The program will run until it reaches line 8, where it will stop. dbx will then display line 8:

```
Running: a.out
stopped in main at line 8 in file "recip.c"
8    printf("This program calculates reciprocals.\n");
(dbx)
```

F.5   Stepping through the Program

At this point, you could resume execution of the program by using the cont ("continue") command, but it is more instructive to step through the program one line at a time. The step command allows you to do this:

(dbx) step (Return)

You should see something like this:

```
This program computes reciprocals.
stopped in main at line 9 in file "recip.c"
9    printf("Enter a number:");
(dbx)
```

Note that the first thing you see is the line that was printed out by the previous statement. Step again, but step two lines this time:

(dbx) step 2 (Return)

The prompt produced by line 9 now appears:

```
Enter a number:
```

Type in a 1 and press (Return):

```
Enter a number: 1 (Return)
```

The program reads the number as it would normally. Then it proceeds to the next line of the program and stops:

```
stopped in main at line 11 in file "recip.c"
11    recip = 1/n;
(dbx)
```

F.6   Printing Expressions

The print command allows you to examine the values of variables. For example, to view the value of n, you would enter

(dbx) print n (Return)

dbx will respond with the current value of n:

```
n = 1
(dbx)
```

Step again:

```
(dbx) step
stopped in main at line 12 in file "recip.c"
12     printf("The reciprocal of %d is %d.\n", n, recip);
```

Use print to check the values of both n and recip:

```
(dbx) print n, recip (Return)
n = 1
recip = 1
(dbx)
```

Use the `cont` command to continue execution of the program; this will run through the remaining lines without stopping:

```
(dbx) cont (Return)
```

You should see something like this:

```
The reciprocal of 1 is 1.

execution completed, exit code is 1
(dbx)
```

The program is now finished running, but you are still inside **dbx**. Leave **dbx** using the `quit` command:

```
(dbx) quit (Return)
§
```

F.7 Tracing Variables and Functions

The `trace` command prints the values of variables as they are changed, as well as the calls to functions in the program. Start up **dbx**:

```
§ dbx a.out (Return)
```

The **dbx** prompt tells you that you are in **dbx**:

```
Reading symbolic information...
(dbx)
```

We want to trace the value of `n` in the `main()` function:

```
(dbx) trace n in main (Return)
```

dbx will confirm that the trace is set up:

```
(2) trace n
(dbx)
```

We also want to trace the value of `recip`:

```
(dbx) trace recip in main (Return)
(3) trace recip
(dbx)
```

Let's trace calls to the `main()` function as well:

```
(dbx) trace main (Return)
(4) trace main
```

Now run the program:

```
(dbx) run Return
```

dbx will run the program, displaying the values of the variables and showing calls to the function:

```
Running: a.out
(process id 3558)
main called from function _start
initially (at line "recip_c":8): recip = -26843620
initially (at line "recip_c":8): n = 0
This program computes reciprocals.
Enter a number:
```

Enter the number 1 at the prompt and note how the values of the variables are printed as they change:

```
Enter a number: 1  Return
after line "recip.c":10: n = 1
after line "recip.c":11: recip = 1
The reciprocal of 1 is 1.
main returns 1

execution completed, exit code is 1
```

Enter the rerun command:

```
(dbx) rerun Return
```

dbx will run the program again:

```
Running: a.out
(process id 3565)
main called from function _start
initially (at line "recip_c":8): recip = -26843620
initially (at line "recip_c":8): n = 0
This program computes reciprocals.
Enter a number:
```

Enter zero to cause an error:

```
Enter a number: 0 Return
termninating signal 8 SIGFPE
```

Leave dbx:

```
(dbx) quit Return
```

Use the ls command to see that a core file was created:

§ ls (Return)

F.8 Using where

You cannot read a core file, but dbx can. In particular, the where command in dbx allows you to find out where in the program the error occurred. Start dbx on the a.out and core files:

§ dbx a.out core (Return)

You might expect to see a few warnings before the dbx prompt appears:

The output on your system may be different.

```
Reading symbolic information...
core header file read successfully.
Reading symbolic information...
Reading symbolic information...
Reading symbolic information...
program terminated by signal FPE (integer divide by zero)
Current function is main
   11        recip = 1/n;
(dbx)
```

This tells you what you already know, namely that the core file was generated by a division by zero. It also shows that this occurred on line 11 in the main() function. Some versions of dbx require that you use the where command to determine where the error occurred:

```
(dbx) where (Return)
[1] .div(0x1, 0x0, 0x4, ...
[2] main(), line 11 in "recip.c"
(dbx)
```

The last line before the dbx prompt tells you that the error occurred on line 11 of the function main().

F.9 Running Shell Commands in dbx

The sh command allows you to run shell commands while you are still inside dbx. Use this command with rm to delete the core file:

```
(dbx) sh rm core (Return)
```

Now use sh and ls to check that the core file has indeed been removed:

```
(dbx) sh ls (Return)
```

G APPENDIX: MAINTAINING PROGRAMS WITH MAKE

The UNIX make program is designed to manage large, multifile projects by keeping track of any changes that are made in the source files. It allows you to modify and recompile one source file without having to recompile the entire program.

G.1 The makefile

The make program looks for its instructions in a file named either makefile or Makefile. For the program in the Trip directory (Sections 3.11 and 32.9), create a file named makefile, and enter the lines shown in Listing G–1.

```
# Makefile for the Trip program

trip: main.o chicago.o indiana.o indy.o
(Tab)cc -o trip main.o chicago.o indiana.o indy.o

main.o: main.c
(Tab)cc -c main.c

chicago.o: chicago.c
(Tab)cc -c chicago.c

indiana.o: indiana.c
(Tab)cc -c indiana.c

indy.o: indy.c
(Tab)cc -c indy.c

clean:
(Tab)rm *.o
```

Listing G–1
Makefile for the
Trip program.

Let's consider some of the interesting features of this file:

- `# Makefile for the Trip program`

This is a *comment line*. `make` ignores anything that follows a pound sign (#).

- `trip: main.o chicago.o indiana.o indy.o`

This is a called a *dependency line*. It indicates that the file `trip` depends on the object files `main.o`, `chicago.o`, `indiana.o`, and `indy.o`. Note that the dependency line must begin in the first column.

- (Tab)`cc -o trip main.o chicago.o indiana.o indy.o`

This is an *action line*. It follows the dependency line and shows how the file `trip` is created from the files `main.o`, `chicago.o`, `indiana.o`, and `indy.o`. In this case, `cc` links the object files and puts the executable into `trip`. Action lines must begin with a tab.

- `chicago.o: chicago.c`

This is another dependency line, showing that `chicago.o` depends on the source file `chicago.c`.

- (Tab)`cc -c chicago.c`

This is an *action line*, showing that `chicago.o` is produced by compiling `chicago.c` using `cc` with the `-c` option.

- `clean:`

This dependency line indicates that "clean" does not depend on any file. It is an example of an *empty dependency*. In this case, "clean" is not the name of a file, but rather a command, which you would run by typing

§ `make clean` (Return)

`make` will then look through `makefile`, find the empty dependency "clean," and run the command on the next action line.

- (Tab)`rm *.o`

This action line will remove any files ending in `.o`—in other words, the object files. This is the action that `make` will perform when you type

§ `make clean` (Return)

G.2 Running make

The first thing to do with make is to remove the executable and object files that were produced when you compiled the Trip program the first time. Try the ls command to see the files in Trip:

§ ls (Return)

You should see something like this:

```
a.out        indiana.c     indy.o     main.o
chicago.c    indiana.o     main.c     makefile
chicago.o    indy.c
```

Now get rid of the old object files:

§ make clean (Return)

The "clean" dependency line in makefile causes the following command line to run:

```
rm *.o
```

Use the ls command now to list the files remaining in Trip:

§ ls (Return)

You should see:

```
a.out        indiana.c     main.c
chicago.c    indy.c        makefile
```

Note that make did nothing to the old executable file a.out, because it was not instructed to do so.

Next, use make to compile the program. Simply type make and press (Return):

§ make (Return)

make then follows the instructions in makefile to compile the program:

```
cc -c main.c
cc -c chicago.c
cc -c indiana.c
cc -c indy.c
cc -o trip main.o chicago.o indiana.o indy.o
```

Note that the files are not necessarily compiled in exactly the same order as they appear in makefile; instead, make figures out which files should be compiled first. Try the ls command to see the files in Trip:

§ ls (Return)

You should see something like this:

```
a.out      indiana.c    indy.o    makefile
chicago.c  indiana.o    main.c    trip
chicago.o  indy.c       main.o
```

`trip` contains the new executable code, which you can run simply by typing `trip`, followed by (Return):

§ `trip`(Return)

The advantage of using `make` to compile the files becomes apparent when you begin making alterations in any of the source files. When you are finished, all you have to do is type `make`, and `make` will automatically recompile only those files that need it. And if you have not made any changes in the program, `make` will take no action. To see how this works, try running `make` again:

§ `make` (Return)

Assuming you have not made any changes in the files, you should see a message such as

`'trip' is up to date.` (Return)

INDEX